Human Rights Transformed

Positive Rights and Positive Duties

SANDRA FREDMAN

OXFORD

UNIVERSITY PRESS

OXFORD
UNIVERSITY PRESS

Great Clarendon Street, Oxford OX2 6DP

Oxford University Press is a department of the University of Oxford.
It furthers the University's objective of excellence in research, scholarship,
and education by publishing worldwide in

Oxford New York

Auckland Cape Town Dar es Salaam Hong Kong Karachi
Kuala Lumpur Madrid Melbourne Mexico City Nairobi
New Delhi Shanghai Taipei Toronto
With offices in
Argentina Austria Brazil Chile Czech Republic France Greece
Guatemala Hungary Italy Japan South Korea Poland Portugal
Singapore Switzerland Thailand Turkey Ukraine Vietnam

Oxford is a registered trade mark of Oxford University Press
in the UK and in certain other countries

Published in the United States
by Oxford University Press Inc., New York

ISBN 978-0-19-953505-7

Printed in the United Kingdom by
Lightning Source UK Ltd., Milton Keynes

To my children
Jem, Kim and Dan,

To my husband
Alan

And to my mother and late father
Naomi and Mike

Preface and Acknowledgements

Transforming human rights is an urgent project. It gains its impetus from the welter of confusing messages about human rights in the modern world. In the name of countering terrorism, Governments in many democratic countries stand prepared to undermine the very human rights they claim to be protecting. Instead of reaffirming the commitment to human rights in the face of threats to democracy, 'rights talk' has been used to undermine rights. Powerful rhetoric about the right to life and security of ordinary people in the face of terrorism is marshalled in support of removing rights to a fair trial and to freedom from torture. In a similar perverse use of rights talk, the preferred method of installing democracy in rogue states is through military might, with no expense spared in lives or money.

At the same time, lack of available resources is quietly stifling the brave hopes of the new millennium. By establishing a universal framework for partnership in pursuit of a shared future for all, the Millennium Development Goals aim to eradicate extreme poverty, empower women, achieve universal primary education, improve maternal health, reduce child mortality and combat HIV/AIDS, malaria and other diseases. But these are 'development goals', which many governments treat as optional acts of benevolence, not fundamental human rights, with first claim over resources. Not surprisingly, the likelihood of reaching the targets by the target date of 2015 is small. While politicians slate human rights as a charter for criminals and terrorists, the rights of young children to live beyond infancy; of mothers to survive childbirth; and of women to literacy, political participation and a healthy life free of poverty, are dubbed mere aspirations.

From a different direction comes the attempt to tie rights to responsibilities, as though fundamental human rights should be earned in return for good behaviour. Recent discourse among policy-makers in Britain is peppered with references to a new charter of 'rights and responsibilities'. But the allusion is to the responsibilities of rights-holders, not of governments: talk of subjecting the State itself to human rights duties is rejected as taking power away from the democratic process. It is true that the post-war Welfare State has been largely, and appropriately, a product of the political process. But the ease with which social rights could be blown away by the icy winds of Thatcherism, demonstrates the perils of resting a human rights edifice on no more than politics.

It is telling that in a recent survey aimed at discovering what ordinary British people would like to see included in a British Bill of Rights, 88% favoured inclusion of a right to free hospital treatment on the NHS within a reasonable time. At the same time, 89% thought that a British Bill of Rights should include the right to a fair trial by jury.[1] It is here that the key lies to transforming human rights. Human rights are more than freedom from State interference, although this a key tenet. They are also about freedom to be and do what one values;[2] the right to the resources and powers necessary to facilitate equal participation in civil, economic and political society. Nor is it correct to view human rights as simply protecting the individual, separate from society. Basic human rights values are essentially communal. Rights to freedom of speech are only valuable within an interpersonal setting; rights to home, family and private life only matter in a context of relationships and the community; the right to life is only possible through shared endeavours. Equally importantly, adequate options for exercising freedom of choice can only be made available through community, coordinated by the State. Transforming human rights therefore entails the recognition that the power of the State needs to be harnessed to securing the genuine exercise of human rights. This in turn means that human rights of all kinds, whether civil and political or socio-economic, can only be fully enjoyed if they give rise to a range of duties on the State. These extend beyond the well-established duty of restraint from interference. Critically, they also include positive duties.

This basic insight was recognized by the drafters of the new South African Constitution. Emerging from decades of persecution and denial of the most basic human rights, they created a Constitution which forged an essential synthesis between protecting individuals against a hostile State and harnessing the power of the State to create the basic conditions for genuine freedom, choice and equality. Thus rights to freedom of speech, to vote, to a fair trial, and to be free from torture, are matched by rights to food, shelter, health care, and social security. Moreover, the State is under a duty to respect, protect and promote all rights in the Constitution, whether civil and political or socio-economic. The existence of such duties has admittedly not yet brought an end to the dire poverty deliberately created by the apartheid regime. But they have required the State to commit itself unwaveringly to their ultimate fulfilment.

Positive human rights duties on the State are frequently caricatured as giving too much power to the State; or creating a Nanny State. This misunderstands the nature of human rights. Human rights duties do not give power to the State to intrude on individuals' lives at its discretion. They oblige the State to act in ways which facilitate the genuine enjoyment of human rights. Nor does a focus on positive duties entail a Nanny State. Human rights duties are essentially empowering, requiring a facilitative State. While this might require the provision of the basic means without which human rights are valueless, it also entails facilitative duties, such as education and health, which empower individuals. This shows too that positive duties are not only for the poor or marginalised: they are for

---

[1] ICM/Joseph Rowntree Reform Trust State of the Nation poll 2006.
[2] A Sen *Development as Freedom* (OUP Oxford 1999).

everyone, whether directly, or through the fact that the community as a whole benefits when all are able to enjoy their rights.

Transforming human rights therefore requires a greater focus on the positive duties to which all human rights give rise. It entails moving beyond artificial distinctions between civil and political rights and socio-economic rights, to recognizing that all rights give rise to the whole range of duties. More pressing still is the need for a much clearer understanding of positive duties, their nature and function. It is to this aspect of the project of transformation that this book hopes to contribute.

There are many people without whose generosity this book could not have happened. My especial thanks go to Cathi Albertyn, Philip Alston, Justice Bannurmath, Daphne Barak-Erez, Upendra Baxi, Jonathan Berger, Stéphanie Bernstein, Geoff Budlender, Justice Edwin Cameron, retired Chief Justice Arthur Chaskalson, Kimberlé Crenshaw, Justice Dennis Davis, Grainne De Burca, Max du Plessis, Jackie Dugard, Judy Fudge, Andrea Gabriel, Beth Goldblatt, Colin Gonsalves, Karthy Govender, Aeyal Gross, Adilla Hassim, Moray Hathorn, Bob Hepple, Murray Hunt, Indira Jaising, Rudolph Jansen, Evance Kalula, Tarunabh Khaitan, Jaina Kothari, Sudhir Krishnaswamy, Justice M Lokur, Patricia Londono, Francie Lund, Chris McCrudden, Manoranjan Mohanti, Justice Yvonne Mokgoro, Justice S Muralidhar, Justice Sandile Ngcobo, Justice Kate O'Regan, Laila Ollapally, Ranjit J Purshotam, Chuck Sabel, Justice Albie Sachs, Sharita Samuel, Kamala Sankaran, Sarah Spencer, Angus Stewart, Susan Sturm, Additional Solicitor General Gopal Subramanium, Faranaaz Veriava, Eric Watkinson, Murray Wesson, Stuart Wilson, and Justice Zac Yakoob. I am also indebted to Gwen Booth and Lucy Stevenson from OUP for all their assistance. My particular appreciation goes to the Leverhulme Trust, who generously funded my three-year research fellowship to carry out this work.

I dedicate this book to my children Jem, Kim and Dan, for all the inspiration they have been to me, and in the hope that they will grow up into a world where fundamental human rights are enjoyed equally and fully by all. I dedicate it too to my husband Alan and to my mother Naomi and my late father Mike, with deep love and appreciation.

Contents—Outline

Contents—Outline

Table of Cases

Table of Legislation

Introduction

Human rights have long been understood as providing protection for individual freedom against an intrusive State. On this view, human rights give rise only to 'negative' duties, preventing the State from interfering with individuals, rather than requiring the State to take positive action. It is widely acknowledged that the modern State has a range of positive functions. However, such responsibilities are generally considered to be a question of politics, rather than rights. Where positive duties are acknowledged, they are usually associated with socio-economic rights. For this reason, socio-economic rights are often considered to be merely aspirational, and their status as human rights doubted.

The distinction between duties of restraint and positive duties sets in motion a cascade of further dichotomies. Civil and political rights are pitted against socio-economic rights, freedom against equality, liberalism against socialism. Duties of restraint are seen as protecting liberty; positive duties as furthering equality. The former are justiciable, the latter non-justiciable. During the Cold War years, this set of distinctions was mapped onto the deep divisions in world politics. Socio-economic rights, associated with communist and socialist regimes, were thought to impose positive duties on the State to further equality at the expense of individual freedom. Conversely, civil and political rights, associated with Western democracies, were said to protect freedom through restraint on the State, thereby reinforcing the fundamental inequalities of capitalist society.[1] One proponent of 'liberty' over 'equality' argues that: 'In short, liberty rights reflect an individualist political philosophy that prizes freedom, welfare rights a communitarian or collectivist one that is willing to sacrifice freedom.'[2] Since the 1970s, these distinctions have also been reflected in the 'North–South' divide, where developing countries argue for a much higher priority to socio-economic rights in order to further goals of equality.[3]

The extent of the divide is reflected in the architecture of both international and European human rights documents. Thus, the International Covenant for Civil and Political Rights (ICCPR) covers civil and political rights whereas the International Covenant for Economic, Social and Cultural Rights (ICESCR) includes socio-economic rights. A similar pattern is evident at European level,

---

[1] See generally HJ Steiner, P Alston, and R Goodman *International Human Rights in Context* (3rd edn, OUP Oxford 2007) 263.
[2] D Kelley *A Life of One's Own: Individual Rights and the Welfare State* (Cato Institute Washington DC 1998) 1.
[3] Steiner, Alston, and Goodman (n 1 above) 282.

where the European Convention on Human Rights (ECHR) covers a separate
set of rights from the European Social Charter. In each case, the former are
justiciable; the latter subject to alternative methods, such as reporting requirements.[4] The result has been to tolerate infringements of basic socio-economic
rights at a level which would never have been acceptable for breach of civil and
political rights. Socio-economic rights, and with them positive duties, remain
the Cinderella of the international human rights corpus. At domestic level,
democratic bills of rights frequently include only civil and political rights to the
exclusion of socio-economic rights. This is true of the US, Canada, and the UK
among others. Where socio-economic rights are included, they tend to give rise
to obligations which are of a different nature from civil and political rights. The
Indian and Irish constitutions distinguish between justiciable civil and political rights, and directive principles of social policy, which create non-justiciable
obligations on the State. Even in the innovative constitutions, such as those
of Finland and South Africa, which include justiciable socio-economic rights,
the latter tend to be formulated differently. While civil and political rights are
immediately effective, socio-economic rights are only realizable progressively
and subject to available resources.

The artificiality of such distinctions has become increasingly clear. There are
many ways in which civil and political rights give rise to positive duties: the duty
to set up an electoral system to secure the fundamental right to democratic elections is a central case in point. Conversely, socio-economic rights can give rise
to duties of restraint as much as to positive duties. For example, the right to be
housed includes a duty of restraint on the State from interfering in home and
family life. Thus, the nature of the duty attached to a right should not depend
on whether it is classified as civil and political or socio-economic. Instead, as
Shue has shown, all rights give rise to a range of duties.[5] These include, not just
duties of constraint, but also duties to establish institutions, to protect individuals against other individuals, and to facilitate, promote, and provide for people's
needs and wants. This approach is specifically endorsed in the 1997 Maastricht
Guidelines, which state: 'Like civil and political rights, economic, social and cultural rights impose three different types of obligations on States: the obligations
to respect, protect and fulfil.'[6] The obligation to *respect* requires States to refrain
from interfering with the enjoyment of rights. The obligation to *protect* requires
States to prevent violations of such rights by third parties. The obligation to *fulfil*
requires States to take appropriate legislative, administrative, budgetary, judicial,
and other measures towards the full realization of such rights.

---

[4] Collective complaints may be lodged under an addition protocol to the European Social
Charter (ETS 158) which entered into force on 1 July 1998.

[5] H Shue *Basic Rights: Subsistence, Affluence, and US Foreign Policy* (2nd edn Princeton
University Press 1996).

[6] 'Maastricht Guidelines on Violations of Economic, Social and Cultural Rights', reprinted in
(1998) 20 *Human Rights Quarterly* 691 (Guideline 6).

The fact that these duties apply to all rights, not just socio-economic rights, is increasingly recognized in domestic and regional law. Thus the Indian Supreme Court has interpreted the civil and political right to life to include a range of positive duties. Even the European Court of Human Rights has recognized positive duties as arising from the avowedly civil and political rights in the ECHR. Most remarkable is the pioneering South African Constitution, which provides expressly that the State has a duty to 'respect, protect, promote and fulfil' all rights enumerated therein, without distinction as between civil and political rights and socio-economic rights.[7]

However, it is not enough to acknowledge the need to transcend the traditional distinctions. There is still much to be done to develop a full understanding of the implications of positive duties triggered by human rights, both from a theoretical and practical legal perspective. This is the aim of this book. Part I establishes the theoretical framework. In Chapter 1, it is argued that the values of freedom, equality, solidarity, and democracy, which underpin human rights, logically entail that the corresponding duties are both positive and negative. In particular, the traditional understanding of freedom as absence of interference requires radical revision. Human rights are based on a far richer view of freedom, which goes beyond absence of coercion and instead pays attention to the extent to which individuals are actually able to use their freedom. Substantive freedom on this understanding draws on Sen's well-known notion of freedom as the ability to be and to do what one has reason to value.[8] Instead of seeking simply to prevent interference in free choice, the role of human rights includes facilitating the exercise of the freedom guaranteed. This necessarily creates a duty to remove constraints on choice and facilitate agency. Thus, the duty of the State goes beyond restraint, to include a positive duty to secure the possibility of rights being exercised. This is reinforced by the recognition that we are essentially social beings, who can only fully realize our human rights through social co-operation. Indeed, it is as part of an interaction with others that personal values and therefore choices are derived and developed. Nor is self-fulfilment achieved only by pursuing self-interested goals. Valuable goals which contribute to self-fulfilment include contributing to a community, through personal relationships of caring as well as civic relationships of solidarity and responsibility.

With the positive view of freedom comes a substantive conception of equality. If freedom is a fundamental value, freedom for some must be freedom for all. However, freedom as non-interference makes it inevitable that some will be in a better position to exercise their freedom than others. Positive freedom therefore places a duty on the State to pay particular attention to those who are not in a position to exercise their rights to the full, even if this entails supplying more resources or providing greater facilitation for these individuals than for others not in the same category.

---

[7] South African Constitution, s 7(2).
[8] A Sen *Development as Freedom* (OUP Oxford 1999).

Nor do positive duties entail an unjustifiable imposition by the State of a particular set of values, thus infringing the basic freedom of each individual to pursue her own autonomously chosen ideal of the good. It is argued here, however, that State neutrality is a myth. The principle of non-intervention is itself based on particular values. Instead, autonomy is protected by placing a positive obligation on the State to provide a range of available options for citizens to pursue, ensuring all have the capacity to pursue their valued options, and that all valued options are treated in the same way.[9]

Finally, Chapter 1 deals with the relationship between rights and responsibilities, examining, in particular, the question of 'who pays?'. It is argued that instead of regarding rights for some as a cost to others, the achievement of rights for all can be viewed as a benefit to all. At the same time, the liberal 'harm' principle need not entail only duties of restraint. Once a positive understanding of freedom is accepted, it becomes clear that social responsibility can ultimately be grounded in the substantive understanding of harm as including omissions to promote others' freedom.

Chapter 2 deals with the nature of the State which carries human rights responsibilities. The first and most important challenge is to reconcile positive duties with democracy. There are many who would endorse a substantive view of freedom, but still maintain that human rights should not give rise to positive duties on the State to take action. Such decisions, it is argued, are best left to the democratic process, where decisions are taken by representatives of the people who are elected and accountable. In particular, positive duties frequently require resources, and allocative questions are, on this view, quintessentially political. The Welfare State in developed countries has therefore developed largely from a political, rather than a rights based ethic. It is argued in Chapter 2 that this makes too many assumptions about the representativeness and accountability of modern democracy, leaving out of account the ways in which power and wealth in society can distort the political process. Properly framed, human rights are necessary to not only establish and maintain democracy, but to ensure that all have the ability to participate equally in democratic decision making. Thus, far from being hostile to democracy, human rights are essential constituents of democracy. Chapter 2 also confronts the argument that it is utopian to consider placing positive duties on the State in an era in which globalization and privatization are undermining the power of the State in the first place. It is argued that globalization is a means to advancing the human rights of citizens, and should not be seen as an end in itself. Globalization has itself created strong international structures, placing a series of duties on the State. These should include and ultimately be subordinate to human rights duties.

---

[9] See J Raz *The Morality of Freedom* (Clarendon Press Oxford 1986) 425.

Part II turns from the theoretical framework to a consideration of the nature of positive duties. Many of the arguments against positive duties focus on their purported indeterminacy and programmatic nature. It is argued as a start that questions of justiciability should not be confused with the underlying question of whether positive duties can have normative content. Chapter 3 aims to delineate a structure of positive duties with normative content independently of whether they are justiciable. The chapter draws on Alexy's useful distinction between rules, which are binding per se, and principles, which are prima facie binding.[10] While rules are either satisfied or breached (or repealed), principles are only binding to the extent legally and factually possible. This means that they may not be determinative in a particular case, but this does not mean that they have no binding character. This analysis is then used to cast light on the debate about the 'minimum core'.

Having established the structure of positive duties, it is possible to turn to the question of justiciability. Chapter 4 argues that positive duties should be justiciable to the extent that they promote participative democracy. Courts have a role in reinforcing accountability of government to the people, in giving a voice to those who are necessarily marginalized in the political process, in ensuring that the material and social preconditions exist for full and equal participation, and ultimately in functioning as a catalyst for deliberative democracy. Chapter 5 then turns to the competence of courts to deal with polycentric and resource intensive duties. This question is tested through a critique of the practical experience of Public Interest Law in India. Chapter 6 moves beyond the courts and considers non-judicial methods of compliance. It concludes by developing a synergistic approach which draws together courts, the political process, local activism, and other regulatory mechanisms to achieve fulfilment of positive human rights through the framework of deliberative democracy.

Part III applies the theoretical framework to substantive rights. Chapter 7, on equality, examines the interaction between equality of status, as found in anti-discrimination law, and distributive equality, as found in the Welfare State and socio-economic rights. It is argued that both these aspects of equality must be integrated within a positive duty analysis of human rights. It then examines positive duties to promote equality in detail. Chapter 8 applies the analysis developed in the book to familiar topics of socio-economic rights, with a particular focus on housing, education, and welfare.

---

[10] R Alexy *A Theory of Constitutional Rights* (OUP Oxford 2004).

PART I

UNDERSTANDING POSITIVE DUTIES

1

Human Rights Values Refashioned: Liberty, Equality, and Solidarity

The function of human rights has traditionally been considered to consist primarily in protecting individuals' freedom against a potentially hostile State. Human rights are therefore presumed to give rise only to duties restraining the State from unjustified interference, rather than positive duties to take action. Behind this view is a set of particular values: a conception of freedom as absence of interference, a characterization of the State as separate from and opposed to the individual, and a principle of State neutrality as far as individual moral choices are concerned. Although there is widespread acknowledgement that the State can play a positive role in modern society, these values are not located in positive duties generated by human rights, but in the political sphere, where contested distributive decisions can be decided through the democratic process.

This chapter contests each of these values, arguing that they produce too limited a view of human rights. First, human rights hold out more than just the promise of freedom from State interference with their exercise. Human rights are based on a much richer view of freedom, which pays attention to the extent to which individuals are in a position actually to exercise those rights. This positive view of freedom carries with it a substantive view of equality. Given that human rights promote freedom by removing constraints, the promise of equality must require all to be in a position actually to enjoy that freedom. Secondly, we are social beings who can only achieve fulfilment through society. While the State needs to be restrained from abusing its power, only the State can supply what is needed for an individual to fully enjoy her human rights. Thirdly, it cannot meaningfully be asserted that the State is neutral in respect of moral or ethical commitments. A clear value commitment is signalled by subscribing to democracy and human rights.

The result is that human rights should be regarded as giving rise to the whole range of duties, including both duties of restraint and positive duties. This in turn collapses the artificial distinctions between civil and political rights on the one hand and socio-economic rights on the other. Chapter 3 examines the implications of the focus on positive duties for the structure of human rights. This chapter gives a detailed justification of the view that the values inherent in human rights as we know them require us to go beyond duties of restraint to positive duties, regardless of whether the right in question is formally classified as civil and political or socio-economic.

A. Positive Freedom and Positive Duties

(i) From non-intervention to enhancing choice

The best-known formulation of the 'negative' conception of freedom as lack of interference is that of Isaiah Berlin. According to this conception, 'I am...free to the degree to which no man or body of men interferes with my activity. Political liberty is simply the area within which a man can act unobstructed by others.'[1] Crucially, it is only interference by others which impinges on liberty: 'Mere incapacity to attain a goal is not lack of political freedom.' This means that I can be free even if I do not actually have the resources or opportunities to fulfil my choices, so long as no one is deliberately interfering with me. Poverty is not viewed as lack of freedom unless it is caused by deliberate acts of others. Berlin accepts that liberty might be curtailed to achieve other goals, such as equality or justice. Nor is the State's only function to protect freedom.[2] However, to make a decision to favour other goals is to accept a loss of liberty. This means that if the State takes positive steps to remove constraints, for example, by alleviating poverty, it must be doing so at the cost of freedom. Ultimately, 'some portion of human existence must remain independent of the sphere of social control. To invade that preserve, however small, would be despotism.'[3] Given, then, that liberty means 'liberty from, absence of interference',[4] it is inevitable that human rights give rise only to duties of restraint.

This emphasis on liberty as absence from coercion has received renewed impetus from modern neo-liberalism, which views the growth of the State as an ever-increasing threat to individual autonomy, and which instead posits the free market as the only way in which individuals can truly be free. This position is best articulated by Hayek, who, like Berlin, sees liberty as the 'state in which a man is not subject to coercion by the arbitrary will of another or others'.[5] For him too, liberty is formal and abstract: the extent to which a person can exercise real choice among a range of acceptable options is irrelevant. 'Liberty describes the absence of particular obstacles—coercion by other men...it does not assure us of any particular opportunities, but leaves it to us to decide what use we shall make

---

[1] I Berlin *Four Essays on Liberty* (Clarendon Press Oxford 1969) 121.
[2] GA Cohen 'Freedom and Money', lecture in memory of Isaiah Berlin (1999).
[3] Berlin (n 1 above) 126.
[4] ibid.
[5] FA Hayek *The Constitution of Liberty* (Routledge and Kegan Paul London 1960) 11.

of the circumstances in which we find ourselves.'[6] Hayek moves quickly from this conception of liberty to an equally narrow definition of the role of the State.[7] Only within a situation in which each individual can make her own choices without direction from the State, is she really free, and such a situation is represented by the spontaneous market order. The very concept of social justice is viewed as a threat to individual liberty. Individuals will only act collectively if they are coerced into doing so, in this case through submitting to the power of coordination necessary to redistribute market allocations.[8] Thus, for a government to act in pursuit of distributive or social justice is an illegitimate use of State power.[9] Inevitably then, the role of human rights is to restrain the State from interfering in individual autonomy within the free market.

However, from a human rights perspective, it is difficult to see why freedom should be seen only as an absence of deliberate State interference. If human rights are to be secured to all, it does not make sense to ignore other constraints on the ability of individuals to exercise their rights. Such constraints can arise as much from poverty, poor health, and lack of education as from tyranny and intolerance. This approach draws on the insights of modern theorists, in particular of Armatya Sen, who see freedom not as absence of coercion, but as agency, or the ability to exercise genuine choice and act on those choices. For Sen, freedom consists in being able to do and be what one has reason to value. As Sen argues: 'What people can achieve is influenced by economic opportunities, political liberties, social powers and the enabling conditions of good health, basic education, and the encouragement and cultivation of initiatives.'[10] Far from being irrelevant, the ability to achieve one's valued goals is essential to this conception of freedom. This necessitates the 'removal of major sources of un-freedom: poverty as well as tyranny, poor economic opportunities as well as systematic social deprivation, neglect of public facilities as well as intolerance or over-activity of repressive states'.[11]

Sen has developed the positive notion of freedom as agency through his 'capability theory'. This theory stresses the importance of considering the extent to which people are actually able to exercise their choices, rather than simply having the formal right to do so. In other words, it is crucial to distinguish between goals an individual might wish to choose, and those which are feasible for her actually to choose. This is captured in the distinction between 'functionings' and 'capabilities'. The goals or things a person might value doing or being, he calls 'functionings'. 'Valued functionings vary from elementary ones, such as being adequately nourished and free from avoidable disease, to complex activities or

---

[6] ibid 19.
[7] Hayek (n 5 above) 207–208.
[8] ibid 64–65.
[9] Hayek (n 5 above) 231.
[10] A Sen *Development as Freedom* (OUP Oxford 1999) 5.
[11] ibid 3.

personal states, such as being able to take part in the life of the community and having self respect.'[12] Not all of these, however, are feasible. A person's capabilities represent the set of functionings which it is actually feasible for her to achieve. Capability is therefore the substantive freedom to achieve alternative functioning combinations. The reason why it may not be feasible for a person to achieve the valued functionings she would otherwise have chosen can be as much due to social, economic, or physical constraints, as to political interference. Thus, in contrast to Berlin, poverty should be seen as the deprivation of basic capabilities and therefore a type of 'un-freedom'.[13]

The logical conclusion of Sen's approach is to require positive action to be taken to enhance individuals' capability sets. However, Sen's work on capabilities has focussed on the goals and measurement of development in developing countries rather than on human rights per se. He remains non-committal on the question of whether positive action to enhance capabilities should be part of a general developmental strategy carried out in the political arena, or whether they should be characterized as positive duties arising from human rights. It is Nussbaum who takes the conceptual apparatus of capability into the heartland of human rights law. Her aim is to articulate an account of how capabilities can provide a basis for central constitutional principles that citizens have a right to demand from their governments.[14] In this sense, she speaks directly to the positive duty of the State. The Kantian ideal that each person is a bearer of value and an end in herself is supplemented with the Marxist perception that the major powers of a human being need material resources to support them. More concretely still, she argues for a threshold level of each capability below which truly human functioning is not available. The social goal is to get citizens above this capability threshold;[15] correspondingly, the rights she advocates give rise to a series of positive duties on the State to ensure the threshold level of functioning.

This approach is strengthened by the recognition that the distinction between non-intervention and positive action is itself elusive. Poverty is always capable of being construed as an act of deliberate intervention by the State: it is the legal regime which creates property rights and protects them from theft and invasion. Bentham famously declared: 'Property is entirely the creature of law ... It is from the law alone that I can enclose a field and give myself to its cultivation ... Before the law, there was no property; take away the laws, all property ceases.'[16] Therefore, as Sunstein argues, if homeless people lack a place to live, it is because the rules of property are enforced. Similarly, there is no law against eating in the abstract; it is the law which forbids a hungry person to eat any of the food which

---

[12] Sen (n 10 above) 75.
[13] ibid 90–91.
[14] M Nussbaum *Women and Human Development* (Cambridge University Press Cambridge 2000) 12.
[15] ibid 5–6.
[16] J Bentham *Principles of the Civil Code* (Simkin Marshall 1898) 1:307–308.

exists in the community.[17] Sen puts it even more strongly. People are hungry if they lack entitlements that enable them to eat; thus, 'the law stands between food availability and food entitlement. Starvation deaths can reflect legality with a vengeance.'[18] To this Cohen adds the further insight, namely that lack of money is itself an act of deliberative intervention by the State. This is because the State has allocated a particular function to money, namely to give people the means to overcome interference with their liberty.[19] Thus, whether poverty is construed as deliberate State intervention, or as an obstacle to freedom which the State has the means to remove, it remains true to say that positive action is required from the State in order to ensure that an individual can exercise her human rights.

It is not only Sen's theory of freedom as agency which demonstrates that the concept of freedom underlying human rights entails positive as well as negative duties. Modern liberal thought, encapsulated by Rawls, has the same result, albeit in an unnecessarily limited form. Rawls' first principle of justice holds that 'each person has the same indefeasible claim to a fully adequate scheme of equal basic liberties, which scheme is compatible with the same scheme of liberties for all'.[20] Basic liberties broadly reflect the catalogue of civil and political rights. Rawls has always stressed the priority of the first principle: if redistributive measures undermine the basic liberties, then the basic liberties must be given precedence. However, in his later work, he is prepared to acknowledge that social and economic inequalities can skew the ability to exercise basic liberties. He thus includes in the first principle the need to secure each citizen fair access to the use of the political process as a public facility.[21] This means that the actual value or usefulness to individuals must be the same regardless of the economic or social opportunities available to a person.[22] This clearly gives rise to positive duties on the State to secure such fair access.

Positive duties play a further role in respect of his second principle, particularly in relationship to the need to secure equality of opportunity in respect of offices and positions. Equality of opportunity in this sense goes beyond mere formal opportunity, to ensure that all have a fair chance to attain them.[23] This means that those with the same level of talent and ability, and the same willingness to use these gifts, should have the same prospects of success regardless of social class. In particular, it requires equal opportunities of education for all regardless of family income. This notion goes beyond natural liberty in that the free market must be regulated to prevent excessive concentrations of wealth, especially those likely to lead to political domination.[24]

---

[17] CR Sunstein *The Second Bill of Rights* (Basic Books New York 2004) 23–24.
[18] Sen (n 10 above) 165–166.
[19] Cohen (n 2 above).
[20] J Rawls *Justice as Fairness* (Harvard University Press Cambridge Massachusetts 2001) 42.
[21] ibid 148–150.
[22] Rawls (n 20 above) 149.
[23] ibid 44.
[24] Rawls (n 20 above) 44–45.

However, Rawls' acknowledgement of the role of positive duties in securing liberty remains limited by his continuing adherence to the priority of negative over positive freedom when there is a conflict. This leads him to deny the need to ensure the fair value of any liberties apart from the political liberties. It is at this point that he sees a conflict with liberty, since this would involve the State in supporting a particular value system of some of its citizens over the others.[25] For example, to ensure the fair value of freedom of religion, he argues, the State would be committed to providing support for such activities as building expensive cathedrals or funding pilgrimages, which would in turn mean that the distribution of resources would be conditional on providing support for individuals' particular conception of the good. It is argued below that State neutrality as to the good cannot, in any event, be sustained. But for Rawls the result of prioritizing negative over positive freedom is to ignore the extent of real constraints on individuals' ability to fully use their rights. To ensure that individuals genuinely have equal opportunities requires a far wider reach of the positive duties on the State than Rawls acknowledges.

(ii) From preference to choice

The rich view of freedom as agency emphasizes the importance of facilitating individuals' ability to fulfil their choices. This requires a closer examination of the social meaning of choice. Economists generally understand 'choice' in highly individualistic terms, denoting the subjective preferences of each individual, which ought to be accepted and respected as essential to her autonomy. The view that freedom is non-interference, and therefore that rights are restraints, is based at least in part on the notion that government should not seek to influence preferences. At first glance, the positive understanding of freedom as agency could equally well be based on this conception of choice. In other words, given an individual's preferences, the State should be under a duty to facilitate their exercise.

However, this ignores the social nature of choice itself. In particular, preferences might themselves be a result of deep-seated constraints within the social structure.[26] Individuals are liable to adapt their preferences to their existing circumstances, to what they perceive is possible, and to power structures in which they find themselves. Part-time female workers are frequently quoted in surveys as expressing a preference for marginal work. But this needs to be seen in the context of a work environment which makes part-time work the only option for women with childcare responsibilities. Similarly, Roma people are often accused of 'choosing' not to send their children to school. But such preferences need to be assessed in the light of a school system which discriminates against them and renders invisible their culture and language. In addition, preferences might directly reflect initial legal and social endowments, instead of vice versa. A person who does not have a legal right in the first place might not express a preference

---

[25] ibid 151. [26] Nussbaum (n 14 above) 65.

for it because it is outside of her field of possibility.[27] Preferences also depend on available information, and are highly malleable, deliberately so in a consumer society which depends on advertising. Even more seriously, some preferences, such as drug abuse, or refusal to wear a seatbelt, may decrease individual welfare despite having been chosen by the subject.

The recognition of adaptive preferences reinforces the argument in favour of positive duties on the State. In order genuinely to enhance freedom of choice, preferences should not necessarily be taken as given. Instead, the State's duty is to increase the range of feasible options. As Sunstein concludes, in such situations, 'the interest in liberty or autonomy does not call for governmental inaction, even if that were an intelligible category. Indeed in many or perhaps all of these cases, regulation removes a kind of coercion.'[28] At the same time, there is the danger that State action might go beyond freeing people from their adaptive strictures and begin to dictate to individuals what they should be choosing. The Marxian notion of 'false consciousness' could either herald a liberating freedom or a patronizing or authoritarian restriction. Sen deals with this issue by focussing not on preferences, but on the things a person *has reason* to value. This leaves open the question of what it means to say that a person has reason to value something or, conversely, that she has no such reason. A more satisfactory answer is to focus on the creation of conditions for the effective exercise of choice.[29] This tackles the underlying problem of adaptive preferences: namely, that individuals cannot exercise effective choice when social, political, or economic conditions limit their horizons of possibility to such an extent that they are unable to even identify the potential choices in the first place. However, it does not dictate which choices should be exercised. The way forward is to provide the conditions which make it possible for individuals to form their choices in genuine freedom as well as act on them. The positive obligation on the State is to secure such conditions, without imposing any particular set of choices on individuals. In this way, the positive obligation can promote freedom by widening spheres of choice without being despotic or paternalistic.[30]

(iii) Choice in context: care, responsibility, and dignity

Sen's normative framework places as its highest value the individual's ability to do or be what she has reason to value. This risks focussing too much attention on what individuals can achieve, giving the impression that the only function of positive duties is to facilitate the ability of individuals to realize their own goals. It is important that this should not eclipse other human rights values, which are not

---

[27] CR Sunstein 'Preferences and Politics' (1991) 20 *Philosophy and Public Affairs* 3, 7.

[28] ibid 10.

[29] Nussbaum (n 14 above) 115.

[30] ibid 160.

based on choice but on interpersonal relationships and interdependence. Central among these is the value of caring, which comes, not as a matter of choice, but of responsibility. In fact, the needs of the person who is cared for might limit, inevitably and appropriately, the capabilities of the person doing the caring. Capabilities theory could wrongly assume that, for the carer, the aim of human rights duties is to open up further feasible choices. But human rights do not only value choices. They also value relationships for themselves. This gives rise to a duty to ensure dignity and respect, and to promote and facilitate responsibility and caring.

This is clearly demonstrated by considering family responsibilities and childcare. Capabilities theory focusses on enhancing the feasible options of the carer, for example, by providing childcare so that mothers can undertake paid work. Those who continue to care are then assumed to have chosen this as an option, and no further policies are considered necessary. This fundamentally misunderstands the nature of responsibility and care. Caring should be valued not because it is chosen as part of an individual quest for self-fulfilment, but because it is in itself a necessary and important social activity. A similar point can be made in respect of situations in which a person is not physically, psychologically, or mentally able to act on her choices. It is not to enhance her achievements that human rights duties are required; but rather to ensure that she is treated with dignity and respect.

B. Individualism and Community

The second major assumption behind the restraints-based theory is that the individual achieves her full freedom only when untrammelled by State and community regulation. This in turn assumes that the individual comes to society fully formed and essentially free. According to the liberal myth, free individuals in a state of nature only submit to State power because of the need for law and order. As Hobbes graphically portrays it, unlimited freedom in the state of nature leads to unlimited warfare, and life is 'nasty, brutish and short'.[31] This makes it necessary to find a way of preserving individual freedom despite the necessity of political authority. For Hobbes, there was no way in which legal limits on sovereign power could be imposed without undermining the ability of the State to maintain order.[32] This is the 'great Leviathan, or rather... [t]hat Mortall God, to which wee owe... our peace and defence'.[33] For Locke, by contrast, there was no more reason to trust the sovereign than to trust one's fellow human beings.[34] He therefore posited a set of 'natural rights' which could not be excluded by the

---

[31] T Hobbes *Leviathan* (Penguin Classics 1985) Part I ch 13.
[32] ibid Part I, ch 14, 190–191.
[33] Hobbes (n 31 above) 227.
[34] J Locke *Two Treatises of Government* (Cambridge University Press Cambridge 1963) 372.

social contract, and which ensured that individual liberty remained impervious to State power. It is as a fully formed person, clothed with 'natural rights', that the individual enters society, and it is only to secure those rights that political authority can use coercion. Such natural rights include the rights of individuals to life and liberty, to govern their own affairs, to dispose of their labour, and to possess property.[35] Rights are therefore essentially constraints on the State, functioning as limits on the extent to which State authority can be imposed.

An alternative view, which dates back to Aristotle, characterizes individuals as essentially social beings. Aristotle argued that a person is by nature a social and political animal, and a fully human life can be achieved only in the context of the polis or the political community. The ultimate aim of politics is to enable individuals to achieve 'self-perfection', and conversely, the life that most fully develops these practical virtues is one of active engagement in political life. Freedom is itself only meaningful in the context of a community or collective life. Similarly, Hegel argues that to insist on an individual as prior to society overlooks the role played by social and political settings in constituting free individuals in the first place. It is only possible to achieve individual freedom through being part of a collective practice of freedom, which allows one to develop the capacities, attitudes, and self-understanding necessary for freedom.[36] Hegel sees it as impossible to develop a sense of self and subjectivity without understanding and recognizing others. An individual derives her own identity from recognizing others and being recognized by them. Therefore, one can only develop and sustain the sense of oneself as free through a process of mutual recognition of other free individuals.[37]

For Hegel, it is only through the State that individuals acquire the capacities to recognize others and accept the responsibilities of the social order. But does this mean, as Hegel suggests, that the individual must be considered to be fully submerged or incorporated into the State? It has been a central challenge for modern political theorists of the liberal tradition to find a synthesis which recognizes the essentially social nature of freedom without extinguishing individual autonomy. Modern liberals, such as Rawls, wholeheartedly accept the social nature of individuals, regarding it as a 'truism that we must live in society to achieve our good'.[38] Indeed, his theory of justice is premised on a concept of society as a fair system of cooperation, and it is through reciprocity that justice can be achieved.[39] While he rejects the view that the sole human good is our engagement in political life, he nevertheless maintains that one of the great goods

---

[35] ibid 123.
[36] GWF Hegel *Phenomenology of Spirit* (OUP Oxford 1977) 104–119; see further A Patten 'Hegel' in D Boucher and P Kelly (eds) *Political Thinkers* (OUP Oxford 2003).
[37] See also A Honneth 'Redistribution as Recognition: A Response to Nancy Fraser' in N Fraser and A Honneth *Redistribution or Recognition* (Verso London New York 2003) 180.
[38] Rawls (n 20 above) 143.
[39] ibid 6.

of human life is that achieved by citizens through engaging in political life. For him, the synthesis is achieved by making such participation voluntary. 'The extent to which we make engaging in political life part of our complete good is up to us as individuals to decide and varies from person to person.'[40]

It is preferable to derive the synthesis from the richer notion of autonomy outlined above. Given an understanding of freedom as agency, it is clear that, instead of regarding society as a limitation on individual freedom, it is the social context which itself enhances autonomy. Individuals need society for more than just law and order. Not only is the individual unable to achieve her full potential without social input, in addition, individual identity is essentially based on inter-personal recognition and relationships. This builds on Hegel's foundational view of individual identity as deriving from inter-subjective recognition within the context of social relations.[41] As a result, rights cannot be seen as a means by which atomistic, estranged individuals are protected against each other. Instead, as Habermas shows, the legal order presupposes collaboration among subjects who recognize each other as free and equal citizens in reciprocally related rights and duties.[42] To have even the wherewithal to enter into a 'social contract', individuals must be able to take the perspective of the other. 'Only then can freedom appear not simply as a natural freedom which occasionally encounters factual resistance, but as freedom constituted through mutual recognition.'[43] Human rights cannot therefore be premised on an understanding of individuals as prior to society.

Thus, society both shapes the individual and makes possible the range of options necessary for full human functioning. As Raz argues, it is only within a social context that personal autonomy can be enhanced, one which not only provides a range of acceptable options, but also includes the institution and networks of human relationships which are essential to human existence.[44] However, the social context needs to be shaped to further such autonomy. This in turn leads directly to an understanding of human rights, which includes positive duties. Freedom of the individual within society directly entails a positive duty on the State to ensure the provision of a range of options, of public goods and the framework within which human relationships can flourish.

C. The Good and the Right: can the State be Neutral?

(i) Theories of State neutrality

Also central to the defence of rights as restraint is the principle that the State should not impose any particular version of the 'good' on its citizens. The

---

[40] Rawls (n 20 above) 144.
[41] Hegel (n 36 above); also Boucher and Kelly (n 36 above).
[42] J Habermas *Between Facts and Norms* (Polity Press 1997) 88.
[43] ibid 91–92.
[44] J Raz *The Morality of Freedom* (Clarendon Press 1986) 124.

right of individuals to make their own decisions as to the good life is seen to be fundamental to liberty, requiring duties of restraint to prevent the State from imposing particular values. It is here that liberalism makes its decisive break from the Aristotelian view that there is an objective 'good' discernible by the rational faculties. Aristotle saw the polis as not only a political entity but also a community based on a commitment to shared values.[45] Nor did he distinguish between moral laws and the positive laws of the polis: the principles of political justice of the polis are also the standard of justice or of right and wrong for its citizens. By contrast, it is a central tenet of much liberal thought that the promotion of the good life is not a legitimate matter for governmental action. As Raz points out, this is inevitably a doctrine of restraint. Government cannot be under a positive duty to act, even if it could improve a state of affairs, because it should remain neutral as between valid and invalid ideals of the good.[46]

It is this argument that Berlin seeks to support in his famous but much misunderstood work on positive and negative liberty. On the surface, Berlin's positive liberty looks very similar to the view argued for in this book.

The 'positive' sense of the word 'liberty' derives from the wish on the part of the individual to be his own master. I wish to be the instrument of my own, not of other men's acts of will. I wish to be a subject, not an object, to be moved by reasons, by conscious purposes, which are my own...I wish to be...a doer—deciding, not being decided for, self-directed and not acted upon by external nature or by other men as if I were a thing, or an animal or a slave incapable of playing a human role, that is of conceiving goal and policies of my own and realising them.[47]

However, Berlin insists that the path of positive liberty is in fact the path to despotism. This is because of the link he draws between positive liberty and the Aristotelian view of an objective 'good' that can be derived from reason. If there is such an objective good, individuals are only un-free when they fail to use their reason and therefore do not perceive the good. Freedom is therefore not the removal of external constraints, but of internal obstacles: the irrational and subjective passions which prevent individuals from attaining true reason. This line of argument has some powerful proponents. Kant argued that the individual must abstract herself from her desires and follow reason in order to be free.[48] Similarly, Hegel maintained that to achieve freedom, it is necessary to liberate the reason, or the real self, from passion, the empirical self. The aim of reason is the agent's own freedom—the will abstracted from all its contingently given desires and purposes

---

[45] Aristotle *Politics* (Random House 1943) 1287, 1280–1282, 1325 and see T Burns 'Aristotle' in D Boucher and P Kelly (eds) *Political Thinkers* (OUP Oxford 2003) 76–77.
[46] Raz (n 44 above) 110.
[47] Berlin (n 1 above) 169.
[48] I Kant *The Moral Law* (Unwin Hyman London 1948) Book I ch viii.

remains committed to its own freedom.[49] For Rousseau, too, freedom requires reason: to be driven alone by appetite or desire is slavery.[50]

It is the next step which takes us to the despotism that Berlin was so concerned with. If individuals are so blinded by their passions as to be unable to see reason, then it is the duty of the State to show them the way. Hegel in particular argued that the State embodies objective reason, to which all owe allegiance. Paradoxically then, as Rousseau famously acknowledged, individuals may need to be forced to be truly free. For Rousseau, citizens who follow reason rather than passion, will all share the same conception of what is in the common good, namely, an equal concern for the well-being of each citizen. When this is embodied in binding law, each can regard the obligations to the common good as self-imposed. Each individual therefore only obeys herself and remains free as before. The conclusion is inexorable. 'Whoever refuses to obey the general will,' maintains Rousseau, 'will be forced to do so by the entire body. This means merely that he will be forced to be free.'[51]

For Berlin, this constitutes not the ultimate step towards freedom, but the yawning chasm of authoritarianism. For him, splitting the self into two, the desires and the reason, is dangerous because very soon the reasonable self becomes identified with a wider 'whole' which imposes its will upon recalcitrant members in the name of higher freedom. Such a view, maintains Berlin, leads us to argue that it is justifiable to coerce people in the name of some goal, such as justice or public health, which it is claimed they would pursue themselves, if they were more enlightened. People can be coerced, bullied, oppressed, and even tortured on behalf of their 'real' selves in the secure knowledge that this will make them truly free by giving them access to their real self and therefore their real choices. This, according to Berlin, leads inevitably to the grossly illiberal view that it is possible to force someone to be free.[52] Berlin concludes that the only way to avoid this conclusion is to reassert the primacy of negative freedom, or freedom as absence of coercion. For this, the State must be strictly neutral as between different particular values or world views. Positive duties arising from human rights would necessarily impinge on the basic individual's freedom to choose her own version of the good.

The problem with this conclusion is the assumption that it is in fact possible for the State to remain value neutral. In practice, however, the illusion of neutrality disguises particular value commitments. Autonomy and individualism are themselves value commitments, as Rawls recognizes in his later work.[53] A similar

---

[49] GWF Hegel 'Philosophy of Right (1942)' in SM Cahn (ed) *Political Philosophy: The Essential Texts* (OUP Oxford 2005) para 149, 153.
[50] JJ Rousseau 'Of the Social Contract (1762)' in SM Cahn (ed) *Political Philosophy: The Essential Texts* (OUP Oxford 2005).
[51] ibid 297.
[52] Berlin (n 1 above) 170.
[53] Rawls (n 20 above) 156.

point could be made about Hayek's basic premise that each individual should be free to pursue her own self-interest as determined solely by herself. Hayek presents this as a neutral principle, triggering a powerful duty on the State to remain impartial as to individual's choices. However, despite masquerading as impartiality, Hayek's premise embodies a particular understanding of human needs and aspirations, one which downgrades collective goals and interpersonal relationships and ignores the ways in which choice is constrained by individuals' initial endowments, their ability effectively to mobilize resources at their disposal and their access to social goods such as education and training.[54]

This raises one of the most difficult modern problems. On what basis can a distinction be drawn between the issues on which the State should not intervene—those areas in which a plurality of values is not only acceptable but essential to maintain equality and freedom in a diverse society—and those areas in which the State is entitled to take positive action to further specific values or prevent the pursuance of what it regards as morally bad goals? This is a problem which political theorists continue to grapple with. One way forward is to distinguish between morality and ethics. Morality is universal and applicable to all, while ethics denotes the particular values relating to the individual or the collective life of the community.[55] Ethical considerations are a matter of choice, for the individual investigating her own cultural history, to choose and continuously reshape. Moral considerations, by contrast, are universal and unchanging, and must be capable of being accepted freely and jointly by all affected.[56] This gives an apparently straightforward demarcation between State and individual moral choices: universal principles of morality can be pursued by the State, since everyone should necessarily agree. But it would be an infringement of individual liberty to intrude on the personal ethical decisions of people.

The difficulty, however, is to determine the content of the universal moral principle. For some modern liberal thinkers, the only principle that can qualify is the principle of universal respect and consideration for each individual. Thus, the space for intervention by the State is limited to this principle. It is only when ethical choices impinge on others' right to equal respect that the moral principle overrides the ethical and the State is entitled to intervene. Nancy Fraser uses this approach to argue for a principle of 'participative parity', which she posits as a moral principle which does not intrude on individual ethics.[57] However, this solution is not always easily sustainable. Most problematically, it assumes that the moral principle of equal respect and consideration has a clear meaning, which can be accepted by all regardless of their ethical perspective. But ethical

---

[54] S Deakin and F Wilkinson *The Law of the Labour Market* (OUP Oxford 2005) 285–286.
[55] Habermas (n 42 above) 97.
[56] ibid.
[57] N Fraser 'Social Justice in the Age of Identity Politics: Redistribution, Recognition and Participation' in N Fraser and A Honneth *Redistribution or Recognition* (Verso London New York 2003) 40.

perspectives clearly have an influence. Ethical choices can lead to the rejection of certain identities, lifestyles, or values. In enforcing the principle of equal respect and consideration, the State may well be impinging on such ethical choices. Conversely, it is not clear that the State should always refrain from intervening in ethical choices, particularly when group decisions might affect individuals.[58]

Rawls has a different approach to how to draw the line between values the State can legitimately impose on individuals and those which individuals should be free to self-define. He does this through his idea of a political conception of justice, which he distinguishes from comprehensive value systems. We need to assume, he argues, that reasonable pluralism of comprehensive value systems is a permanent condition of democratic society. If the State were to attempt to enforce continuing adherence to a single comprehensive doctrine, coercive power would be required. Yet in a democratic State, coercive force can only be exercised with the consent of all the people.[59] These two requirements are reconciled through his notion of an overlapping consensus: 'a public basis of justification that all citizens as reasonable and rational can endorse from within their own comprehensive doctrines'. The aim is not to achieve a single comprehensive doctrine, moral or religious, but to find a political conception of justice, which all can affirm, even if for different reasons.[60] The result is only neutral in that everyone can accept it, regardless of his or her particular world view.[61] It is not neutral in the sense of being value free. Indeed, Rawls acknowledges that one cannot expect a political conception of justice not to favour some doctrines over others.[62] Any reasonable political conception must impose restrictions on permissible comprehensive views; and basic institutions set up in accordance with just principles inevitably encourage some ways of life and discourage others.[63]

Rawls' claim to neutrality depends on the possibility of finding an overlapping consensus to which all can agree. Most importantly, it is central to his claim that the overlapping consensus should be one that is acceptable by citizens who are both rational and reasonable. Rationality denotes the pursuit of self-interest, but reasonableness goes further and accepts that there is a need to specify principles which would be honoured because they are reciprocal, even if this is at the expense of one's own self-interest. It would be reasonable to honour these principles even at the expense of one's own interests provided others do too.[64] This central notion of reasonableness is clearly not one which is in itself value-neutral. Rawls acknowledges that any reasonable political conception must impose restrictions on permissible comprehensive views.[65] Dworkin further challenges Rawls' attempt to separate political values from comprehensive moral convictions. In particular, the principles of justice which emerge from Rawls'

---

[58] JG Finlayson *Habermas* (OUP Oxford 2005) 96–97.
[59] Rawls (n 20 above) 33–34.   [60] ibid 32.
[61] Rawls (n 20 above) 152.   [62] ibid 154.
[63] Rawls (n 20 above) 153.   [64] ibid 6.
[65] Rawls (n 20 above) 153.

discussion could be seen to depend on controversial moral principles. Moreover, it might be impossible to achieve unanimity on some central political questions, simply because no overlapping consensus exists.[66] The result is to dissolve the attempted distinction between issues in which the State cannot intervene and those in which it can intervene without breaching the principle of neutrality, even when neutrality means only consensus.

(ii) The perfectionist State and positive duties

The above argument has demonstrated that the view that the State should not interfere with individual choices of the good is based on the myth that the State can indeed be neutral. This leads us to ask why we should aspire to neutrality at all. The usual answer is that no one is in a better position than anyone else to decide on the meaning of the good, least of all the State. Therefore, to impose any particular vision of the good on any individual is to fail to treat her with the respect and concern which is essential to her humanity. However, this approach relies on moral relativism, while at the same time contradicting it. This is because it espouses at least one moral principle, namely that individuals should be allowed to choose their own version of the good. Even within this moral principle is a further contradiction, which is the assumption that individuals can ever be entirely free to choose their own version of the good. However, individuals' choices are not independent of their social context. On the contrary, choice is intensely situated within a social context, which influences what choices are available, and the values and penalties attached to different choices. Choices also depend heavily on other people's choices, and on choices made earlier in the same individual's life. Most importantly, it is impossible to exercise choice unless adequate options exist, and only the State can provide these. Therefore, positive duties cannot simply be rejected on the grounds that they are bound to infringe on individuals' ability to choose the good for themselves. Instead, the central challenge is expressly to recognize and continually engage with the ways in which the State does and should actively infuse a particular kind of public morality into the lives of individuals.

The most convincing solution to these problems is that provided by Raz. Raz not only rejects the possibility of a neutral State, he views it as a positive attribute of the State to promote a public morality. Nevertheless, this does not entail the coercive imposition by the State of a particular world view. This is because of the way in which he derives political freedom from his foundational notion of personal autonomy or the ability to be part author of one's own life. Raz recognizes that personal autonomy cannot be an individualistic enterprise. Instead, it requires an adequate range of available options, which includes the possibility of choosing mutually incompatible moral positions. Thus, Raz's perfectionist State

---

[66] R Dworkin 'Rawls and the Law' [2004] 72 Fordham Law Review 1387, 1397–1398.

is not only consistent with a plurality of valuable and mutually exclusive forms of life, but positively requires them.

This leads directly to a theory of positive duties. People can only be fully autonomous if the State creates the conditions for valuable autonomy.[67] The State's duty to promote personal autonomy requires it to create the conditions of autonomy. Crucially, this includes positively encouraging the flourishing of a plurality of incompatible and competing pursuits, projects, and relationships.[68] This does not mean that the State can never reject the moral choices of citizens. The State may also have a positive duty to sanction measures which encourage the adoption of valuable ends and discourage the pursuit of base ones. How then does one avoid the charge of paternalism? In fact, Raz's theories readily embrace various paternalistic measures, provided they are confined to the creation of conditions of autonomy. Although morally bad options can be autonomy enhancing, choosing a morally bad option makes one's life worse than a comparable non-autonomous life.[69]

Raz's endorsement of positive duties on the State depends centrally on his distinctive interpretation of the harm principle, that is, the principle that the State can only legitimately interfere with individuals' freedom in order to protect others from harm. For Raz, harm includes omissions, or the failure to provide the conditions of autonomy for people who lack them. In this sense, the harm principle is far from a principle of restraint. It allows the State to use coercion to stop people from taking action which would diminish people's autonomy. Equally importantly, it permits the State to force people to take action required to improve people's options and opportunities. The harm principle does, however, require the State to be restrained in respect of the means it may legitimately use to promote morally valuable opportunities and eliminate repugnant ones. Although the State can legitimately pursue moral ideals by political means, it cannot use coercion to prevent individuals from making repugnant choices. The only situation in which coercion might be justified is when repugnant choices cause harm, and even then, not all uses of coercion are justified.[70]

This approach does not on its own address the difficulty of permitting too much power to the State. However, the answer is not to create an illusion of State neutrality. Instead, it is necessary to consider other checks and balances. Most important for our purposes is the normative character of positive duties arising from human rights. Positive duties arising from human rights do not give governments carte blanche in their use of their power. By requiring the State to act, positive duties give no more latitude to governments than duties which require them to refrain from acting. Nor are they legitimate unless they further the goals of substantive freedom, solidarity, equality, and democracy advocated here. Thus, positive duties arising from human rights are themselves an important means of

---

[67] Raz (above n 44) 426.   [68] ibid 425.
[69] Raz (above n 44) 410.   [70] ibid 409–423.

preventing the State from abusing its power. What they add to traditional doctrines of restraint is the perception that failure by the State to act can limit freedom as much as action by the State.

D. Who Pays? Reconceptualizing Responsibilities

The discussion thus far has proceeded as if the State were an autonomous entity. In fact, of course, the State is only the medium through which the community operates. This immediately raises the question of who bears the burden of providing the resources to fuel the State's positive duties. Will some have to sacrifice their right to pursue and achieve the fulfilment of their own capabilities in order to ensure that others achieve the minimum? In other words, must the State interfere with the freedom of some in order to provide freedom for others, so that positive freedom is won at the expense of negative freedom? This section addresses these issues by interrogating the question itself. By asking who bears the cost, we immediately cast the issue in terms of an inevitable conflict between burdens and benefits. Rights are characterized as a bundle of goods which benefit only the individual rights-holder, while correlative duties are born by others who must surrender some of their freedom. This conflict can be avoided by reconceptualizing rights and responsibilities in the light of the richer understanding of the individual as embedded in society. Three different solutions are discussed here: reciprocity focuses on the mutuality of benefit generated by the interaction between rights-holders; republicanism emphasizes the broader self-fulfilment of all through exercising civic virtue; while the reconstructed harm principle directly engages with responsibility. Each is considered in turn. It should be noted that this question is not just about 'horizontal' effect, the principle that holds that it is not only the State but also individuals who can be held directly responsible for discharging human rights obligations. Even on a 'vertical' model, which limits such responsibility to the State, positive duties would require citizens to contribute, both in effort and financially, to the discharge of such duties.

(i) Reciprocity

The first way to address the issue is to argue that burdens can be justified when directly linked to benefits. At its narrowest, this approach mirrors that of the private contract: duties to contribute to others' welfare are only legitimate when those contributing can be repaid with reciprocal benefits. However, the private contractual model of mutual exchange is too limited because it requires a one-to-one mapping of benefits to burdens, so that contributions to others are directly rewarded or paid for. Positive duties do in fact benefit all members of society, including those who contribute. But because benefits are diffused throughout society, responsibility should extend beyond an individual exchange of benefit for burden. Nor should burdens in society necessarily be proportionate to the benefits received by a particular individual. Reciprocity must therefore move beyond this transactional framework if it is to explain the structure of responsibility in society.

A more complex understanding of reciprocity is put forward by Rawls, who places it at the basis of his theory of what amounts to a fair system of social cooperation. For Rawls, members of society are prepared to accept terms of cooperation on the basis that they know others will do the same.[71] Thus, reciprocity can only be achieved through a set of principles of justice that both the advantaged and the disadvantaged can accept. It is usual to highlight Rawls' emphasis on what the disadvantaged could accept, but for our purposes his treatment of the advantaged is more relevant. For Rawls, the advantaged have no inherent right to retain their advantaged position, because there is no link between individual moral desert and the distribution of native endowments. Neither the better endowed nor the less endowed deserve their place in the distribution of native endowments. The same is true for contingencies of social position and good and bad luck.[72] The better endowed therefore can only take advantage of their position by reciprocal contribution to the good of the less endowed. This is encapsulated in the 'difference principle', which states that inequality is justifiable provided it is to the benefit of the least well-off. Social institutions should be established in such a way that no one can take advantage of contingencies of native endowment, or initial social position, or good or bad luck over the course of life except in ways that benefit everyone, including the least favoured.[73]

Rawls' theory arguably takes the reciprocal element one step further than he needs to. For Rawls, the requirement to contribute to society arises not from the simple fact of advantage, but only when the advantaged wish to acquire further benefits. As Rawls puts it, the better endowed, who have a fortunate place in the distribution of native endowments they do not morally deserve, are encouraged to acquire still further benefits on condition they train their native endowments and use them in ways that contribute to the good of the less endowed, who do not deserve their lesser place either.[74] Yet if, as Rawls argues, the distribution of native endowments is a common asset and no one has a moral claim on what they gain as a result of their natural endowments, there seems no reason why they should not have a duty to reinvest those fruits into the social endeavour without being rewarded by further advantages. Hutton argues that property should not be seen as an absolute right, but a 'concession, made by the society of which it is part, that has to be continually earned and deserved'.[75] Those who own property are members of society 'to which necessarily they must contribute

[71] Rawls (n 20 above) 6.
[72] ibid 124.
[73] Rawls (n 20 above) 124.
[74] ibid 76.
[75] Rawls (n 20 above) 84.

as the quid pro quo for the privilege of exercising property rights'.[76] However, Rawls is reluctant to take this radical step. Instead, he uses the idea of reciprocity as a way of justifying the greater advantages which the better endowed can obtain from social life.

Rawls' theory aims to provide the criteria for assessing whether a system is just, rather than the details of particular systems. Nevertheless, this approach to reciprocity raises several questions, whose resolution would lead to very different models of social contribution. One is that that he does not spell out what the reciprocal duties of the better-endowed entail, apart from the requirement that they train their native endowments in order to lead productive lives.[77] It is not clear whether his criteria would be fulfilled simply by requiring the better-endowed to maximize their own self-interest in the market, in the expectation that benefits will 'trickle down' to the less well-endowed. A second is how the State's contribution to initial endowments are factored in. Those who achieve highly in the market do not generally do so only because of their natural endowments but because the State has already endowed them with the possibility of doing so. A third is whether caring and other unpaid work would be regarded as productive in his sense.

But the most problematic part of Rawls' theory of reciprocity is its assumption that the only way in which individuals can be expected to contribute to society is through creating incentives which ultimately serve their self-interest. The difference principle, although it is centred on improving the situation of the disadvantaged, is ultimately a justification for inequality, holding that the more advantaged can legitimately expect still greater benefits on condition they use their advantage in order to lead productive lives. Yet most people would acknowledge that there is an ethic of solidarity and caring in most societies, which the State is in a position to foster.

(ii) Solidarity and civic virtue

The reciprocity notion remains grounded in the assumption that society is composed of individual rights-bearers who enter into relationships with other rights-bearers in order to 'trade' benefits and burdens. It was argued above that instead individuals should be understood as embedded in society, in the sense that individual identity and even survival cannot be conceived of outside of the social framework. Responsibilities for social arrangements are an obligation of everyone in society, not as a payment for a social benefit, or of a one-to-one relationship between responsibility and benefit, but because everyone needs society in order to flourish. This goes beyond the notion of reciprocity to a richer notion of social solidarity. Sen captures this broader sense of responsibility when he states

---

[76] W Hutton *The World We're In* (Abacus 2002) 63.
[77] Rawls (n 20 above) 126.

that 'individual freedom is quintessentially a social product, and there is a two-way relation between (1) social arrangements to expand individual freedoms and (2) the use of individual freedoms not only to improve the respective lives but also to make the social arrangements more appropriate and effective'.[78]

The republican view of civic virtue takes a step beyond this. Drawing on the Aristotelian view of the individual as achieving perfection through social and political participation,[79] this approach views social participation as an end in itself, and an essential part of the development of the self.[80] This makes it possible to move away from the spectre that positive freedom for some encroaches on the freedom of others from State interference. Contribution to society is a part of civic virtue and therefore contributes to the development of the self as much as to the development of others.

In essence, civic republicanism re-casts obligation as self-fulfilment. This can be problematic in two related ways. First, self-fulfilment as civic virtue must be conceived of as an objective concept, which can be achieved even if the individual does not consider herself to be fulfilled. This blurs the borderline between freedom and obligation. Even if she feels that she is unfairly burdened or her freedom is wrongly curtailed, the individual is not truly being coerced but is being assisted to be free. Civic republicanism gives too little guidance on how to set limits on individuals' duty to contribute. In Oldfield's words, civic republicanism is 'a hard school of thought... Citizens are called to stern and important tasks which have to do with the very sustaining of their identity.'[81] Secondly, in its pure form, civic republicanism can presume a homogeneity of social purpose which threatens to undermine the pluralism that is essential for a free and active understanding of rights.

Thus, many who support the republican values of community orientation and active citizenship stop short of viewing the duties imposed as obligatory. Lister, for example, distinguishes between being a citizen and acting as one.[82] Citizenship as participation is the expression of human agency; but the citizen should be free to decide against participation without risking withdrawal of her citizenship.[83] The requirement to contribute to society is therefore a moral rather than legal one. As Cohen puts it, while the individual retains her personal prerogative to 'be something other than an engine for the welfare of other people', there is also a personal obligation to have regard to that welfare.[84] The way forward then is to create a society in which individuals value and are valued for the extent to which they fulfil their personal or moral responsibilities to society. Rather than

---

[78] A Sen *Development as Freedom* (OUP Oxford 1999) 31.
[79] Aristotle *Politics* (Random House 1943) Book I ch 3 1253a 19–41.
[80] R Lister *Citizenship: Feminist Perspectives* (2nd edn Palgrave 2003) 13, 15–16.
[81] A Oldfield *Citizenship and Community, Civic Republicanism and the Modern World* (Routledge London 1990) 5.
[82] Lister (n 80 above) 41–42.
[83] ibid 37.
[84] Cohen (n 2 above).

creating material incentives, as Rawls suggests, the positive duties of the State should include the duty to foster a sense of personal and ethical self-fulfilment. However, this leaves open the question of whether or not there should be a compulsory element. It is here that the reformulation of the harm principle to include positive duties is pivotal. It is to this we now turn.

(iii) The harm principle and positive duties

The 'harm principle' is the classic liberal statement of the scope and legitimacy of the State's authority to limit individuals' freedom. As formulated by Mill, it states that government is only entitled to use coercion to restrict one person's individual freedom to prevent her causing harm to another. As we have seen, Raz widens the traditional notion of harm to include failing to improve the situation of another. The primacy of individual autonomy can only be asserted on the basis that autonomy should be equally available to all. Given the rich definition of autonomy used here, failure to promote the autonomy of others in society is just as much a manifestation of harm as intruding on their legitimate area of autonomy. This insight allows us to derive the duty to contribute positively to society directly from the duty not to harm others. Since the State can legitimately restrain individual freedom to the extent that it is causing harm to others, it can justifiably impose duties to contribute in order to ensure that those who are in a position to promote the autonomy of others do in fact do so.

Moreover, Raz argues that it is possible to cause harm even if not to an identifiable person. This decouples responsibility from fault. It is legitimate to impose a responsibility on members of the community to contribute to the promotion of others' autonomy even if the person who has the duty cannot be blamed for harming the person who actually suffered, for example, because the allocation of the loss was determined elsewhere. This in turn means that the State can use coercion to require individuals to take actions which are necessary to improve people's options and opportunities.[85] Thus, he concludes, a government with responsibility to promote autonomy of its citizens is entitled to redistribute resources, and provide public goods on a compulsory basis provided its laws merely reflect and make concrete autonomy-based decisions. If coercion is used to ensure compliance with these laws, it is legitimated by the harm principle as here understood.[86]

The challenge has been to find an understanding of civic responsibility which retains space for differing value judgements and personal autonomy but at the same time legitimates the imposition of compulsory duties on citizens. This can be achieved by a synthesis of the milder version of civic responsibility with the wider account of the harm principle. This synthesis also permits the reconciliation of positive and negative freedom. Once individuals are seen to gain fulfilment by being active members of society, the duty to contribute to society can

---

[85] Raz (n 44 above) 415–417.   [86] ibid.

be viewed as enhancing rather than detracting from the freedom of those who contribute. Secondly, to the extent that it does infringe on negative freedom, the duty to contribute can be seen to be a legitimate limit on negative freedom when that freedom causes harm. By recognizing that harm includes failing to promote another's autonomy, it can be seen that the harm principle legitimates limits on negative freedom in order to promote positive freedom.

E. Conclusion

This chapter has set out the main argument in favour of a conception of human rights which give rise, not just to a duty of restraint on the State, but also to a series of positive duties on the State. This draws on the values implicit in the commitment to human rights: a conception of freedom which entails not just absence of interference with rights, but genuine ability to exercise these rights; a recognition of the role of society and the State in enhancing freedom; and a substantive view of equality which insists that everyone be able to exercise their rights. While the insights of Sen's capabilities theory are central to the positive notion of freedom, it was also argued that individual achievement is not the only value behind human rights. A positive view of human rights as giving rise to positive duties also draws on other human rights values, in particular, those of solidarity and dignity. The chapter also rejected the argument that positive duties require the State to intrude on individuals' moral decisions, arguing that moral neutrality is a myth, but that a commitment to human rights signals a moral commitment by the State which both enables and constrains State action. The framework developed in this chapter does more, however, than support the view that human rights give rise to positive duties. It also gives a set of criteria by which to assess and evaluate the ways in which positive duties are being developed in different arenas, whether judicial or political. Not all positive duties are necessarily acceptable within a human rights framework; only those that specifically advance human rights values.

2

The Nature of the State: Democracy, Globalization, and Privatization

The first chapter argued that human rights give rise to positive duties on the State, without interrogating the nature of the State itself. A closer look at the modern State demonstrates that this approach could be challenged in three different ways. The first arises from the democratic nature of the modern State. There are many who would have no difficulty in accepting the argument that the State has a positive role in facilitating and promoting freedom and equality. They would argue, however, that this is not the function of human rights, but of the democratic process. Given that the democratic State is representative of and accountable to the electorate, the type and extent of intervention by the State in society should be determined by the democratic process and not by human rights pre-commitments. Moreover, if the aim of human rights is to restrain a potentially overwhelming State, then, arguably, this purpose is better achieved by democracy. As Bentham wrote: 'A democracy...has for its characteristic object and effect...securing its members against oppression and depredation at the hands of those functionaries which it employs for its defence.'[1]

The second challenge to the argument for positive duties is concerned with the diminishing strength of the State in the face of globalization. On this view, the imposition on the State of positive duties to secure human rights overestimates the ability of the modern State to make autonomous policy decisions. To impose such duties is either unrealistic and fanciful, or is positively counterproductive, since it makes it impossible for a given country to compete effectively in the world. The third and related challenge is based on the shifting boundaries of the State through privatization and contracting out. Not only does this represent further evidence of the attenuated nature of the State; in addition, the imposition of positive duties on the dwindling State creates a range of anomalies and boundary disputes.

It will be argued in this chapter that far from detracting from democracy, human rights are necessary to constitute and maintain democracy, and that

---

[1] Bentham *Constitutional Code* Bk 1 ch 9 quoted in D Held 'Central Perspectives on the Modern State' in G McLennan, D Held, and S Hall (eds) *The Idea of the Modern State* (Open University Press Milton Keynes 1984) 42.

positive duties on the State are essential to the ensure that human rights fully fulfil this role. Similarly, the argument from globalization strengthens the case for positive human rights obligations. In fact, the trade liberalization regime places obligations of many kinds on individual States, obligations which are enforced internationally to an unprecedented degree. There is no reason why trade obligations should be legitimate but positive duties to secure human rights should be thought to be beyond the capacity of governments. Instead, positive human rights duties are all the more necessary. Finally, privatization and the fragmentation of the State can be addressed through a system of positive obligations which continue to tie private bodies exercising public functions into the human rights regime. In addition, there are clear precedents for imposing equivalent positive obligations on private actors.

A. Positive Duties and Democracy

The statement that the positive function of the State belongs with the democratic process gives the impression that democracy is a clear concept. In fact, both the theory and practice of democracy throughout history have been deeply contested. While all agree that democracy entails participation by the people, the extent and nature of participation is controversial. This is complicated further by the ease with which prescriptive theories are intertwined with descriptive approaches. The practice of democracy generally falls short of democratic aspirations; but does this mean that the practice should be improved or the aspirations modified? This chapter does not attempt to present a fully fledged theory of democracy; but instead to demonstrate that the dichotomy between positive human rights duties and democracy is misconceived. This is because human rights and particularly positive human rights duties are essential to achieve the participation which is at the core of all democratic theories.

(i) Justiciability distinguished

It is very common for the unaccountable or inexpert nature of the courts to be used to support the argument that positive human rights duties are anti-democratic. Waldron, for example, argues that there is no reason why a decision by a majority of nine judges should be given more weight than a decision by a majority of the electorate.[2] Although arguments from democracy and questions of justiciability are indeed closely bound up, it is argued here that they should be kept separate. It is certainly possible to frame human rights and to specify corresponding duties, both negative and positive, without necessarily giving judges the last word on their scope or enforcement. Human rights have an expressive and educational

---

[2] J Waldron *Law and Disagreement* (OUP Oxford 1999) 15.

role, signalling the values a society stands for, regardless of the method for their enforcement. Human rights also constitute a focus for political and grass-roots campaigning, giving a specific and authoritative legitimacy to demands for their fulfilment.

Equally important is their proactive function, guiding political and executive decision-making so that legislation, policy, and administration are formulated to meet human rights demands. Within a 'human rights culture', there is an expectation that legislation and executive action are shaped by the demands of human rights, rather than waiting for complaints of breach. The UK Human Rights Act 1998 (HRA 1998) requires all legislation to be assessed for its human rights compatibility before enactment, and the Secretary of State responsible for any new bill must include a statement of compatibility as part of the legislation.[3] A parliamentary committee scrutinizes all legislation for its potential human rights impact. A different way of stressing the proactive normative role of human rights in decision-making is through the mechanism of directive principles of social policy, as in the Irish and Indian constitutions, which declare that the State is bound to carry out certain duties, but specify that these are not justiciable.

Nor is the courts' role an 'all or nothing' one—courts can have an input into human rights enforcement without having the final say. Under the HRA 1998, for example, courts can make a declaration that legislation is incompatible with the European Convention on Human Rights, but this does not invalidate that legislation. The responsibility returns to Parliament to take further action to comply with its human rights obligations. Finally, there is a range of non-judicial methods of enforcing rights. This chapter therefore aims to consider the democratic legitimacy of human rights as giving rise to positive duties, leaving the question of justiciability to be dealt with in the next chapter.

(ii) 'We the people': participation and democracy

At first glance, the democratic argument against positive human rights duties seems self-evident. In a democracy, it is for the people to decide fundamental issues, without human rights pre-commitments. This is particularly true for positive duties, which inevitably require the State to make distributive allocations. This presumes that the people actually do make such decisions. But in what sense can it be said that democracy means decision-making by the people? The closest to this ideal is the model of direct democracy, derived from the Athenian paradigm, according to which all decisions are directly made by the people, through a majority vote. However, no one would nowadays consider this to be a feasible approach. Even in Classical Greece, it is well known that direct democracy did not include all the people. Women, slaves, and foreigners were all excluded. Even if everyone could be included, it has been questioned whether it is appropriate

[3] HRA 1998, s 19.

to have decision-making by the people with no rights-based constraints. Critics dating as far back as Plato and Aristotle argued that decision-making by the demos is undesirable without further constraints, since the crowd is easily swayed by the passion of the moment, manipulated by opinion-formers and lacking the expertise necessary to make consistent and sustained decisions.[4] Illustrations from ancient Greece to fascist Germany support this view. As MacLennan puts it, 'classical democratic theory never did provide a utopian scenario in which equal citizens actively, knowledgeably and collectively decide upon the rational course of action for their society'.[5]

The modern State necessarily requires representative government, requiring more sophisticated theories to root decision-making in the will of the people. One such is republicanism, which retains sovereignty in the people by insisting that representatives are mandated by voters to carry out certain policies rather than exercising their free judgement.[6] In this way, the vote remains a full equivalent of direct participation in decision-making. As in classical democracy, there is no strict division between the State and civil society; instead, civil society in effect directs government.[7] In its pure form, this approach is problematic for two reasons. First, it is impossible in a complex modern society for the electors to mandate every aspect of policy. Secondly, it depends on what Habermas calls an unrealistic assumption of a citizenry capable of collective action towards a common cause. Presupposing such a common good belies conflicts of interests, a plurality of value systems, and inequalities of power.[8]

The reality of modern democracy is that casting a vote in periodic elections gives barely any real participative power to individual voters. But does this mean, as Schumpeter argues, that representative democracy inevitably entails 'rule by elites'? Schumpeter regards the demos as too inexpert, uninterested, or ill-informed to make detailed governmental decisions. Instead, he characterizes democracy as a process of elite teams seeking popular endorsement by any means at their disposal. Power is exercised by a coalition of elites, with relative autonomy of decision-making between elections. Participation by ordinary people is necessarily tenuous, and even accountability is attenuated, since 'popular opinion' is as much shaped by political representatives as a response to it. The voices of the media, big business, and other powerful bodies drown out that of ordinary people.

Schumpeter's description of democracy is depressingly close to our current experience. Nevertheless, the aspiration of popular participation remains a valid one. One potential alternative to Schumpeter's view is that of political pluralists.

---

[4] See Plato *The Republic* (Penguin Harmondsworth 1974) 282; Held (n 1 above) 19–27.
[5] G McLennan 'Capitalist state or democratic polity?' in Held (n 1 above) 82.
[6] There are many formulations of republicanism; this is just one aspect of it. See CR Sunstein 'Beyond the Republican Revival' [1988] 97 Yale Law Journal 1539.
[7] D Held *Models of Democracy* (3rd edn Stanford University Press Stanford 2006) 268–269.
[8] J Habermas *Between Facts and Norms* (Polity Press 1997) 300.

Pluralists agree that individuals on their own cannot exercise real power in modern democracies. Nevertheless, individuals can effectively augment their power and achieve real political participation by combining into interest groups. Thus, political pluralists recast democracy as a process of negotiation and contest between organized interest groups for power. It is democratic in that any group should be able to protect itself by entering into the give and take of the political marketplace. Oligarchy and rule by elite is avoided because alliances are continually reconfigured, ensuring that power is not concentrated for too long in any particular set of elites.

Political pluralism is premised first on the assumption that individuals are able to organize around common interests, and secondly, on the possibility of equality of access by different interest groups. As a descriptive model, it is clearly inaccurate. Concentrations of wealth and power inevitably skew the decision-making process in favour of interest groups made up of those with power in society. It is a short distance between this and Schumpeter's description of rule by elites. For a pluralist model to be democratic, the background requirements for fair bargaining require that all parties have equal opportunities to influence each other.

This tendency to reinforce concentrations of power and inequalities among various competing groups is now readily acknowledged[9] and the need for balancing measures accepted. However, even if equality of bargaining power could be achieved, political pluralism is a limited model. This is because it assumes that all political cooperation takes the form of interest bargaining. Habermas usefully distinguishes between 'interest governed' and 'value-oriented' coordination. Interest bargaining is communication for the purpose of forcing or inducing the opponent to accept one's claim. Success depends on factual power rather than on good reasons or the power of the better argument. Interest bargaining presupposes that each person's or group's interests are fixed and unchangeable; and the solution is either victory, surrender, or compromise. This contrasts with coordination based on values. Instead of factual power, such coordination is based on the ability to adduce reasons which can convince all the parties. The parties enter the process aiming to justify their position by appeal to reasons that all parties can accept, and willing to be persuaded by arguments put forward by other parties. In place of defeat or victory, therefore, coordination takes place through rationally motivated consensus.[10]

The desire to increase the role of value coordination over interest bargaining is reflected in the recent surge of interest in deliberative democracy. Democratic decision-making, on this view, is a situation in which citizens 'share a commitment to the resolution of problems of collective choice through public reasoning'.[11]

---

[9] JH Ely *Democracy and Distrust: A Theory of Judicial Review* (Harvard University Press 1980) 135.

[10] Habermas (n 7 above) 139–40, 165.

[11] J Cohen 'Deliberation and Democratic Legitimacy' in A Hamlin and P Pettit (eds) *The Good Polity* (Blackwell Oxford 1989) 22.

Deliberative democracy contests the assumption that preferences are fully formed prior to the political process. Arguing that preferences are heavily influenced by social circumstances, theorists in this school conclude that the process of decision-making can itself play a central part in shaping those premises. This in turn means that initial preferences may be revised in the course of deliberation in a way which encompasses not only one's own perspective, but also those of other members of an association. Deliberation enables participants to see the extent to which their preferences are adaptations to their own limited circumstances.[12]

Nor is the aim of the process simply to reach a compromise or to aggregate those preferences. Instead, the aim is to arrive at a decision which is capable of being justified by reasons which participants sincerely expect to be persuasive to others. Attempting to justify a position by resorting to self-interest alone is unlikely to be successful. In addition, taking the deliberative commitment seriously requires a willingness to revise one's own preferences and convictions.[13] This is particularly true for preferences which a participant discovers cannot be justified. The result is to open up the possibility of resolving disagreements by reasoned persuasion. Moving from a bargaining model to a deliberative model therefore requires a substitution of interest-governed action by value-oriented action. Particularly important is the function of disciplining political representatives, by requiring them to justify decisions by reference to the public interest, not to preferences (their own or voters) which could be distorted or self-seeking.[14] At the same time, deliberative democracy is postulated as being a pluralistic association, whose members have diverse preferences, convictions, and ideals. Apart from sharing a commitment to deliberative democracy itself, participants need not share a conception of the good.[15] This in turn necessitates explicit discussion of what values should be the basis of community aspirations.[16]

Habermas draws on these insights to develop his discourse theory of democracy. He aims to transcend the liberal view of the democratic process as exclusively a form of compromise among interests. At the same time, he does not follow the republican view of democratic will formation as a process of discovering the common ethical community. For Habermas, the key lies in the procedure of communication, rather than in a prior commitment to a particular ethical or universal ideology. Democracy requires procedures and conditions aimed to guarantee a flow of communication between informally developed public opinion, on the one hand, and legislative and executive institutions on the other. Through these procedures, the influence of communicative power is transformed into legislation which in turn shapes administrative power. Thus, democracy goes beyond the legitimation of the exercise of political power to include the programming of political power. At the same time, given the need for action and expertise,

[12] ibid 27.   [13] Cohen (n 11 above) 25–26.
[14] Sunstein (n 6 above).   [15] Cohen (n 11 above) 23.
[16] ibid 24.

he recognizes that the communicative structure cannot rule itself, but acts as a network of sensors which point administrative power in the right direction. In this way, he retains the distinction between the State and civil society, which republicanism merges.

The deliberative democracy approach is not without its difficulties, both in principle and in practice. In particular, it is difficult to see how consensus can always be achieved through deliberation, and at what point closure is declared. One way forward is to use Sunstein's notion of incompletely theorized agreements. This involves distinguishing between different levels of agreement. People might disagree at one level of abstraction, but agree on a more particular application. This allows agreement on outcomes without agreeing on the most general theory that accounts for it. There may be no need to achieve consensus on the fundamental principle if the outcome can be agreed.[17] For example, people might agree on a redistributive policy because they believe in charity for the poor, or because they believe that property is theft, or because they believe in equality. This may work in both directions: there may be general consensus on the principle but not on the particular application; in which case, the principle could be agreed and the specification left for another time. Sunstein sets out a series of benefits of incompletely theorized agreements about constitutional principles and cases. Most important is the background value of mutual respect: even if there is no detailed agreement, people agree on the need for reciprocity, harmony, and respect. Such agreements reduce the political cost of enduring disagreements, while at the same time allowing the consensus to evolve over time.

Incompletely theorized agreement modifies deliberative democracy to the extent that, in putting forward their reasons, participants are not aiming to convince others of the soundness of their reasons, but only of their plausibility, so that the background value of mutual respect permits agreement to be reached. Even in this form, however, it is clearly unrealistic to expect that all decision-making fulfils the criteria of deliberative democracy. Instead, the insights of deliberative democracy fulfil the more partial function of acting as a discipline on decision-makers. Deliberative democracy requires decision-makers to justify their decisions by reference to reasons that all can regard as sound, even if they cannot command a consensus. Thus, self-seeking or biased reasons are flushed out and regarded as unacceptable.[18] Similarly, reasoned persuasion might still have a role in the context of a debate in which more than one reasoned solution is possible. In such a case, majority voting may be necessary. But this does not mean that the majority votes simply to advance its own personal interests. Instead, it is a way of deciding between various reasonable alternatives on the basis of the numbers of those who find one set of reasons more persuasive than another. In such cases, even if consensus cannot be achieved, it is possible to

---

[17] CR Sunstein *Designing Democracy What Constitutions Do* (OUP Oxford 2001) 50–65.
[18] CR Sunstein 'Beyond the Republican Revival' [1988] 97 Yale Law Journal 1539.

establish a reasonable set of policies which cannot be bargained away through the use of factual power.

At the same time, deliberative procedures will always co-exist alongside interest bargaining. Habermas concedes that in complex societies, it is often the case that interests are sufficiently diverse that consensus is not possible.[19] In such cases, resort must be had either to majority voting or to bargaining between success-oriented parties who are willing to cooperate. Similarly, Sunstein describes the legislative process as a continuum, at one pole of which interest group pressures are determinative, while at the other end, legislators engage in deliberation in which interest group pressures play little or no role. Along the continuum, outcomes depend on an amalgam of pressure, deliberation, and other factors.[20] Even for those decisions in which interest bargaining is unavoidable, deliberative procedures are necessary to establish the background procedural requirements. This is particularly important to ensure that all interested parties are provided with equal opportunities to influence one another.[21]

Thus far, the discussion has been concerned with democratic participation in what Held calls its 'protective' sense, that is, aiming to prevent domination by a single group or ruler. Recently, there has been a renewed focus on democracy from a 'developmental' perspective, where participation is not just a means to an end, but is part of the self-fulfilment of citizens. This has reawakened interest in the developmental perspective of the republican tradition, which, as we saw in Chapter 1, regards rule by the people as the fulfilling of civic virtue through taking part in the activities of the State. For republicans, the political good can only be achieved through political interaction and deliberation. Its key aim is to revitalize the public sphere,[22] reversing the trend towards, in Arendt's views, the drab 'substitution of [politics by] bureaucracy, the rule of nobody, for personal rulership'.[23] Freedom is not the same as licence; freedom consists as much in not being subject to others as in not dominating others.

(iii) Enhancing democracy through positive duties

The above discussion has suggested that modern democracies are a complex amalgam of individual representation, interest group bargaining, and deliberative procedures. Against this background, it becomes clear that to counterpoise democracy with human rights is a false contradiction. Instead, positive human rights duties should be recognized as necessary to constitute democracy and ensure that it functions properly. As a start, positive duties are necessary to ensure

---

[19] Habermas (n 7 above) 166.
[20] CR Sunstein 'Interest Groups in American Public Law' (1985) 38 Stanford Law Review 29, 48–49.
[21] Habermas (n 7 above) 166.
[22] ibid 300.
[23] H Arendt *The Human Condition* (2nd edn University of Chicago Press Chicago 1998) 45.

that elections take place and individuals are free to vote. In addition, the State may need to take positive steps to protect individuals against other individuals' interference with the right. The existence of a universal suffrage does not mean that everyone can in fact exercise their rights, as the de facto disenfranchisement of people of colour in the US before the Civil Rights Act demonstrates.

Even when blatant exclusionary practices are not in place, it is clear that, as Rawls acknowledged, social and economic inequalities in a modern democratic State are so large that those with greater wealth and position usually control political life and enact legislation and social policies that advance their interests.[24] Even more to the point is TH Marshall's approach. For him, political citizenship is not sufficient. To ensure full and democratic citizenship, it is necessary to go beyond liberal and political rights, to the granting of social rights. These in turn enlist the positive contribution of the State.[25] Nor is it sufficient to resort to collective organization, as the pluralists would have it. Interest group bargaining inevitably entrenches existing balances of power. Therefore, to the extent that decision-making is a result of interest bargaining among groups in society, democracy can only be sustained if there is a positive duty on the State to ensure that all are equally able to exercise their democratic rights and participate in society.

The same is true for deliberative democracy. To secure the conditions for effective exercise of deliberative democracy, participants must be both formally and substantively equal. This in turn means that the distribution of power and resources should not obstruct their chances to contribute to deliberation.[26] All of these require positive input from the State to create the appropriate arenas for deliberation. Cohen sees it as central to a deliberative model of democracy that the existence of such arenas should be considered a public good to be funded by public money, not because this is the most efficient way to do it, but because it expresses the 'basic commitment of a democratic order to the resolution of political questions through free deliberation among equals'.[27] To the extent that deliberative democracy is thought to be desirable, there is a clear role for human rights duties to facilitate deliberation, and to channel decision-making away from interest bargaining towards deliberation. It will be argued in Chapter 4 that judicial reasoning constitutes a hybrid of deliberation and rights-based decision-making, which together reinforce the role of deliberation and lessen that of interest bargaining in the application and development of the law.

Thus all the models of democracy discussed here, namely political pluralism, deliberative democracy, and developmental democracy, have elements of both

[24] J Rawls *Justice as Fairness* (Harvard University Press Cambridge Massachusetts 2001) 148–150.
[25] TH Marshall 'Citizenship and Social Class' in TH Marshall and T Bottomore (eds) *Citizenship and Social Class* (Pluto 1992) 7.
[26] Cohen (n 11 above) 23.
[27] ibid 25.

description and aspiration. Each reflects a partial reality of modern democracies, but none are fully realized. It is to bridge the gap between the description and the aspiration that positive human rights duties can play a role. The detailed nature of this role will be developed throughout this book.

B. Globalization and Positive Duties

The discussion so far may seem utopian in the face of a globalized world, which signals both the diminishing ability of the State to make autonomous decisions, and the supremacy of utilitarian trade-based values over human rights. It is argued here, however, that globalization strengthens the argument in favour of positive human rights duties, rather than undermining it. This is because globalization should not be seen as an end in itself, but only as a means of enhancing welfare, where welfare is not simply defined in consumerist and utilitarian terms, but in the deeper sense understood in this book. It has to be acknowledged that globalization itself is not reversible. It therefore needs to be firmly directed towards actually enhancing welfare. But it can only do so if combined with strong governance by States and international institutions which regard themselves as bound to implement human rights obligations and not just trade and free-market imperatives.

To develop this argument, it is necessary first to specify what is meant by globalization. The salient characteristic of globalization is the drive towards liberalization of trade and capital markets through the lifting of regulatory barriers. Facilitated by the explosion of information technology, globalization has led to the opening up of new trading markets as well as an unprecedented movement of capital across national boundaries. With this has come the growth of increasingly powerful transnational actors. Multinational corporations, with more economic power than many individual States, are able to use their new-found mobility to exercise considerable political pressure on national governments anxious to attract and maintain inward investment. This freedom of movement of capital has not been matched by equivalent freedom of movement of labour. Not only have immigration restrictions remained in place, in addition, people do not necessarily consider themselves as simply units of labour, able to move from their families and culture to new places of work.

Also of key importance has been the creation of new transnational modes of governance, with increasing power to intervene in domestic policies. Trade liberalization operates through the medium of multilateral treaties, such as the well known General Agreement on Tariffs and Trade (GATT). At first, the focus was on reducing tariffs or import taxes. However, as GATT became more successful at lowering border tariffs, domestic policies with indirect trade implications became a growing preoccupation. Subsidies, dumping (selling products at below cost to gain market share),[28] and technical barriers to trade[29] quickly came within its purview. In 1995, the GATT was transferred to a permanent institution, the World Trade Organization (WTO). The WTO claims to stand for a trading system which is free, predictable, and competitive: free in that barriers should come down through negotiation; predictable in that foreign companies, investors, and governments should be confident that trade barriers (including tariffs and non-tariff barriers) should not be raised arbitrarily; and more competitive by discouraging 'unfair' practices such as export subsidies and dumping.[30] It has an even wider remit than the GATT, including services,[31] intellectual property rights,[32] government procurement,[33] and investment measures.[34] Unlike the broad approach of the original GATT, WTO agreements generally take the form of a detailed legal code. The WTO has its own disputes procedure, with power to give binding interpretations of the relevant treaties. A finding that a provision has been breached triggers the right to retaliate against the offending party. Whereas under the old GATT, rulings of the dispute panels required adoption by the membership of the organization, the WTO dispute procedure is binding, unless opposed by consensus of the membership.[35]

Globalization is not intrinsically opposed to human rights. Recognizing that a free market cannot operate in situations of autocratic power, the globalization ideology endorses democratic rights and freedoms which restrain State action. However, by the same token, positive human rights duties on the State are an anathema. This opposition to positive duties has been articulated in three ways. The first derives from the powerful free market ideology which drives globalization. Secondly, it is claimed that the free market is the best means of enhancing human welfare. Positive human rights duties are said to obstruct the process of globalization and therefore make things worse for the very people they set out to protect. The third and more pragmatic argument is that globalization has weakened the power of the State to take autonomous decisions, and therefore it is unrealistic to expect the institution of positive human rights duties. Each will be dealt with in turn.

---

[28] 'Dumping' refers to the act of a manufacturer in one country exporting a product to another country at a price which is either below the price it charges in its home market or is below its costs of production.

[29] R Howse and M Mutua 'Protecting Human Rights in a Global Economy: Challenges for the World Trade Organisation" International Centre for Human Rights and Democratic Development, Policy Paper 6.

[30] See <http://www.wto.org/>.

[31] General Agreement on Trade in Services (GATS).

[32] Trade-Related Aspects of Intellectual Property Rights (TRIPS).

[33] This is one of only two optional agreements: the others are obligatory.

[34] Trade-Related Investment Measures (TRIMS).

[35] Rulings are subject to appeal to a standing appellate body. Note that only governments can bring disputes to the WTO Dispute Settlement Body.

(i) The 'free market' and positive duties

Globalization is driven by a free-market ideology which regards State intervention as an obstruction of freedom and an impediment to the proper workings of the market. Globalization therefore by its nature seems to militate against positive human rights duties. However, the claim that the free market requires absence from State intervention is only superficially credible. Outside of pure rhetoric, there are few who believe that a spontaneous market free of regulation is a real possibility. Not only is there a need for enforceable laws of contract and property, regulation is also necessary to protect competitive markets from monopolistic tendencies. Moreover, markets are known to function better with the input of public goods, not just in the form of transport, infrastructure, and information technology but also in training, health provision, and education.[36] Yet competitive markets themselves do not provide such public goods: indeed, globalization has led to a fiscal squeeze, which in turn has made it difficult for governments to provide the very goods necessary for a well-functioning market.[37] The paradoxical truth is that a 'free market' can only be created and sustained with a high degree of regulation. The choice is therefore not between regulation and non-regulation, but between different kinds of regulation. Proponents of the free market in the global arena cannot consistently argue against positive human rights duties on the grounds that they constitute State interference with the market. They can only disagree with the kind of intervention.

The contradictions within the position of free-market advocates are even more conspicuous at international level. As a start, free-market ideology is not applied evenly or consistently through the WTO. The former World Bank Chief Economist Joseph Stiglitz described the pattern whereby: 'As developing countries take steps to expand their exports and open their economies, they . . . quickly run up against dumping duties (when no economist would say they are really engaged in dumping) or they face protected or restricted markets in their areas of natural comparative advantage, such as agriculture or textiles.'[38] More fundamentally, as Brazilian President Enrique Cardoso argues, it is a serious mistake to think of globalization as the result of market forces alone: 'The boundaries within which the market operates are defined *politically*, in direct negotiations between governments in multilateral forums, such as the World Trade Organization. *The power game is always present in such negotiations*.'[39]

---

[36] See, for example, S Deakin and J Browne 'Social Rights and Market Order: Adapting the Capability Approach' in T Hervey and J Kenner (eds) *Economic and Social Rights under the EU Charter of Fundamental Rights* (Hart Oxford 2003).

[37] United Nations Development Programme *Human Development Report 1999* (OUP Oxford 1999).

[38] J Stiglitz 'Trade and the Developing Work: A New Agenda' *Current History* (November 1999) 387.

[39] FE Cardoso 'Globalization and International Relations: Public Address to the South African Institute of International Affairs' (Johannesburg 26 November 1996) 5–6, cited in J Oloka-Onyanga

Even if it were consistently applied, the free-market ideology has been repeatedly shown to be self-destructing unless carefully regulated. Instead, strong governance is essential for a globalized market to function. This was demonstrated in 1997, when the sudden and massive capital outflow from the 'Asian tiger' economies[40] led to a financial crisis with serious long-term repercussions. Having opened their economies in 1990, these countries experienced rapid growth, including capital inflows of as much as $93bn. In 1997, this was reversed overnight, with an outflow of $12bn, constituting 11% of GDP. The Human Development Report of 2000 argues that this was not an isolated incident, but is a systemic feature of globalized capital markets, which can lead to rapid build-ups and reversals of short-term capital flows with little clear logic or predictability beyond the whim of the market. The report concludes that one of the chief problems was that there were not sufficient structures of governance in place. Instead, the expansion of the market outpaced governance.[41]

The claim that globalization requires non-intervention is further contradicted by the WTO itself. The WTO is far from a hands-off institution. It has created a tight system of international regulation which is unprecedented in its reach and effectiveness. It has powers to intervene in the decision-making powers of sovereign States on issues which may impact on trade, but also have many other social functions. For example, the TRIPS[42] agreement introduced in 1995 requires States to have in place legislation permitting the registration of patents which give exclusive intellectual property rights over inventions to those claiming to have invented them. Developing countries, many of which had no intellectual property laws, were given five years (to 2000) to introduce such laws, extended to 2016 for pharmaceutical patents. This has constituted a highly intrusive regulatory mechanism, particularly in respect of drugs combating the AIDS virus. Countries such as Brazil and India, which had produced cheap generic forms of these drugs to combat the rapid spread of the virus in their populations, have come under increasing pressure to register patents, which would exponentially increase the price of the drugs. Such interventionism is true too of the other Bretton Woods institutions, namely the World Bank and the International Monetary Fund. Through making financial aid and loans conditional on the implementation of economic policies dictated by the institution, both these bodies exercised overwhelming powers over developing States. Yet none of these institutions is democratic or accountable.

It cannot therefore credibly be argued that globalization stands for de-regulation. Regulation is a necessary feature of a stable market economy, whether domestic or global. What is at issue is the type of regulation. The

and D Udagama 'The Realisation of Economic, Social and Cultural Rights: Globalisation and Its Impact on the Full Enjoyment of Human Rights' (Preliminary Report submitted to the United Nations Economic and Social Council, E/CN.4/Sub.2/2000/13, June 2000) para 7.

[40] Thailand, Indonesia, Malaysia, South Korea, and the Philippines.
[41] *Human Development Report* (n 37 above) 2–3.
[42] Trade Related Aspects of Intellectual Property Rights.

current regulatory structure includes the imposition of a range of positive duties on Member States, but these are of a kind which can fundamentally damage basic human rights, both in the sense of infringing on the democratic rights of the people to decide their own governance and by interfering with their substantive freedom to be and do what they have reason to value. TRIPS in particular imposes duties on States to protect corporate bodies' property rights, at the expense of the duty to protect and fulfil the rights to life and health of human subjects. There is no reason why rights to property and trade should trump other rights, nor why regulation should be permitted in order to promote trade and not to promote human rights. Indeed, the international community has made higher order commitments to human rights, which include the duty to secure those rights to all individuals. This requires the whole range of duties: the duty to respect rights by refraining from interfering with them, to protect rights against multinationals and other private parties, and to facilitate and fulfil rights directly.

(ii) Free global markets are the best means to advance human welfare

Even if it is conceded that regulation is necessary in a globalized market, there is a second way in which advocates of globalization argue against positive human rights duties. This is the familiar claim that the free market is the best means of enhancing human welfare. Human rights, on this view, are only desirable to the extent that they advance the globalization project. While duties of restraint arising from human rights may well fulfil this criterion, State intervention through positive duties is costly, artificially elevates labour costs above market value, and prevents companies from competing on equal terms with others in the globalized world who are not subject to such regulation. Positive human rights duties therefore obstruct the process of globalization and make things worse for the very people they set out to protect.

There are two aspects to this claim. The first is that globalization on its own advances human welfare. The second is that positive human rights duties impede such advances. Neither of these withstands closer scrutiny. The claim that globalization on its own advances human welfare achieves coherence largely because of its specific definition of welfare as the satisfaction of individual preferences. Such preferences are treated as fixed and beyond interrogation on the ostensible grounds that they are an expression of the individual's right to choose. However, they are predominantly defined in market terms. The result is that welfare is simply equated with the availability of a wider range of consumer goods and services. As one commentator puts it:

Why do multinationals want to spread all over the world? . . . they do it so that you and I can walk down the street and buy a cheaper car. We can talk about other social preferences, and we can use fancy Latin describing why we do it. But each and everyone of us goes and buys the cheapest car...We are each of us the agents of globalisation, because we are the consumers.[43]

Equally problematic is the assumption that welfare should be measured according to a utilitarian calculus, which gives an average per capita score derived from the greatest good for the greatest number. The same commentator sums up this method as follows: 'The gains from trade...by having things produced where they can be produced most cheaply and by allocating them to the people who want them more, result in an increase in global welfare. That means there is more money available for us to buy more things and if we don't want to buy things, then we can buy leisure.'[44] But who are 'we'? This reflects the familiar flaw in utilitarian measurement, namely, that as long as it maximizes the welfare of the greatest number, it is irrelevant that some bear a disproportionate burden of the cost. By simply aggregating the benefits across a whole population, distributional inequalities are obscured.

It is to address these flaws that Sen created his capabilities analysis. Welfare is not simply defined in terms of uncontested consumer preference. Instead, welfare should reflect the extent of substantive freedom by increasing the range of feasible options. This means that average income is an unsatisfactory way of measuring welfare: the same income can bring very different sets of functionings to different individuals depending on social factors such as access to education and health, personal factors such as disability, parenthood, or age, and environmental factors such as climatic conditions. Welfare needs therefore to measure a range of factors in addition to per capita GDP.

Once this more sensitive understanding of welfare is applied, it can be seen that globalization on its own does not achieve the claimed advances in human welfare. As evidence of the effects of globalization mount up, it has become clear that it has not resulted in the expected convergence of the poorer countries with their richer counterparts. Instead, globalization has been accompanied by increases in inequality both between countries and within countries.[45] As Jeffrey Sachs concluded in 2000, 'globalisation by itself hardly guarantees that much of the developing world will be able to achieve rapid economic growth'.[46] Some countries might benefit from the capital inflows and access to technologies and markets made possible by globalization, but others are unable to reap such benefits, because they are too geographically isolated, too subject to diseases, or too dependent on a few principal commodities. Measures necessary to achieve change depend on the particular economy. However, in all cases, the need for strong positive input from the State is identified by Sachs as a primary

[43] M Warner 'Globalisation and Human Rights: An Economic Model' [1999] 25 Brooklyn Journal of International Law 99, 99, 100–101.

[44] ibid 101.

[45] *Human Development Report* 1999 (n 37 above).

[46] J Sachs 'Globalisation and Patterns of Economic Development' [2000] 136 Weltwirtschaftliches Archiv/Review of World Economics 579, 597.

measure. Countries with high population growth require a major investment in improved public health and education, especially for girls. Countries dependent on primary commodity exports need major investments in human capital to make diversification profitable. Economically isolated countries need substantial investment in transport and communications infrastructure.[47] In effect then, far from retarding development, positive State intervention is necessary to facilitate and advance it.

More problematically, still, there are aspects of globalization that clearly impede human welfare. The TRIPS agreement is a case in point. Rather than permitting free competition to bring down prices, the TRIPS agreement protects intellectual property rights so that prices are kept high. The ostensible reason is to protect the incentive on major companies to continue to conduct research and development and thereby to produce new drugs. However, it has been shown that the profits received far outstrip the investment in research and development; less protection would hardly stifle ongoing innovation.[48]

The argument that positive human rights duties impede globalization also assumes that rights associated with positive duties are necessarily inefficient. Against this are increasingly persuasive bodies of argument demonstrating that such regulation, far from undermining competition, is a valuable aspect of comparative advantage. Social rights such as labour rights can contribute to efficiency by encouraging investment in workers' human capital, giving workers the necessary framework for committed, productive, and where necessary, innovative work.[49] Hepple concludes that different national labour laws impose no competitive disadvantage where they enhance the efficiency of the employment relationship.[50] More generally, it is clear that well-educated, well-nourished, and self-respecting individuals will contribute to development; and this is particularly true of gender equality. Positive human rights duties should not therefore be dismissed on the ground that they obstruct development.

Demonstrating that rights can be productive factors is an important contribution to the ideological battle for positive human rights in the face of globalization. However, this insight should not lead to the conclusion that rights are merely instrumental, in the sense that they are only legitimate if they can be proved to be 'productive'. This risks inverting the means–end relationship: globalization is seen as the end and human rights as merely the means to ensuring that trade is in fact liberalized and that capital can move freely. This leads inevitably to a bias in favour of negative duties. It is crucial to reassert that

---

[47] ibid 598–599.

[48] E Cameron *Witness to AIDS* (IB Tauris & Co London, New York 2005).

[49] S Deakin and F Wilkinson *The Law of the Labour Market* (OUP Oxford 2005); S Deakin and J Browne 'Social Rights and Market Order: Adapting the Capability Approach' in T Hervey and J Kenner (eds) *Economic and Social Rights under the EU Charter of Fundamental Rights* (Hart Oxford 2003).

[50] B Hepple *Labour Laws and Global Trade* (Hart Oxford 2005) 256.

globalization is no more than an instrument to advance human welfare in the sense understood by Sen and developed in Chapter 1. Where it does not achieve those goals, it should be modified and limited. Rights, on the other hand are an aspect of human welfare.

(iii) The hollowing out of the State

The final argument against positive human rights duties does not contest the worth of positive duties, but instead argues that the State has been so undermined by globalization that it is unable to bear such a burden. The threat of a flight of capital means that the State cannot, even if it wished to, insist on securing human rights if this is perceived to go against the interests of big business. The State's weakness is underscored by the unprecedented strengthening of international trade regulation through the WTO. International trade law prohibits States from taking a wide range of economic and regulatory decisions which might have the effect of protecting domestic businesses from exposure to international competition. This is particularly problematic where this prohibition incorporates non-trade-related decisions which are construed as having indirect protectionist effects. This includes providing public subsidies or promoting public health.

This argument has been used extensively to oppose social rights generally. Given the ease with which companies can relocate, outsource, or move to capital-intensive production, it is claimed to be utopian to suggest more regulation. Many have predicted a regulatory race to the bottom, as States dismantle their employment protection, social security, and environmental regulation in order to compete in a globalized world. However, evidence shows that international competitiveness does not depend on absence of positive State programmes. In fact, the bulk of capital movement is from one high-income country to another.[51] This is no coincidence. According to the World Bank:

countries with better investment climates—as indicated by the level of corruption, voice (political openness), rule of law, quality of regulatory regime, government effectiveness and political stability—tended to receive an increasing share of total foreign direct investment (FDI) over the 1990s.[52]

Particularly important is the finding that, as Wolf explains:

the great bulk of direct investment continues to go to countries with high labour costs and strong regulatory regimes. But these are more than offset, in the eyes of investors, by the benefits of political stability, personal security, excellent institutions, highly skilled workers and large markets.[53]

---

[51] M Wolf *Why Globalization Works* (Yale Nota Bene New Haven and London 2004) 114–115, 242, 233.
[52] World Bank *Globalisation, Growth and Poverty: Building an Inclusive World Economy* (2002) 118–119.
[53] Wolf (n 51 above) 233.

Conversely, unregulated economies do not offer either the public goods or the merit goods necessary for modern industry, including infrastructure, skill, properly regulated financial markets, and the social stability necessary for safe investment. Low wage costs often mean low productivity, so that only highly labour intensive industries, using unskilled labour, will seek out the cheapest labour. As soon as productivity rises and labour markets tighten, these industries move on.[54]

Nor has there been a race to the bottom. Instead, high-income countries have maintained or strengthened their comparative advantage and there remains considerable variation in detail of both regulatory and welfare provision across different jurisdictions.[55] Although the exponential growth of the welfare state has stabilized, it remains in a 'steady state'.[56] There is also clear evidence that countries do not gain a competitive advantage by attempting to undercut each other through the removal of social rights. Thus, Hall and Soskice argue, nations prosper, not by becoming more similar, but by building on their 'comparative institutional advantage'.[57] Companies rarely make decisions to relocate simply on the basis of the cheapness of labour: labour may be cheap because it is unproductive, and if it is cheap but productive, market forces will soon drive up wages to their market value. Comparative advantage also entails the provision of public goods and cultural and community values.

The demands of globalized free trade do not therefore constitute a good reason for opposing the possibility of regarding human rights as imposing positive duties on the State to protect, promote, and fulfil those rights. States which fulfil their positive human rights duties can be seen to maintain their comparative advantage, to attract inward investment, and to enhance the welfare of the citizens. This does not dictate any particular economic or political strategy for carrying out such duties. It merely makes the point that, rather than viewing positive human rights duties as unobtainable in a globalized world, such duties should be seen as a necessary part of such a world.

(iv) The WTO and human rights

More threatening to the possibility of positive human rights duties are the rules of the WTO. The WTO regime clearly has the potential to interfere seriously with the ability of Member States to pursue positive human rights duties where this is construed as interfering with free trade. This can be seen by examining the

---

[54] ibid 179.

[55] F Castles, *The Future of the Welfare State* (OUP Oxford 2004); Wolf (n 51 above); P Hall and D Soskice 'An Introduction to Varieties of Capitalism' in P Hall and D Soskice (eds) *Varieties of Capitalism: The Institutional Foundations of Comparative Advantage* (OUP Oxford 2001); Hepple (n 50 above) 252.

[56] Castles (n 55 above) 157.

[57] Hall and Soskice (n 55 above) 60.

two central principles of the WTO. The first is that a country should not discriminate between its trading partners. This is known as the most favoured nation principle, because it requires a country to give all its trading partners equal 'most-favoured-nation' (MFN) status.[58] Secondly, once foreign goods have entered the market of a Member State, the State should not discriminate between its own and foreign products, services, or nationals. This is known as the national treatment principle, because it requires countries to give foreign goods the national treatment which domestic goods are given.[59] The prohibition on discrimination is not confined to express discrimination. It also refers to indirect effects of domestic policy. An example would be a requirement that companies use products of domestic origin. Although this applies to all companies, whether foreign or local, it would in practice be more difficult for foreign companies to comply. Similarly, a policy restricting access to foreign exchange would make it more difficult to import products. Thus, Mauritius has argued that enforcement of WTO trade rules undermines its duty to provide guaranteed access to adequate food in pursuance of the right to be free from hunger.[60]

Even more interventionist is the agreement on intellectual property, TRIPS. TRIPS has directly impinged on the ability of States not only to decide their own patenting regime, but also to pursue important policies in promotion of the rights to life, health, and food. We have already seen how the duty to fulfil the right to life through the provision of medical care is threatened by the patenting requirements of TRIPS. The scale of the problem was recognized to some extent in the Doha agreement of 2001 which permits countries to issue a compulsory licence, permitting the production of drugs despite a patent, if the drug treats any disease causing a severe health emergency in the country, or if the patent owner abuses its rights, for example, by offering the product at a price too high for potential buyers to afford. However, even this apparent lightening of the regulatory stranglehold is far from uncomplicated, as both Brazil and Thailand discovered when exercising their rights to issue compulsory licences in 2006 and 2007. In these cases, multinationals threatened to cut off investment to the country in question unless the licence was revoked.[61] Similarly, in 2001, 39 major pharmaceutical companies tried to prosecute the South African government for passing a law which they claim breached TRIPS regulations because it allowed easy production and importation of generics, principally in order to deal with the AIDS pandemic that devastated the country. Fortunately, international pressure forced them to back down, but the risks remain.

---

[58] General Agreement on Tariffs and Trade (GATT), Article 1; General Agreement on Trade in Services (GATS), Article 2; Agreement on Trade-Related Aspects of Intellectual Property Rights (TRIPS), Article 4.

[59] GATT, Article 3; GATS, Article 17; TRIPS, Article 3.

[60] Document G/AG/NG/W/36/Rev.1; G Marceau 'WTO Dispute Settlement and Human Rights' (2002) 13 European Journal of International Law 753 text to footnote 111.

[61] See generally Oloka-Onyanga and Udagama (n 39 above).

A particularly problematic example of the potential of WTO law to interfere with positive duties arising from human rights relates to the duty to promote equality. This can be seen in relation to the South African Black Economic Empowerment (BEE) legislation. A central plank of the South African government's strategy of transformation has been to promote economic empowerment and particularly to achieve a representative share in the economy for the black majority who were forcibly excluded during the apartheid era. There is a range of strategies but chief among them are preferential procurement and investment in enterprises that are owned or managed by black people.[62] A detailed scorecard has been produced which rates a business according to its black empowerment achievements.[63] Businesses are rated according to criteria which include the extent of black ownership, management control, and employment equity. Every organ of state and public entity must take the scorecard into account and apply it as far as is reasonably possible, in determining qualification criteria for the issuing of licences or other authorizations; for the sale of State-owned enterprises; and for developing criteria for entering into partnerships with the private sector.[64]

Notably BEE is not just based on considerations of equity. It also expressly aims to enhance market efficiency. The preamble to the Broad Based Black Economic Empowerment Act of 2003 declares that the exclusion of the vast majority of South Africans from ownership of productive assets and the possession of advanced skills has led to the under-performance of the economy. Steps to increase effective participation are necessary for the future prosperity of all South Africans, irrespective of race. This virtuous combination of efficiency and equity within a positive human rights framework should not be open to challenge by those seeking only self-interest through international trade law.

Nevertheless, there is a risk of challenge under WTO rules. BEE applies equally to domestic and foreign producers and therefore does not directly discriminate against foreign businesses. However, it may be construed as indirectly discriminating, in that it is more difficult for a foreign company than a local company to comply with requirements such as black majority ownership, or black management control, given that 'black' is defined in terms of those who were oppressed under apartheid.[65] Similarly, direct procurement by the government is not at risk, since the GATT principle of National Treatment does not apply to procurement by governmental agencies and the South African government has

---

[62] Broad Based Black Economic Empowerment Act 53 of 2003, s 1.

[63] DTI 'The Codes of Good Practice on Broad Based Black Economic Empowerment—Phase One: A Guide to Interpreting the First Phase of the Codes' (2005).

[64] Broad Based Black Economic Empowerment Act 53 of 2003, s 10.

[65] J Mortensen 'WTO v BEE: Why Trade Liberalisation May Block Black South Africans' Access to Wealth, Prosperity or just a White Collar Job' Danish Institute for International Studies Working Paper no 2006/30.

not signed the Agreement on Government Procurement which brings procurement within its purview. However, BEE does not only apply to direct procurement: a company will improve its score when tendering for government contracts if it requires black empowerment measures from its subcontractors or trades with BEE compliant companies. This creates a chain of BEE influence, with the conceivable possibility of an international company further down the chain of procurement arguing that it was indirectly discriminated against.

There has in fact been a complaint reported, not under the WTO system but under a bilateral investment treaty.[66] The claim is brought by European investors whose rights to mineral extraction under the treaty in question are in the process of being expropriated. Compensation for expropriation of mineral rights depends on the investors' progress in meeting black empowerment targets in terms of the Mining Sector Black Economic Empowerment Charter. According to the European investors, the requirements of appointing black managers and selling 26% of its shareholding to Black individuals are very onerous for small, family-held companies.[67] The claim is to be adjudicated under the World Bank investment dispute procedure;[68] but it has been suggested that there is a risk that a similar claim might come before the WTO.

The vulnerability of a major social programme based on positive human rights duties to attack on purely trade-related grounds demonstrates the seriousness of the problem posed by the WTO. The Preamble to the WTO agreement does not mention human rights, although it does refer to the aim of raising standards of living and the need for sustainable development. Nor does the GATT test explicitly list human rights as a potential reason why a State may be permitted to take measures which directly or indirectly discriminate against foreign products in its own market. The only relevant explicit provision is Article XX, which permits non-trade public values to prevail in the event of conflict with free trade rules. According to this article, nothing in the GATT shall be construed to prevent the adoption or enforcement by any contracting party of measures, inter alia, 'necessary to protect public morals'; 'necessary to protect human, animal or plant life or health'; 'essential to the acquisition of or distribution of products in general or local short supply'; 'relating to the conservation of exhaustible natural resources if such measures are made effective in conjunction with restrictions on domestic production and consumption'; or 'relating to the products of prison labour'. However, this clause was interpreted highly restrictively under the GATT disputes procedure. In their opinion in the *Tuna Dolphin* cases, the GATT panels developed the concept that a measure would only be 'necessary' and therefore justified under Article XX if it was impossible to imagine an alternative to achieving

[66] The South Africa–Italy Bilateral Investment Treaty.
[67] Reported by R Geldenhuys 'South Africa's BEE Policy in Trouble' (26 February 2007); see <http://www.tradelaw.co.za/news/article.asp?newsID=133> and <http://www.tradelaw.co.za/news/article.asp?newsID=90>.
[68] International Centre for Settlement of Investment Disputes (ICSID).

the public purpose which was less restrictive on trade.[69] This standard is clearly impossible to meet.

The detailed application of WTO rules and jurisprudence is beyond the scope of this book. However, it needs to be stressed that international trade law should not be allowed to develop autonomously in a way which gives it preference over human rights commitments. Howse and Mutua argue that the creation of the WTO gives an opportunity to reinterpret Article XX in the light of norms of international human rights law.[70] According to Article 31(3) of the Vienna Convention, when interpreting treaty obligations, such as those of the WTO Agreement, 'there shall be taken into account, together with the context . . . (c) any relevant rules of international law applicable in the relations between the parties'. The GATT should therefore be interpreted in the light of Member States' commitments to international human rights law; and in particular, to the UN Charter, which has priority over all other obligations. The Charter expressly commits Member States to promote universal respect for and the observance of human rights and fundamental freedoms, as well as to promote higher standards of living, full employment, and conditions of economic and social progress and development.[71] Thus, the GATT should not be interpreted in a way which interferes with Member States' duties to promote human rights.

An analogy is found in respect of environmental protection. In the *US–Shrimp* case, the WTO Appellate Body accepted that international environmental law had to be used as an appropriate benchmark for the meaning of 'exhaustible natural resources' in the Article XX exception.[72] This, together with the WTO preamble which sees environmental protection as a goal of national and international policy, allowed the Appellate Body to interpret the term in an evolutionary sense, to include endangered species. The result was to permit an exception to the free trade regime for rules protecting endangered species. The analogy is not perfect in that the environment, but not human rights, is mentioned in the WTO preamble. Nevertheless, the reference in the preamble to the aim of raising standards of living and the need for sustainable development, interpreted according to the definition of welfare used in this book, should encompass positive human rights duties such as the duties to respect, protect, and provide health, food, security, and equality.

The Doha agreement of 2001 goes some way to recognizing this. Thus, it states that, recognizing the gravity of the public health problems afflicting many developing and least-developed countries:

[69] *Thailand-Restrictions on Imports of Tuna* (1991) 30 ILM 1594; *United States-Restrictions on Imports of Tuna* (1994) 33 ILM 936.
[70] Howse and Mutua (n 29 above) 11.
[71] Charter of the United Nations (1945) Articles 55 and 56.
[72] WTO Report of the Appellate Body, *United States—Import Prohibition of Certain Shrimp and Shrimp Related Products* (12 October 1998) WT/DS58/AB/R.

We agree that the TRIPS Agreement does not and should not prevent members from taking measures to protect public health. Accordingly, while reiterating our commitment to the TRIPS Agreement, we affirm that the Agreement can and should be interpreted and implemented in a manner supportive of WTO members' right to protect public health and, in particular, to promote access to medicines for all.

However, because it is framed in terms of an exception to the rules, which will inevitably be restrictively interpreted, it does not go far enough. In particular, by requiring Member States to issue a compulsory licence if they wish to take measures to protect public health, this approach puts a government on the defensive, requiring it to justify its decision as an exceptional matter, rather than the converse, which would put the onus on those pursuing the right to patenting protection to justify their position.

This in turn shows that the decision as to whether there is a conflict between trade rules and human rights should not rest with the WTO disputes machinery. Human rights obligations are frequently drafted in general terms, whose applicability in particular situations may be contested. The adjudicative panels of the WTO are made up of trade experts and lawyers, without any broader judicial training or human rights expertise. This is compounded by the lack of transparency of the process: oral and written pleadings remain secret unless States party to the dispute agree to their being open. A small step in this direction was taken in 1996, when Ministers of the WTO Member States renewed their commitment to internationally recognized core labour standards, but declared that the ILO should be the competent body to set and deal with these standards.[73] However, there is no mechanism for coordinating the two decision-making bodies. The danger is that the more focussed and powerful disputes procedure of the WTO will inevitably take precedence. Instead, there needs to be a procedure whereby the WTO is required to refer cases which have implications for human rights to a human rights body with superior decision-making powers, either on request of the parties, or of NGOs, or of another Member State.

There are important precedents for the interpenetration of trade rules by human rights duties. The most significant of these is the EU, which is in many ways a microcosm of international globalization. It is therefore worth turning briefly to the experience of the EU.

(v) Globalization and the EU

The EU owes its origin to a profound commitment to free trade and the free movement of capital as the means to secure both peace and prosperity. The EU differs from the international arena in that the legal order which binds the EU

---

[73] Ministerial Conference of the WTO (3 December 1996), Singapore Ministerial Declaration, adopted 13 December 1996 (1997) 36 ILM 218.

is much stronger and more sophisticated than that represented by the WTO. Nevertheless, the way in which the EU has developed social rights in dynamic tension with freedom of trade and capital sheds important light on the globalization argument.

The development of the EU since its founding clearly illustrates two of the features noted in respect of globalization. The first is that the promotion of a free market is far from a deregulatory exercise. The debate is not between regulation and non-regulation, but between different types of regulation. The second is that it is essential to include social freedoms and positive human rights duties in a regime which advances economic freedoms. The EU's genesis as a free trade zone has always threatened to privilege economic freedoms over social rights, endangering social law in Member States. It is thus of crucial significance that the EU has come to recognize its own role in the protection and promotion of social rights. Because of the unique powers of the EU to bind its members, the EU has the potential to operate as a powerful buttress for social rights against the 'race to the bottom' created by competitive forces.

The EU was originally established for the purpose of creating a common market. Political union was eschewed, and no charter of human rights was incorporated. Rights at EU level had to be justified in market creating terms. This has meant that the fundamental rights of the EU have not been the familiar civil and political rights but basic market freedoms: freedom of movement of goods, services, and labour. The absence of social rights was justified by the belief that social progress would follow as a natural by-product of the proper functioning of the market. Hence, Article 2 of the Treaty of Rome stated that the 'promotion of an accelerated raising of the standard of living' is to be achieved 'by establishing a common market and approximating the economic policies of the member states'.[74] Nor was harmonization of social law thought necessary to prevent distorted competition.[75] Only one social right was included and this was wholly on market grounds. Since France was in advance of all the other Member States in providing for equal pay for equal work regardless of gender, it was able to secure the adoption of Article 119 (now Article 141), on equal pay for men and women doing equal work, on the grounds that otherwise it would find itself at a competitive disadvantage.

The absence of fundamental human rights at EU level did not mean that there were no such rights. The EU system is superimposed upon well-developed social and industrial relations systems of Member States, which States had no desire to relinquish to the EU. As Collins maintains, each member 'prided itself on its advanced welfare system, its union traditions, its dedication to social progress, and to have asked them to dismantle their cherished edifices would have met with

---

[74] See also Art 117 and 118 of the Treaty of Rome.
[75] ILO 'Social Aspects of European Economic Cooperation: Report of a Group of Experts' [1956] 74 International Law Review 99, 104–105.

no response'.[76] Thus, 'efficiency' concerns were for the EU, while redistribution remained in the hands of Member States. On this view, the 'goal is to increase societal net gain through market integration without concern as to how such wealth is distributed'.[77]

However, this division of labour did not reckon with the inextricable enmeshment of economic and social freedoms. Instead, the guarantee of market freedoms without social freedoms gave the EU the power to disrupt social law at Member State level. As at international level, prohibitions on direct trade preferences were soon augmented by indirect prohibitions, with ever more intrusive effects on domestic policy. On the grounds that market freedoms are fundamental rights,[78] the ECJ has held that EU law precludes any measures which have the effect of hindering intra-Community trade. This is true whether the effect is direct or indirect, actual or potential.[79] Thus, challenges have been mounted to legislation regarding working hours, the organization of work, public systems of labour procurement services, and price regulations. In a provision similar to Article XX of GATT, the Treaty on the EU expressly permits restrictions on market freedoms if necessary on public policy grounds.[80] However, the ECJ has held that such measures cannot be justified if the same result could have been achieved by less restrictive means.[81] The result is that social considerations were seen not as rights in themselves, but as derogations from economic rights, to be narrowly interpreted. 'Obstacles' to movement within the community can only be accepted if they are necessary in the public interest.[82]

The parallels with the developing WTO system are obvious. However, while the WTO remains at this stage of development, the EU has moved beyond it. Most important has been the express acknowledgement that economic advancement needs to be twinned with social progress. This shift was signalled in 1976, in *Defrenne (No 2)* where the ECJ declared that the Community 'is not merely an economic union, but is at the same time intended . . . to ensure social progress and seek the constant improvement of the living and working conditions of their peoples'.[83] The expansion of EU competence to legislate in the social field has been admittedly halting and often controversial, resulting in sporadic and somewhat haphazard forays into the area. Nevertheless, the EU has now gained competence

---

[76] D Collins 'Social Policy' in J Lodge (ed) *Institutions and Policies of the European Community* (Pinter London 1983) 98.

[77] M Maduro 'Striking the Elusive Balance Between Economic Freedom and Social Rights in the EU' in P Alston (ed) *The EU and Human Rights* (OUP Oxford 1999) 468.

[78] Case C-55/94 *Gebhard v Consiglio* [1995] ECR I-4165 (ECJ) at para 34.

[79] Case 8/74 *Procureur du Roi v Dassonville* [1974] ECR 837 (ECJ).

[80] Article 31 EC.

[81] C-155/82 *Commission of the European Communities v Kingdom of Belgium* [1983] ECR 531 (ECJ).

[82] Case 120/78 *Cassis de Dijon* [1979] ECR 649 (ECJ).

[83] Case 43/75 *Defrenne v Sabena* [1976] ECR 455 (ECJ).

to legislate over a wide range of social issues although some basic rights are still excluded.[84]

Key to the changing attitude has been the increasing acceptance of the view that rights are not necessarily burdens on business but should be viewed as productive factors. The 'modernised European Social Model' regards social policy as a 'productive factor',[85] an essential contribution to the economy, while economic policy should promote social objectives.[86] This synthesis of competitiveness and social rights is summed up Article 3 of the draft Constitutional Treaty, which provides that the EU is committed to 'the sustainable development of Europe based on balanced economic growth, a social market economy, highly competitive and aiming at full employment and social progress'.

On a strategic level, the alliance between social and economic rationales has led to progress which might not have been achieved without the economic partner. However, clothing fundamental rights in the vocabulary of efficiency runs the risk of simply disguising their subordination. A good example is in the field of gender. The impetus to integrate women into the workforce is often presented as the achievement of gender equality. However, integration frequently takes the form of precarious work: low status, low paid, and with little job security. This ties in well with the drive towards flexible labour markets with consequent profitability gains for employers, but could scarcely be considered consistent with gender equality. This points again to the need to avoid viewing rights as instrumental. The power of the market will always subordinate social rights where there is a conflict with efficiency, unless there is a bedrock of fundamental rights which owe their genesis to fairness and justice for its own sake.

In fact, the EU is slowly reaching beyond the purely economic approach to rights, to include a commitment to fundamental rights for their own sake. This can be seen in the form of the EU Charter of Fundamental Rights. In deciding to initiate a process of establishing such a Charter, the EU as a collectivity was clearly signifying that its *raison d'être* extended beyond the original economic aims. The drafters of the Charter were ambitious, both in their attempt to create a genuinely participative and deliberative process, and in their unified vision of human rights. The resulting Charter organizes rights under the titles of dignity, equality, solidarity, and citizenship rather than the traditional categories of civil and political or socio-economic rights. This is not to say that the process has been smooth. As Miguel Maduro points out, the Charter reflects two opposing perspectives: for some, it reinforces limits on the power of the EU and reasserts the control of States; while for others, the Charter is the starting point of a 'truly constitutional deliberative process and the construction of a European political identity'.[87] This

---

[84] Article 13, 136–148 EC.
[85] *Social Policy Agenda,* para 1.2.
[86] ibid, para 1.2.
[87] MP Maduro 'The Double Constitutional Life of the Charter of Fundamental Rights of the European Union' in T Hervey and J Kenner (eds) *Economic and Social Rights under the EU Charter of Fundamental Rights* (Hart Oxford 2003).

ambivalence is reflected in three ways. First, there has been intense controversy over the legal status of the Charter. Although solemnly proclaimed in 2000, it took until 2007 for the European Council to agree that the Charter should have 'the same legal value as the Treaties', and even this is subject to an opt-out by the UK.[88] Secondly, traditional civil and political rights are expressed in the form of a right: 'everyone has the right' to life, to freedom of speech and religion, or to respect for private and family life. But socio-economic rights are formulated as a 'duty to recognise and respect' rights such as the rights of the elderly and disabled people; or the right to social security benefits and social services.[89] Thirdly, the Charter also draws a distinction between rights, which are justiciable, and principles, which may be implemented by Member States or the EU, but which are not 'judicially cognisable' except in the interpretation of legislative or executive acts. Although there is no specific link between 'principles' and socio-economic rights, the intention was to limit the justiciability of the latter.[90]

Nevertheless, the Charter plays an important role in ensuring that the creation of a single market does not undermine the positive duty on Member States and the EU to secure human rights. Although presented as weaker than a justiciable right, in fact the duty to recognize and respect rights can be far-reaching. As a start, such a duty clearly prevents the EU from interfering with Member States' provision in the social sphere. Particularly important is Article 34, which states: 'In order to combat social exclusion and poverty, the Union recognises and respects the right to social and housing assistance so as to ensure a decent existence for all those who lack sufficient resources...' The duty to respect and recognize is more than just a duty of restraint. It also imposes a proactive duty on the EU to scrutinize all policies and legislation to be sure that the latter are recognized and respected. In fact, in 2005, the European Commission committed itself to systematically screening all legislative proposals for compatibility with the Charter of Fundamental Rights.[91] It is even arguable that the duty to recognize and respect requires positive action to be taken in cases where such rights are not protected by Member States; but the extent to which this can be a vehicle for positive policy initiatives is limited by the fact that the Charter creates no new competences. The Charter also imposes express positive duties. Clearest is Article 23 on gender equality, which states that 'equality between men and women *must be ensured* in all areas, including employment, work and pay'.[92] Finally, although duties to respect and recognize may not in themselves create justiciable rights, courts should take them into account. This means that economic freedoms cannot be imposed in the form of duties of restraint preventing States or the EU from fulfilling positive human rights duties.

[88] Presidency Conclusions, Brussels, 21/22 June 2007.
[89] Charter of Fundamental Rights of the Union OJ C310/41 16.12.2004 Article II-85, 86 and 82.
[90] Charter of Fundamental Rights of the Union OJ C310/41 16.12.2004 Article II-112.
[91] IP/05/494 Brussels, 27 April 2005.
[92] Emphasis added.

Although the EU's unique positioning between national and international facil-itates the creation of a mechanism such as this, there is no doubt that the lessons learned at EU level are generalizable to the brave new world of globalization.

C. Privatization and Positive Duties: whose Responsibility?

So far, this chapter has considered the nature of the State in two respects: its democratic relationship to its people, and its relationship to other State and inter-national actors. Both contexts create particular challenges for the understanding of human rights as giving rise to positive duties. In this section, a third challenge is considered: that arising from the increasing fragmentation of the State. The Welfare State in its prime years took responsibility for a wide range of functions in respect of the provision of the basic means of social citizenship. However, under the influence of neo-liberal policies, recent decades have witnessed a powerful move towards privatization of such functions. As in the case of globalization, the prime motivations have been 'efficiency' and 'cost-effectiveness', the under-lying assumption being that exposure to competition in the marketplace will lead to efficiency gains not available in an allegedly bloated and complacent public sector. The process of 'rolling back the State' has taken place in many countries, whether as a result of local political initiatives, such as those in the UK under Margaret Thatcher, or as a result of conditions on foreign loans imposed by the World Bank and International Monetary Fund. Privatization has reached deep into the traditional confines of the State. In the UK, such traditional State func-tions as law and order have been privatized, through the use of private security firms to run prisons and detention centres for asylum seekers; and of private com-panies to be responsible for probation.[93]

This creates a major challenge for the theory of positive human rights duties proposed here. Traditionally, human rights have only been enforceable against the State, both domestically and internationally. Positive human rights duties appear particularly inappropriate for private actors because the obligation to take action could potentially conflict with other freedoms. If this approach applied to the privatization situation, it would have serious consequences for human rights protection. As the boundaries of the State shrink, so does the reach of human rights duties. This process can even be accelerated by limiting positive human rights duties to the State, since there is a clear incentive to opt out of those duties by privatizing.

However, the arguments against imposing positive duties on private individu-als are only tangentially relevant to privatization. The subjects of the duties are not private individuals but corporate bodies or unincorporated associations and

[93] Joint Committee on Human Rights *The Meaning of Public Authority under the Human Rights Act* (The Stationery Office 2007) para 64, 65.

it is not obvious that they have freedoms or rights in the same sense as private individuals. The real arguments against applying human rights duties to private contractors are market based: that they would be costly, impede competitiveness, and undermine the 'efficiency' gains that privatization sets out to achieve. The UK government for example has argued that in the arena of social housing provision in particular, human rights obligations would 'be likely to have an effect upon the availability of affordable housing for some of the most disadvantaged in society', and create a disincentive for other private housing providers to enter the social sector.[94]

There is little actual evidence that private providers have left the market as a result of the imposition of positive duties to promote human rights.[95] More fundamentally, this argument assumes that there is a necessary contradiction between efficiency and positive human rights duties. This is only the case if efficiency is defined narrowly to cover only the utilitarian measurement of consumer preferences. Once welfare is seen to include the ability to exercise human rights, then this contradiction disappears.

There are several methods of bringing privatized functions within the scope of human rights law. First, the State may remain liable even if it has contracted out a particular function. The European Court of Human Rights has expressly held where the State relies on private organizations to perform essential public functions, in particular those necessary for the protection of Convention rights, it retains responsibility for any breach of the Convention that arises from the actions of those private organizations.[96] Thus in *Costello-Roberts*,[97] the Court reiterated the principle that the responsibility of a State is engaged if a violation of a Convention right results from non-observance by that State of its duty to secure those rights and freedoms in its domestic law to everyone within its jurisdiction. It could not absolve itself of its Convention obligations by delegating the fulfilment of such obligations to private bodies or individuals. This approach is also endorsed in UK legislation imposing a positive duty to promote equality on grounds of gender or disability. The duty expressly applies to a public authority in relation to services and functions which are contracted out, which means that a public body which has contracted with another body is still bound by the duty in relation to that contract.[98]

Secondly, contractual means can be used to enforce positive duties against private contractors entering into procurement arrangements with public bodies. The use of public contracting has long been recognized as a powerful vehicle by which to fulfil positive duties in equality and other fields.[99] However, contract

---

[94] ibid para 84.
[95] Joint Committee on Human Rights (n 93 above), para 88.
[96] *Van der Mussele v Belgium* (1984) 6 EHRR 163 (European Court of Human Rights).
[97] *Costello-Roberts v UK* (1995) 19 EHRR 112 (European Court of Human Rights).
[98] SDA 1975, s 76A; DDA 1995, s 49A.
[99] See further C McCrudden *Buying Social Justice Equality, Government Procurement, & Legal Change* (OUP 2007).

is a private, bipolar and consensual legal mechanism. There are inevitably limits in the extent to which it can deliver human rights, which are mandatory and generally applicable. For a start, the consensual nature of contract means that its content is a matter for negotiation and may not accurately reflect the scope of the human rights duty. In addition, only the parties to the contract are bound. Since the individual rights-holder is not a party, it is difficult for her to enforce it in her own right; indeed, she may have no way of knowing whether it exists and what its contents are.[100] Only the authority, who is a party, can enforce it, which means that the duty is only as effective as the authority's ability and willingness to monitor and enforce it. The simple act of privatizing could therefore deprive an individual of a right which was previously enforceable against the authority. Thus, although there is clearly a role for the enforcement through contract, the UK Joint Committee on Human Rights (JCoHR) rightly concluded that this could never provide fully comprehensive, consistent, and equal human rights protection for all recipients of public services.[101]

A third solution is to place the obligation directly on the body carrying out the privatized function. The HRA 1998 provides that human rights duties should apply to private or voluntary sector bodies when performing functions 'of a public nature'.[102] For example, if a private security firm provides security to a prison as well as private commercial operations such as a supermarket, it would be required to comply with Convention rights in its running of the prison, but not of the supermarket.[103] Although the aim was to construe this widely,[104] domestic courts have adopted a restrictive interpretation of the meaning of public authority, resting the definition on the relationship of the body to the government, rather than the function itself. The result has been to exclude important providers of public functions, such as housing providers or care homes.[105] Instead, as the JCoHR has proposed, the key test for 'public function' should be whether the relevant 'function' is one for which the government has assumed responsibility in the public interest.[106]

Even on this definition, the fluid boundary between public and private will always make it difficult to reach a consistent and sufficiently robust definition of 'public'. A more wide-ranging solution could be to provide that everyone, public or private, be bound by human rights duties. One such solution is found in the South African Constitution, which provides: 'A provision of the Bill of Rights

---

[100] Joint Committee on Human Rights 'The Meaning of Public Authority under the Human Rights Act' Seventh Report of Session 2003–2004 (The Stationery Office 2003) para 115.

[101] ibid para 125.

[102] HRA 1998, s 6(5).

[103] The example comes from Lord Chancellor, HL Deb, 24 November 1997, col 811.

[104] See, for example, HC Deb, 16 February 1998, col 773 (Home Secretary); HC Deb, 17 June 1998, cols 409–410, 433 (Home Secretary), HL Deb, 24 November 1997, col 800, 811 (Lord Chancellor).

[105] YL (By her litigation friend the Official Solicitor) v Birmingham CC [2007] UKHL 27; [2007] 3 WLR 112 (HL).

[106] JCoHR (2007) (n 93 above) para 7.

binds a natural or a juristic person if, and to the extent that, it is applicable, taking into account the nature of the right and the nature of any duty imposed by the right.'[107] In the certification proceedings, the Court rejected the argument that private persons should not be bound because this would limit their other freedoms: all rights can in principle be limited in appropriate circumstances.[108] Given that, in a privatization situation, the respondent will be a juristic rather than a private person, there seems even less reason to hold that the respondent is not bound. Conversely, the invasion of the rights of the victim is potentially serious. Thus, it is arguable that a private operator carrying out a privatized function should certainly be bound. This is born out by the criteria applied by the Court to enforce the applicability of the right to free speech in defamation proceedings between private individuals. These criteria expressly include 'the intensity of the constitutional right in question, coupled with the potential invasion of that right which could be occasioned by persons other than the state'.[109]

Even without an express horizontality provision, there is no simple dichotomy between vertical and horizontal applicability.[110] This is because courts, as public bodies, are bound by human rights obligations, and therefore are required to take human rights duties into account in their interpretation of private law. The clearest manifestation of such an approach would be a refusal to enforce private agreements which, although lawful in themselves, are in breach of human rights. In the US case of *Shelley v Kraemer*,[111] the Supreme Court was faced with a case in which a black American couple had bought a property which was subject to a restrictive covenant requiring the seller to sell only to whites. The Court reiterated that the equality guarantee in the 14th Amendment did not apply to private conduct. However, it did bind the court and judicial officials. This meant that the discriminatory covenant could not be enforced by the courts. Similarly, under HRA 1998, courts as public bodies are bound to develop the common law consistently with the Convention rights enacted therein.[112]

D. Conclusion

This chapter has considered in more detail the nature of the State which is the bearer of positive human rights duties. Three major conclusions can be drawn.

---

[107] South African Constitution, s 8(2).
[108] *Ex Parte Chairperson of the Constitutional Assembly: In re Certification of the Constitution of the Republic of South Africa* 1996 (4) SA 744 (South African Constitutional Court) para 56.
[109] *Khumalo v Bantubonke Harrington Holomisa* Case CCT 53/01 (South African Constitutional Court) para 33.
[110] For a thorough review of the comparative case law see *Du Plessis v De Klerk* Case CCT 8/95 (South African Constitutional Court).
[111] *Shelley v Kraemer* 334 US 1 (1948) (US Supreme Court); cf *Retail, Wholesale & Department Store Union, Local 580 v Dolphin Delivery* (1987) 33 DLR (4th) 174 (Canadian Supreme Court).
[112] HRA 1998, s 6(3).

First, positive human rights duties, far from impeding democracy, are essential to the achievement of a democratic system which aspires to full and equal participation, both in decision-making and in constraining power. In particular, the conditions for fair interest bargaining as well as for proper deliberative decision-making require positive input from the State to ensure both equality and genuine participation. Secondly, globalization does not constitute a good reason for opposing positive human rights duties or considering them unobtainable. Instead, positive human rights duties should be an essential part of globalization in a world which has expressly committed itself to human rights. Finally, the State should not be able to escape its positive duties through privatization.

PART II

JUDGING AND ENFORCING: COURTS AND COMPLIANCE

3

The Structure of Positive Duties

Part I of this book advanced the theoretical case for positive human rights duties. It demonstrated that the basic values behind human rights, namely freedom, equality, solidarity, and democracy, support the need to ensure that human rights are not just formal entitlements but can in fact be enjoyed by all rights-holders. This part considers the nature of positive duties in more detail. This chapter closely examines the structure of positive duties, while Chapter 4 turns to the role of the courts in enforcing positive duties. Chapter 5 briefly considers alternative or complementary methods outside of judicial enforcement.

The current chapter begins by demonstrating that it is artificial to attempt to distinguish between rights according to the nature of their correlative duties. Instead, all rights can be seen to give rise to a range of duties, including both duties of restraint and positive duties. There is now some measure of recognition of this indivisibility of positive and negative duties. But the struggle it has taken to achieve this small victory has meant that few analyses go beyond this and consider the nature of positive duties in detail. This is the aim of the second part of the chapter. In this section, I examine the question of whether positive duties are sufficiently determinate to be truly normative. Rejecting the charge of indeterminacy, I argue that positive duties are best understood by using the concept of principles, developed by German constitutional lawyer Alexy. A principle is a norm which must be realized to the greatest extent possible given the legal and factual possibilities. Principles do not lose their prima facie binding force when they are outweighed in particular circumstances by other principles. The issue then is not indeterminacy, but orders of priority. This analysis can also explain why positive duties retain their normative force even when they are not immediately fulfilled. I argue that the charge of indeterminacy wrongly assumes that, to be determinate, a duty must specify precise standards to be met. Instead, I suggest that it is sufficient to meet specific parameters, namely, effectiveness, participation, accountability, and equality. This approach is then applied to the controversy over the minimum core obligation. The chapter concludes with an examination of the relationship between the right-holder and the duty bearer.

A. The Indivisibility of Duties

(i) Civil and political rights v socio-economic rights

The traditional approach draws a bright line around a cluster of concepts: duties of restraint are attached to freedom-protecting civil and political rights while positive duties attach to equality-promoting socio-economic rights. The former are justiciable, the latter aspirational. The link between the nature of the right and the nature of the duty is embedded in the definition itself. Thus, civil and political rights are generally thought to refer to rights which protect individuals against intrusion by the State; while socio-economic rights are rights to protection by the State against want or need. These sets of distinctions are given apparent solidity by the architecture of international and European human rights law. The International Covenant on Civil and Political Rights (ICCPR) includes civil and political rights, giving rise to negative duties of restraint, which are enforceable through the courts. Conversely, the International Covenant on Economic, Social and Cultural Rights (ICESCR) consists of socio-economic rights, giving rise to positive duties which are monitored through regular reporting requirements.[1]

Despite this separate architecture, much rhetoric has been expended on asserting the indivisibility and equality of the two sets of rights. The preamble of the ICCPR states: 'The ideal of free human beings enjoying civil and political freedom and freedom from fear and want can only be achieved if conditions are created whereby everyone may enjoy his [or her] civil and political rights, as well as his [or her] economic, social and cultural rights.' A parallel provision is found in the ICESCR. This indivisibility was reiterated by the Vienna World Conference in 1993 which stressed that all rights are 'indivisible and interdependent and interrelated'.

Such assertions are largely a rhetorical flourish. The reality is that there is a clear hierarchy in international human rights protection and in domestic human rights law in Western democracies. As the UN Committee on Economic, Social and Cultural Rights stated in 1993:

The shocking reality ... [is] that States and the international community as a whole continue to tolerate all too often breaches of economic, social and cultural rights which, if they occurred in relation to civil and political rights, would provoke expressions of horror and outrage and would lead to concerted calls for immediate remedial action.[2]

---

[1] There are ongoing discussions on the possibility of an optional protocol to the ICESCR allowing NGOs or individuals to bring complaints or communications to the Committee.

[2] HJ Steiner, P Alston, and R Goodman *International Human Rights in Context* (3rd edn OUP Oxford 2007) 264.

(ii) Beyond the boundaries

The first step is to recognize that there are important interactions between the two sets of rights. Without basic socio-economic entitlements, civil and political rights cannot be fully exercised. Freedom of speech or assembly are of little use to a starving or homeless person. Equally problematically, those without resources will find it hard to access the legal system to redress breaches of their rights. This means that even the most fundamental rights, such as the right not to be detained without trial, or subjected to torture, may be less available to those without socio-economic means than others.

The interaction also works in the other direction. Political and civil rights, including freedom of speech, can be highly instrumental in preventing or ameliorating poverty. As Sen has argued, if leaders are not accountable to the population, and are insulated from the effects of famine or drought, they have no incentive to take action to protect the population from such disasters. Freedom of the press, a free opposition, and freedom of information 'spread the penalty of famine to the ruling groups'. They also contribute greatly to dissemination of information which can assist in the prevention of such disasters. Moreover, he argues: 'Political rights, including freedom of expression and discussion, are not only pivotal in inducing political responses to economic needs, they are also central to the conceptualisation of economic needs themselves.'[3] Equally importantly, measures taken to ameliorate need can only be legitimate and effective with democratic participation.

Acknowledging the interaction between the two sets of rights is an important first step. We need to go further still and recognize that rights cannot coherently be distinguished by the kind of duty to which they give rise. Instead, the ideological lens through which a right is viewed determines which kind of duties are in focus. Civil and political rights are only regarded as limited to duties of restraint because they are viewed though the lens of freedom as non-intervention. The richer conception of freedom as the ability to exercise one's rights immediately reveals that these rights also entail positive duties. This can be illustrated by considering the right to life. If we assume that freedom consists of absence of State intervention, the right to life appears merely as a duty that the State refrain from deliberately taking life. A very different interpretation follows from viewing freedom as the ability to act and fulfil oneself. Seen in this light, the right to life is not genuine unless it can be exercised by the rights-bearer. This necessarily includes the right not to die of preventable causes, such as starvation, exposure, or reasonably avoidable illnesses, which in turn gives rise to a range of positive duties on the State. The result is a substantial overlap with socio-economic rights to food, health care, and shelter. This has been the perspective of the Indian courts,

---

[3] A Sen 'Freedoms and Needs' *The New Republic* (10 and 17 January 1994) 31, 32, cited in Steiner, Alston, and Goodman (n 2 above) 371.

which have held that the right to life includes the right to emergency health care, the right to be housed, the right to livelihood, and even the right of an isolated community to a road.[4]

A similar overlap has emerged between the civil and political right not to be tortured or subject to inhuman treatment or punishment and the socio-economic right to minimum subsistence. Even in the UK, which has no justiciable socio-economic rights, the right not to be subject to inhuman treatment has implied a right to minimum subsistence.[5] The right to personal security could also be interpreted either as merely preventing the State from interfering with security, or as requiring the State to take positive measure to provide security. The two perspectives are clearly found in recent Canadian jurisprudence. The majority judgment in a recent case endorsed the established view that the right to life, liberty, and security of the person in section 7 of the Canadian Charter gave rise only to a duty restraining the State from depriving people of their life, liberty, or security, rather than a positive duty to ensure that each person enjoys this right.[6] By contrast, the dissenting opinion of Arbour J moved from the richer conception of freedom directly to a positive duty on the State. Thus, she declared:

Freedom from state interference with bodily or psychological integrity is of little consolation to those who... are faced with a daily struggle to meet their most basic bodily and psychological needs... theirs is a world in which the primary threats to security of the person come not from others, but from their own dire circumstances. In such cases, one can reasonably conclude that positive state action is what is required in order to breathe purpose and meaning into their s. 7 guaranteed rights.[7]

Not only do civil and political rights give rise to positive duties. Many socio-economic rights give rise to duties of restraint in addition to positive duties, thereby overlapping with civil and political rights. The right to be housed includes a restraint on the State from unlawful evictions,[8] covering the same ground as the civil and political right to respect for privacy, home, and family life. Spanning both negative and positive duties is the right to equality. Traditionally, equality has been a classic civil and political right, requiring only that the State refrain from discriminating. However, through the lens of substantive equality and freedom, it can quickly be seen to entail positive duties to promote equality. Even more interesting is the way that equality can turn negative duties into positive duties. The State need not provide social benefits. But if it does, it must do so without discrimination.[9]

---

[4] See Chapter 5.
[5] *R (on the application of Limbuela) v Secretary of State for the Home Department* [2005] UKHL 66 [2006] 1 AC 396 (HL).
[6] *Gosselin v Quebec* 2002 SCC 84 (Canadian Supreme Court) para 81.
[7] ibid para 377.
[8] Committee on Economic, Social and Cultural Rights (CESCR), General Comment 4, The right to adequate housing (Sixth session, 1991) para 8(a).
[9] *Ghaidan v Godin-Mendoza* [2004] UKHL 30, [2004] 2 AC 557 (HL) See Chapter 7.

Positive duties need not be confined to the overlap with socio-economic rights. They also include the State's duty to provide the basic legislation and institutions to secure human rights. This is implicit in Article 1 of the ECHR, which states that the State has the duty to secure to everyone within its jurisdiction the rights and freedoms guaranteed in the Convention. This means at the very least that the State must enact laws to create the rights. There would be no right to marry without laws about marriage; no right to free enjoyment of one's possessions without property laws.[10] (The fact that these laws might already exist should not mask the existence of the positive duty: if they did not exist, there would be a positive duty to enact them.[11]) Beyond this, rights require institutional backing. There could be no right to a fair trial without positive action to set up courts and a criminal justice system.

(iii) Redrawing the boundaries: the nature of obligations

The above discussion has shown that it is impossible to distinguish between rights on the basis of whether they give rise to positive duties or duties of restraint. Far more useful is to consider each right as giving rise to a cluster of obligations, some of which require the State to abstain from interfering, and others which entail positive action and resource allocation. In his seminal work, Shue argues that there are no one-to-one pairings between kinds of duties and kinds of rights. Instead, 'the complete fulfilment of each kind of right involves the performance of multiple kinds of duties'. He therefore goes beyond the 'usual assumption that for every right there is a single correlative duty', and suggests instead that for every right, 'there are three types of duties, all of which must be performed if the basic right is to be fully honoured, but not all of which must necessarily be performed by the same individuals or institutions'. He classifies these three types of duty as duties to avoid, duties to protect, and duties to aid. Applied to the basic right of security, this would impose on the State the duties to *avoid* eliminating a person's security, duties to *protect* people against deprivation of security by other people, and duties to aid by providing for the security of those unable to provide for their own.[12]

This three-fold classification has been adopted and developed in the ICESCR. Using the ICESCR terminology, all rights can be seen to give rise to at least three types of correlative obligation: the duties to *respect, protect*, and *fulfil*. The duty to *respect* requires the State to refrain from interfering directly or indirectly with the enjoyment of the right. The obligation to *protect* requires State parties to prevent third parties from interfering in any way with the enjoyment of the right. The duty to *fulfil* requires the State either to provide the right directly or to facilitate the

---

[10] R Alexy *A Theory of Constitutional Rights* (OUP Oxford 2004) 324.
[11] ibid 326.
[12] H Shue *Basic Rights* (Princeton University Press Princeton 1980) 51.

provision by assisting individuals and communities to make their own provision. It also requires the State to promote the right by disseminating information and educating people as to their rights.[13] Alexy adds to this three-fold classification by noting the State's duty to enact the norms which are indispensable to protect the right in question. These he calls rights to organization and procedure. These are duties on the State to enact laws, such as property law and marriage laws, without which it would be impossible meaningfully to have the right. Similarly, the State must put in place procedures to permit individuals to exercise their right to vote and to enjoy the right to a fair trial.[14]

Focussing on different types of duties rather than different types of rights gives us a more sophisticated tool for analysis and implementation.[15] The tripartite distinction is particularly important in allowing us to go beyond the debate as to whether or not positive duties arise from a right, and instead to begin to understand what such positive duties entail. It is to this we now turn.

B. Understanding Positive Duties

There are three ways in which positive duties are usually contrasted with duties of restraint. Duties of restraint are said to be determinate, immediately realizable, and resource free. Positive duties are said to be indeterminate, programmatic, and resource intensive. While duties of restraint must be fulfilled immediately, positive duties are said to require only progressive realization as resources become available.[16] It is argued here that these contrasts are overdrawn. Nevertheless, positive duties pose specific challenges, which need to be met. To do so requires much closer attention to the nature of positive duties.

(i) Indeterminacy and incommensurability

To say a duty is indeterminate is to assert that it is impossible to define what a body has to do to fulfil the duty. Indeterminacy could denote vagueness, or incommensurability and radical disagreement. Vagueness means that the content of the duty cannot be derived from the framing of the right. For example, asserting a duty to provide for rights such as social security, protection against poverty, health, or housing does not, on its own, tell us what standard of living is the

---

[13] See also CESCR, General Comment 12, Right to adequate food (Twentieth session, 1999), UN Doc E/CN.12/1999/5, reprinted in Compilation of General Comments and General Recommendations Adopted by Human Rights Treaty Bodies (2003) UN Doc HRI/GEN/1/Rev.6 at 62, para 13.
[14] Alexy (n 10 above) 126, 324.
[15] See Chapter 8.
[16] Compare ICCPR, Article 2(1) with ICESCR, Article 2(1). See further the discussion of progressive realization below.

minimum commensurate with human dignity and freedom. Incommensurability is even more problematic, since it means that different values or goods cannot be measured by the same metric.[17] This in turn entails that the question cannot be resolved by reasoned deliberation but must be subject to another mode of decision-making, such as interest bargaining.[18] Alternatively, it could mean that the question simply has no answer. Either response deprives the duty of its normative content. If the body subject to the duty can do whatever it wishes, then clearly it is not truly under any duty.

The claim that positive duties are indeterminate is generally used to support the argument that judicial resolution is inappropriate. Kelley argues that since there is 'no universal and non-arbitrary standard for distinguishing need from luxury', it is for the political process to draw the line.[19] Judges, on this view, have no greater capacity for resolving disputes based on indeterminate standards than anyone else. A closer examination of this claim reveals that a similar challenge could be posed to duties of restraint. Most duties of restraint are subject to limitations in the public interest. In such a case, the State can interfere with an individual's rights if its action is justifiable as necessary for the public interest or to balance the rights and freedoms of others. There is similarly no universal standard for determining the public interest or its weight relative to the right in question. Alder goes so far as to argue that this involves balancing incommensurables, with the result that resolution of human rights disputes 'depend substantially upon emotional attitudes not susceptible to legal rationality'.[20] If he is correct, then there is no basis for making any human rights decisions at all. But it also means that there is no good reason why politicians are any better at making such decisions than judges. If there is real indeterminacy, politicians too will have difficulty settling on a standard or valuing incommensurables, reducing political decision-making to favouritism or arbitrariness. The problem with this view is that it takes us further than opponents of positive duties wish to go.

This sense of radical instability and indeterminacy can be steadied, however, by using the distinction between rules and principles drawn by Alexy. Rules are fixed points: they are either fulfilled or breached. Principles are not binary in the sense of being fulfilled or breached, but instead can be satisfied to varying degrees.[21] Their normative force lies in the requirement to realize their content to the greatest extent possible, given the legal and factual possibilities. In Alexy's terminology, principles are 'optimisation requirements'. Unlike rules, principles are always prima facie binding, but they may be outweighed in particular

---

[17] Contrast J Alder 'The Sublime and the Beautiful: Incommensurability and Human Rights' [2006] Public Law 697–721.

[18] See Chapter 1 above. Cf Alder (n 17 above) who argues that vagueness can be resolved through reasoned argument.

[19] D Kelley *A Life of One's Own: Individual Rights and the Welfare State* (Cato Institute 1998) 1.

[20] Alder (n 17 above).

[21] Alexy (n 10 above) 45–57.

circumstances by other principles. Thus, whereas it is possible to enumerate in abstract the conditions under which a rule has been breached, the actual (as against prima facie) binding force of a principle can only be determined in the context of competing principles.

The argument from indeterminacy assumes that all norms[22] must be rules. However, once we recognize that many positive duties are principles rather than rules, it can be seen that it is not the principles themselves which create problems of determinacy, but the process of weighing them, or determining which takes priority in particular circumstances. Alexy argues that it is possible in a particular situation to establish determinate relationships of precedence between principles which have equal weight in abstract. By enumerating the circumstances in which one principle takes priority over another, it is possible to formulate a determinate rule. In other words, when those conditions apply, principle A always takes precedence over condition B. This of course does not fully resolve the problem of indeterminacy, because the process of weighing principles requires background principles which are determinate. If background principles are themselves only optimization requirements, this potentially leads to an infinite regress. This is particularly problematic if principles are incommensurate, in that there is no common metric against which to weigh them.

It is acknowledged here that there is frequently an irresolvable element of indeterminacy, which means in effect that some autonomy always remains to the decision-maker as to the content of a positive human rights duty. Moreover, the order of priority decided on continues to be revisable in the light of future argumentation. As Habermas argues, decision-making (whether by a majority of judges or majority of legislators) represents only a 'caesura in an ongoing discussion. It records the interim result of a discursive opinion-forming process.' Once there has been a competent discussion of disputed issues, the decision can be viewed as the 'rationally motivated yet fallible result of a process that has been interrupted because of institutional pressures to decide but is in principle resumable'.[23] Thus, minorities give consent only with proviso of retaining the opportunity in future of winning over the majority with better arguments. Similarly, dissent in a court records arguments that might convince a majority in future.[24] It is this which allows constitutional rights to be regarded as a living tree. There may also come a point where decisions are reached simply as a result of commitment to basic values.

None of these caveats, however, deprive the duty of all normative content—if they did, no decisions could be reached on anything. Nor does it make it impossible to reach decisions as to whether the duty has been fulfilled. As will be recalled, principles are optimization requirements: they must be achieved to the

---

[22] Norms are deontic modes, that is commands, prohibitions, or permissions (ibid 23).
[23] J Habermas *Between Facts and Norms* (Polity Press 1997) 179.
[24] ibid.

greatest extent possible given legal and factual constraints. But the optimization requirement does not assume that the answer given is 'right' in the sense that other arguments cannot be brought to bear in the future. Such arguments may take the form of principles which previously had not been relevant; but they may also re-value existing principles in the light of changing beliefs and social commitments. The fact that the resolution is revisable does not mean that it does not have some stability. There is an independent principle requiring stability and certainty. Revisability denotes a situation in which the stability principle is displaced in the course of maximizing other principles, and needs to be openly justified in these terms. In effect, revisability means that the rule of priority settled in previous situations has been repealed and a new order of priority established. There is also a principle allocating the decision-making power to an institution, such as the court, legislature, or executive. In the following sections, this analysis is applied to duties to protect, and duties to fulfil in turn.

(ii) Duties to protect

The duty to protect requires the State to protect individuals against breach of their human rights by other individuals. In other words, the State has a duty to restrain others in the same way as it restrains itself. At first glance, there should be no difficulty in giving a determinate content to the duty, since it merely transposes onto private individuals the State's own duty not to interfere. However, this is not so straightforward, since the rights of the private individual must also be taken into account. In protecting A's rights against invasion by B, it is necessary always to keep in mind that B has rights too. Thus, the duty to protect introduces a three-way relationship, between the State, the right-holder (A) and the perpetrator of the breach (B). Protection of A cannot be achieved at the cost of undue coercion of B. As a result, the duty to protect may not guarantee that the exercise of the right in question is wholly free of disruption, because total restraint might entail an unacceptable level of coercion of B. In addition, other factors might need to be taken into consideration, including the cost of protecting A against B relative to other demands on the public purse.

This tangled interaction is much more easily analysed using Alexy's approach. The duty to protect A's exercise of the right is the first of several relevant principles. In addition, there is a principle preventing the State from using undue coercion on individuals, and thereby infringing other rights. There is also a third relevant principle: the institutional principle which requires that decisions as to appropriate measures be made by those with acceptable expertise and legitimacy. Further relevant principles include other State duties requiring resources. Once the principles have been clearly identified, it is necessary to optimize each of them in a transparent and justifiable way. The resulting order of priority establishes a rule for equivalent future circumstances. An advantage of this approach is that it permits partial implementation of a principle. For example, even if full protection cannot be provided to A, a reasonable level of restraint might be imposed on B.

The usefulness of this approach in identifying the relevant principles can be seen in the light it casts on the way in which the European Court of Human Rights has formulated a positive duty to protect. Dealing initially with the right to assembly, the first step is to identify the relevant principles. The right to assembly gives rise to a *duty to protect* lawful demonstrators (A) against counter-demonstrators (B). But the right to counter-demonstrate simultaneously invokes a *duty of restraint* on the State not to interfere unjustifiably with B. As well as these two competing principles, a third principle consists of other duties, constituting competing claims on State resources. Finally, the principle that the decision must be made by the competent and legitimate body means that there may need to be a measure of deference to the State or its senior police officers. The role of the court is then to optimize each of these principles to the extent legally and factually possible.

This analysis makes sense of the European Court of Human Rights decision in the case of *Plattform*,[25] in which an anti-abortion demonstration in Austria had been disrupted by pro-abortion demonstrators. The demonstrators (A) claimed that the Austrian government had failed to protect their right against the counter-demonstrators (B). The first principle identified by the Court is the *duty to protect* demonstrators against others. 'In a democracy the right to counter-demonstrate cannot extend to inhibiting the exercise of the right to demonstrate. Genuine, effective freedom of peaceful assembly cannot, therefore, be reduced to a mere duty on the part of the State not to interfere.'[26] The first principle must then be optimized in the light of the second principle, which is the *duty of restraint* preventing the State from interfering with B's right to demonstrate. Here the Court held that the State 'cannot guarantee [the right] absolutely'. Also identifiable is the principle of institutional balance, requiring a level of autonomy in the executive to determine which means are most effective. The Court held that the authorities 'have a wide discretion in the choice of the means to be used'.[27] Optimizing all these principles led to the finding that the duty is to take reasonable and appropriate measures to enable lawful demonstrations to proceed peacefully.

A similar analysis can be applied to Article 2, the right to life. The European Court of Human Rights has had no hesitation in holding that Article 2 is not confined to restraining the State from taking life itself. The right can also trigger a positive obligation on authorities to safeguard the lives of those within its jurisdiction, including taking preventative measures to protect an individual (A) whose life is at risk from the criminal acts of another individual (B).[28] At

---

[25] *Plattform 'Ärzte für das Leben' v Austria* (1991) 13 EHRR 204 (European Court of Human Rights).
[26] ibid para 32.
[27] *Plattform* (n 25 above) [34].
[28] *Osman v United Kingdom* (2000) 29 EHRR 245 (ECHR) para 115.

the same time, A's prima facie right to be protected against criminal actions by B must be optimized in the light of the competing duty of restraint on the State not to infringe on B's rights in the investigation and prosecution of crime. The conflict between these two principles is clearly illuminated in *Osman*,[29] which concerned the murder of the applicant's husband by the obsessed teacher of their son. The applicant complained that the authorities had failed to protect them from the murderer despite a series of clear warning signs that the former teacher represented a serious threat to the physical safety of the boy and his family. Here the court identified all the major principles. The first was the *duty to protect* A against B by taking preventative measures. The second was the *duty of restraint* in respect of B's rights. The State must 'fully respect the due process and other guarantees which legitimately place restraints on the scope of [the authorities'] action to investigate crime and bring offenders to justice'.[30] Both of these principles must be optimized in the light of factual constraints, such as 'the difficulties involved in policing modern societies, [and] the unpredictability of human conduct'. The Court also refers to the principle of institutional competence and competing resources so that the decision must be made in the light of 'the operational choices which must be made in terms of priorities and resources'.[31]

Article 3, the right not to be subjected to torture or inhuman or degrading treatment or punishment, requires a somewhat different analysis, since it is expressed as an absolute right under the ECHR. This means that any competing principles are given minimal weight. This can be seen in *Z v UK*,[32] which concerned a claim that the State had failed in its duty to protect children against inhuman and degrading treatment inflicted by their parents. In this case, the Court stressed that 'Article 3 enshrines one of the most fundamental values of democratic society'. This leads to a strong duty to protect, deriving from the obligation under Article 1 of the Convention to secure to everyone within their jurisdiction the rights and freedoms defined in the Convention. This obligation is to take measures 'designed to ensure that individuals within their jurisdiction are not subjected to torture or inhuman or degrading treatment, including such ill-treatment administered by private individuals'. These measures should provide effective protection, in particular, of children and other vulnerable persons and include reasonable steps to prevent ill-treatment of which the authorities had or ought to have had knowledge.[33]

Identification of relevant principles is, however, only the first step. More difficult is to show that the principles can be ordered in a way which gives sufficient determinacy to the norm. Here the Court has implicitly given different weightings to the principles at stake. The right to freedom of assembly carries less weight

---

[29] ibid.
[30] *Osman* (n 28 above) para 116.
[31] ibid para 116.
[32] *Z v United Kingdom* (2002) 34 EHRR 3 (ECHR).
[33] ibid para 73.

than the right to life, whereas the right not to be subjected to torture or inhuman or degrading treatment or punishment has such weight that it is very difficult to displace. This can be seen in the standard expected of the State in order to justify the action that it took to protect the right. Thus, to protect freedom of association the State is under a duty *to take reasonable and appropriate* steps, whereas to protect the right to life the State is under a duty to do *all that could be reasonably expected*. So far as Article 3 is concerned, the Court in *Z v UK* reiterated that Article 3 prohibits in absolute terms torture or inhuman or degrading treatment or punishment. The obligation under Article 3, therefore, requires States to take measures designed to *ensure* that individuals within their jurisdiction are not subjected to torture or inhuman or degrading treatment, including such ill-treatment administered by private individuals.

This is not to say that the duty is entirely determinate. Deference to the State's institutional expertise leaves a core area of indeterminacy, in that it remains to be determined which measures are reasonable and appropriate. However, this autonomy is structured by the requirement that the State's decision meets the standard of justification required. In the case of the right to freedom of assembly, the State is required to give appropriate and reasonable protection to demonstrators without undermining the right of counter-demonstrators. In *Plattform*, the Court had to be satisfied that the State had provided a level of policing which was capable of such justification, before it could hold that the duty had been fulfilled. By contrast, it rejected the justification offered in *Osman*. In that case, the UK government argued that a duty to protect is breached only if the failure to take preventive measures is tantamount to gross negligence or wilful disregard of the duty to protect life. The Court held that 'such a rigid standard must be considered to be incompatible with the requirements of Article 1 of the Convention and the obligations of Contracting States under that Article to secure the practical and effective protection of the rights and freedoms laid down therein, including Article 2'. Instead, the authorities must do 'all that could be reasonably expected of them to avoid a real and immediate risk to life of which they have or ought to have knowledge'.

It can be seen from these cases that it is possible to formulate and apply a positive duty to protect without incurring insurmountable problems of indeterminacy. Once analysed in terms of competing prima facie principles, each of which requires optimization in the light of legal and factual possibilities, then it is possible to identify areas of relative determinacy and areas which are inevitably discretionary or indeterminate. The discretionary areas can themselves be explained by determinate principles such as the separation of powers as between executive and judicial decision-makers. This means that discretion is not wholly indeterminate but bound by the requirements of legitimacy and accountability through public and reasoned justification. What indeterminacy is left is no different from the kind of indeterminacy found in many other legal norms when applied in situations in which several principles need to be reconciled.

(iii) The duty to fulfil: specifying the duty

It is against the duty to fulfil that the charge of indeterminacy is most often levied. In rebutting the charge, it is important as a start to keep the duty and the right separate. The right is the goal; the duty is to realize the goal. The right may not be capable of immediate fulfilment, either because other principles have priority or because the resources are not available. This does not, however, reduce the right to a mere aspiration. There is still a duty to realize the right: the fact that the duty is complex and subject to competing factors is not a reason for downgrading the right. In Alexy's terms, the principle constituting the right remains prima facie binding. The task is to optimize it to the extent legally and factually possible.

The spotlight therefore turns to the task of determining how and when such a duty is fulfilled. The charge of indeterminacy generally assumes that to be determinate requires a predetermined level of provision. Kelley in his rejection of the legitimacy of welfare rights argues that welfare rights are 'entitlements to have certain goods'.[34] However, the right need not lie in a bundle of goods. It can also be a right to an act, such as the creation of institutions, enabling or facilitative powers, or programmes of further action. Nor is it necessary to specify precise steps to be taken for a duty to be determinate. This would preclude any autonomous input from domestic decision-makers, giving no space for the distribution of decision-making required by the principle of institutional competence. Instead, the question of whether a duty is fulfilled can be answered according to criteria deduced from the underlying principle behind the implication of positive duties in the first place. Positive duties aim to secure to all the ability to exercise their rights. This requires the removal of constraints, as well as the provision of resources or the facilitation of activities which ensure that all are substantively equal in the ability to participate fully as citizens in society. Four parameters can be deduced from this broad aim. The first is effectiveness. Whatever actual level of provision is made at any particular time, or whatever steps are taken to facilitate self-provision, these must be appropriate and aimed at achieving the right. The second is participation. The involvement of those affected in the process is essential for the result to be meaningful. The third is accountability. Authorities must be in a position to explain and justify the view taken of the steps taken to optimize the right. Accountability is a necessary aspect of the autonomous space for the State to decide what specific measures should be taken. While those measures cannot be predetermined, the State must be accountable for the measures actually taken. The final parameter is equality. The focus of the positive duty to fulfil is on the disadvantaged, those who are under more constraints in their ability to enjoy the right than others. This means that it goes beyond equality of treatment to substantive equality, which might include giving the less advantaged a greater share of resources. These criteria are not all-or-nothing standards,

---

[34] Kelley (n 19 above) ch 2.

but permit degrees of fulfilment. They also leave the precise action to be taken to be determined in a context-dependent manner.

This value of this approach can be demonstrated by analysing the duty to fulfil in a relatively straightforward situation, namely the right of access to court. Without the provision of legal aid, this right might be of little use to those who cannot afford to pay legal fees. This means that to secure its exercise, the State should be under a duty to provide legal aid. But this does not mean that the precise amount of legal aid needs to be specified before the duty could be said to be determinate. Instead, the State's actions can be judged according to whether it has taken steps which are effective, whether they advance participation; whether they are justifiable; and whether they advance substantive equality in the sense of ensuring that all are equally capable of having access to court.

The European Court of Human Rights case of *Airey*[35] is a helpful demonstration of this approach. The Court recognized that the right of access to court, although a civil and political right, can in certain circumstances give rise to a positive duty to provide legal aid. But in enforcing this duty, it did not feel the need to specify the amount of legal aid needed. Instead, the criteria outlined above can be discerned within the Court's judgment. Most important was effectiveness. The Irish government argued that there was no duty to provide legal aid because the applicant could exercise her right to access to court by appearing in person. The Court rejected this argument, focussing instead on whether such formal freedom was effective: 'The Convention is intended to guarantee not rights that are theoretical or illusory but rights that are practical and effective.'[36] This meant that the chief question before the Court was whether 'Mrs Airey's appearance before the High Court without the assistance of a lawyer would be effective, in the sense of whether she would be able to present her case properly and satisfactorily'. In the light of the complexity of the case, it was improbable that the applicant would be able effectively to conduct her own case. Therefore, the State was required to take positive action to fulfil the right. Importantly, the provision of legal aid was only one possible means to make the right effective. The Court held that the State could take other measures, such as simplifying the procedures, provided it had the same outcome.

The other three criteria are implicit in the judgment. The participative criterion was pivotal: legal aid was essential for the applicant to be in a position to participate in legal decisions affecting her; and the court also emphasized the centrality of the right to a fair trial in a democratic society. The Court stressed that it could not dictate which measures should be taken: 'All that the Convention requires is that an individual should enjoy [an] effective right of access to the courts.' Implicit in this is that the State should be in a position to explain and justify the measures taken. Finally, equality is at the heart of the decision. The duty

---

[35] *Airey v Ireland* (1981) 3 EHRR 592 (European Court of Human Rights).
[36] ibid para 24.

to provide is clearly essential to equalize the chances of the disadvantaged to have the same access to the court as those who can afford to. Here the Court stressed that the applicant would be at a disadvantage if her husband were represented and she were not.

The duty to provide legal aid did not strike the Court as posing insurmountable difficulties as to determinacy. From the familiar terrain of civil and political rights, it seemed relatively easy to strike out in the direction of the positive duty to fulfil. Socio-economic rights are generally considered to pose more difficult problems, leading to the familiar dismissal of such rights as mere aspirations. However, on closer inspection a similar analysis to that in *Airey* is available. The right to health is the most challenging of these rights. The right to the 'highest attainable standard of physical and mental health'[37] appears intrinsically indeterminate, since what can be attained in terms of health depends on a wide variety of polycentric factors, including medical science, available resources, environmental conditions, and political will. Nor is it a right which can be provided to the individual alone. It requires the promotion of conditions in which people can lead a healthy life, and therefore extends to the underlying determinants of health, such as food, housing, access to safe water and adequate sanitation, safe and health working conditions, and a healthy environment. It is therefore dependent on the realization of a host of other rights, such as the right to food, housing, work, education, life, human dignity, equality, freedom of information, and the right against torture.[38]

How then can the duty to fulfil the right to health be formulated in a way which is sufficiently determinate to retain its normative content? It is clearly impossible to set a specific standard, in the same way as it was impossible to set a standard for legal aid. Nevertheless, although much more complex, the duty can be defined according to the parameters of effectiveness, participation, accountability, and equality set out above. These can all be seen in the analysis of the normative content of Article 12 in the General Comment by the ICESCR Committee. The first and central requirement is effectiveness. For there to be an effective right to health, there is a duty to make available in sufficient quantities the basic determinants of health, including safe and potable drinking water, adequate sanitation facilities, hospital, clinics and other health-related buildings, trained medical and profession personnel, and essential drugs. The second is participation. The Committee stresses the importance of participation of the population in all health-related decision-making at the community, national, and international levels. Participation is also essential to ensure that health provision is respectful of culture and sensitive to gender. Accountability is found in the requirement that the State justify any violation of the duty by showing that despite a shortage

[37] ICESCR, Article 12.
[38] See CESCR, General Comment 14, *The Right to the Highest Attainable Standard of Health* (Twenty-second session 2000) para 3–4.

of resources every effort has been made to satisfy the obligations attendant on the right.[39] Finally, equality requires not only physical accessibility, but also affordability to all, especially the most vulnerable or marginalized sections of the population, so that poorer households are not disproportionately burdened with health expenses. The Committee stresses the special obligation of the State to provide those without sufficient means with the necessary health insurance and health care facilities and to prevent discrimination on prohibited grounds.

(iv) The duty to fulfil: progressive realization

The second main challenge for the duty to fulfil relative to the duty of restraint concerns the timescale for compliance. Negative duties are said to be immediate, requiring the State simply to desist from an action. Duties to fulfil take time to realize. In the case of socio-economic rights, recognition of the fact that resources may not be immediately available to fulfil the right has led to an explicit formulation of the duty in programmatic terms. Thus, the principal obligation in the ICESCR is expressed in Article 2(1) as the duty 'to take steps...to the maximum of its available resources, with a view to achieving progressively the full realization of the rights recognized in the present Covenant by all appropriate means'. As the ICESCR Committee itself acknowledges, 'in this sense the obligation differs significantly from that contained in article 2 of the International Covenant on Civil and Political Rights which embodies an immediate obligation to respect and ensure all of the relevant rights'.[40] A similar formula is used in the South African Constitution: 'The state must take reasonable legislative and other measures, within its available resources, to achieve the progressive realisation of this right.'[41]

Again, Alexy's analysis is helpful. The duty is to optimize the right so far as legally and factually possible. Its immediate realization may be delayed by factual impediments such as the lack of resources, or the existence of competing principles which must justifiably be given relative priority at any particular time. However, the principle encapsulated in the right remains prima facie binding. This also highlights the dynamic and continuing nature of the optimization requirement: the principle must be continually realized as resources become available or as other principles are satisfied. The duty to fulfil therefore operates along two axes: one referring to the level of provision and one to the time taken to achieve the right.

Approaching the duty in this way makes it possible to see that not all duties to provide are progressively realized. In some contexts, the right must be fulfilled

---

[39] ibid para 47.
[40] CESCR, General Comment 3, The nature of States parties obligations (Fifth session 1990) UN Doc E/1991/23, Annex III, para 9.
[41] South African Constitution, ss 26(2), 27(2).

immediately because there are no competing principles with sufficient weight to displace them. Duties to fulfil civil and political rights are often of this nature; but this might be true too of duties to fulfil socio-economic rights. Thus, the South African Constitution gives every child the right to basic nutrition, shelter, basic health care services, and social services.[42] This gives rise to a duty to immediately realize the right. No other principles, nor demands on resources, have sufficient weight to displace it. Similarly, the duty might not require extra resources, so that there are no factual impediments to its immediate fulfilment. A better allocation of existing resources might make the right immediately available.[43]

Even where the duty to optimize the right is progressive, it is not the case that the whole obligation is postponed.[44] First, the State is under an immediate obligation to take action towards achieving the goal so far as current circumstances permit, striving to ensure the widest possible enjoyment of the relevant rights under the prevailing circumstances even where the available resources are demonstrably inadequate.[45] In particular, resource constraints have no effect on the duty to devise strategies and programmes for the fulfilment of the duty. Clearly retrogressive steps should not be taken except where fully justified and in the context of full use of maximum available resources. Secondly, there is an immediate obligation to monitor the extent of the realization.[46] Thirdly, there is an immediate duty to guarantee that the relevant rights will be exercised without discrimination. This entails extending existing provision to excluded groups, whether in the form of housing,[47] social security,[48] or health care.

It is when it is accepted that the duty may be progressive and the right may take time to be realized that the real challenges arise. In an influential article in 1996, Chapman demonstrated the difficulty in demonstrating that a State had failed to fulfil its obligations under the ICESCR.[49] This is because progressive realization means that obligations cannot be uniform or universal, but vary according to levels of development and available resources. This necessitates a multiplicity of performance standards.[50] Even more difficult is to determine the meaning of 'maximum of its available resources'. As Robertson wryly notes: ' "Maximum"

---

[42] South African Constitution, s 28 (1)(c).
[43] A Chapman 'The Status of Efforts to Monitor Economic, Cultural and Social Rights' Economic Rights: Conceptual, Measurement and Policy Issues Conference University of Connecticut (2005) 17.
[44] CESCR, General Comment 3 (n 40 above).
[45] ibid para 9.
[46] CESCR, General Comment 3 (n 40 above) para 11.
[47] *Ghaidan v Godin-Mendoza* [2004] UKHL 30, [2004] 2 AC 557 (HL).
[48] *Khosa and Mahlaule v Minister for Social Development* 2004 (6) BCLR 569 (South African Constitutional Court).
[49] A Chapman ' "A Violations Approach" for Monitoring the International Covenant of Social, Economic and Cultural Rights' (1996) 18 Human Rights Quarterly 23, 23–66.
[50] ibid 31.

stands for idealism; "available" stands for reality. "Maximum" is the sword of human rights rhetoric. "Available" is the wiggle room for the State.'[51]

However, a decade later, Chapman reported that significant progress had been made.[52] Of particular importance has been the progress in assessing whether maximum available resources have been used. In a groundbreaking publication, *Dignity Counts*, it was demonstrated that it is possible to assess three elements of government investment: the sufficiency of government investment, the equity of patterns of expenditure, and the efficiency of spending. Sufficiency is assessed by comparing actual expenditure with a benchmark figure, such as the proportion of GDP, or of total government spending.[53] The World Health Organization has suggested that health spending should comprise 5% of GDP.[54] A State which spends less would be in violation of the duty to utilize maximum available resources. Also of importance is the way in which budgeting has changed over time. If government spending has been dropping, relative to GDP or other government spending, it strongly suggests that there are available resources but the duty has not been prioritized. This is particularly true where a government reduces spending on realization of a right but increases its budget overall.

Efficiency of spending is more difficult to assess. But where a sum has been clearly budgeted and not used, a very strong argument can be made to compel a government to fulfil its obligations. For example, in India, when starvation deaths were occurring even though adequate food was being held in storage, it was clear that the duty arising from the right to life had been breached.[55] The duty was similarly breached where a budget had been allocated for a road to a small hilltop town, but never used. In an analysis of the right to health in Mexico, *Dignity Counts* demonstrates the Health Ministry had significantly under-spent its budget, while Tourism and Defence had over-spent (indeed, their overspend was more than the whole health budget). Mexico could be held to have breached the duty. Similarly, in South Africa, it is clear that available resources are not being used to fulfil rights, as demonstrated by under-spending of budgets both at municipal and provincial level.

The third criterion to be considered is equity. Equity is also measurable. If spending is inequitable as between genders, classes, regions, or ethnic groupings, the government would be in breach of its duty. This too can be illustrated by the Mexican example, in which it was shown that the richest regions in Mexico had received significantly more of the health spending than the poorest. The analysis

    [51] R Robertson "Measuring State Compliance with the Obligation to Devote Maximum Available Resources to Realising Economic, Social and Cultural Rights' (1994) 16 Human Rights Quarterly 693, 694.
    [52] A Chapman 'The Status of Efforts to Monitor Economic, Cultural and Social Rights' Economic Rights: Conceptual, Measurement and Policy Issues Conference University of Connecticut (2005).
    [53] H Hofbauer, A Blyberg, W Krafchik *Dignity Counts* (Fundar 2004) 36.
    [54] Chapman (n 52 above) 18.
    [55] See Chapter 5.

was also able to consider spending on different aspects of the right, such as reproductive care, preventive care, and hospital care.

Progress has also been made in giving more determinate content to the duty
progressively to realize a right. Again, the key is not so much to specify precisely
the steps to be taken, but the process whereby decision-makers should identify
those steps. Effectiveness, participation, accountability, and equality can again
be used to assess whether the steps fulfil the duty. Effectiveness is the most
complex, because, as Hunt points out, progressive realization means that what
is expected of a State will vary over time. This variable dimension can, however,
be measured along the two axes mentioned above, namely, level of provision at
a particular time. This is done by setting targets or benchmarks to which the
State must direct its efforts within a set timetable. When the particular target
has been achieved, the duty is fulfilled at that time; but progressive realization
means that there should then be continuing movement towards the next target
on the road to ultimate fulfilment. Where the right is complex, it is useful to set
benchmarks in respect of three types of indicators necessary to realize the right:
key structures and mechanisms ('structural indicators'); programmes, activities,
and interventions ('process indicators'); and outcomes ('outcome indicators').[56]
Given the difficulty in collecting data, Hunt emphasizes that it is crucial that
indicators are relatively straightforward and can be measured from data which
is commonly available or without considerable extra expense.[57] The criteria of
accountability and participation require this process to be transparent and fully
participative. This is particularly facilitated by the immediate obligation to draw
up a clear and detailed plan, setting both goals and timetables; and by the continuing obligation to monitor. An interesting example comes from South Africa,
where children themselves have been consulted in an attempt to flesh out priorities for fulfilling children's rights under the Constitution.[58] Finally, the criterion of equality requires that progressive realization must be sure to prioritize
the needs of the most disadvantaged and marginalized. Thus the South African
Constitutional Court held in *Grootboom* that the duty progressively to realize the
right to housing was breached because it did not pay sufficient attention to the
rights of the most disadvantaged.[59]

An example of this process can be seen in respect of the duty to reduce maternal
and infant mortality which arises from the right to health. One way of achieving
this is to improve the proportion of births attended by skilled health personnel.
The State should begin by finding out the current position, in order to determine

---

[56] Economic and Social Council 'Report of the Special Rapporteur on the right of everyone
to the enjoyment of the highest attainable standard of physical and mental health, Paul Hunt'
(GENERAL E/CN.4/2005/51, 11 February 2005) paras 54–56.

[57] ibid Annex, para 5.

[58] Institute for Democracy in South Africa (IDASA).

[59] *Republic of South Africa v Grootboom (1)* 2001 (1) SA 46 (South African Constitutional
Court).

where the right is being denied and therefore where effort needs to be made. Once the baseline has been established, a target or benchmark for improvement is set. This requires baseline statistics of the number of births currently attended by skilled health personnel. To ensure that the equality dimension is taken into account, these figures need to be disaggregated on grounds of gender, race, ethnicity, rural/urban and socio-economic status. For example, the baseline statistics, suitably disaggregated, might reveal that the average is 60%, but that this rises to 70% in urban areas and drops to 50% in rural areas. Further disaggregation might show that in the rural areas the dominant ethnic group enjoys a coverage of 70% but the minority of only 40%. Faced with these figures, the State will need to set a target, say 70%, to be achieved over the next five years, where all relevant groups reach this target. The State must then set in place policies and programmes to achieve this target, with specific emphasis on reaching the minority groups in rural areas.[60] If after five years the target has been reached, then a higher target should be set, covering the subsequent five years, until the right has been fully realized. If the target has not been reached, then the reasons for this need to be considered. It may be that the State has deliberately neglected its duty, in which case it will be in violation. Alternatively, there may be factors outside of its control, such as a natural disaster, the AIDS pandemic, etc. On the other hand, the programme might have been less than fully efficient, in which case it should be reviewed and corrected. It should be noted that the duty extends across borders, so that countries in the developed world have a duty to provide appropriate aid to those without adequate resources to realize the right.

(v) The minimum core obligation

One way of responding to the charges of both indeterminacy and lack of immediacy is to specify a core obligation which is determinate and requires immediate fulfilment. The ICESCR Committee has sought to pin down a set of core obligations for each right which constitute the minimum essentials of the right. State parties 'must demonstrate that every effort has been made to use all resources at its disposition in an effort to satisfy, as a matter of priority, those minimum obligations'.[61] This concept has proved highly controversial. Most striking is the rejection of the concept by the South African Constitutional Court.

To understand the issues, it is useful to consider the South African Court's objections to the applicability of a minimum core within South African jurisprudence. There are several different dimensions of the problem. The first is the difficulty in defining a minimum core. The Court held that this needed so much contextual information about the needs of those affected and the available opportunities that, given the institutional limits of a court, it could not be

---

[60] Hunt (n 56 above) paras 39–43.
[61] CESCR, General Comment 3 (n 40 above).

expected to determine this.[62] This assumes that a minimum core must consist of predetermined standards, which can be precisely measured in abstract. However, as argued above, the content of the duty, whether it be the minimum core or the final duty, cannot be established by setting detailed thresholds. Instead, it is specified through parameters, including effectiveness,[63] participation, account-ability, and equality.

This demonstrates that the problem associated with the minimum core is not truly one of setting standards, but one of priorities and timing. Here the UN Committee seems at first sight to insist that the minimum core are those obli-gations which need to be fulfilled immediately, requiring 'all resources at its disposition' to be used to satisfy these minimum obligations, 'as a matter of priority'.[64] This led to the second objection by the South African Court. If the minimum core is an immediate obligation, and the State must use not just avail-able resources but all resources at its disposal, it would seem that 'everyone can demand that the minimum core be provided to them'.[65] However, according to the judgement in *Khosa*, 'it is impossible to give everyone access even to a core service immediately. All that is possible and all that can be expected of the State, is that it act reasonably to provide access to the socio-economic rights…on a progressive basis.'[66]

However, this is to take the UN Committee's statement out of context. Read as whole it can be seen that the obligation is one of optimization, but that the State faces a much higher burden of justification when it relies on alleged lack of available resources to justify failing to meet the minimum core obligations. Thus, the statement reads: 'In order for a State party to be able to attribute its failure to meet at least its minimum core obligations to a lack of available resources *it must demonstrate that every effort has been made* to use all resources that are at its dispos-ition in an effort to satisfy, as a matter of priority, those minimum obligations.'[67] This means that the State is not required to do more than is possible given its resources; but it must be able to show that it could not do more than it has done, given its resources.

It could be retorted that this does not avoid the need to decide which parts of the obligation are urgent in this way. It is here, once again, that Alexy's use of principles as optimization requirements is helpful. Dealing with the general question of whether a principle can be absolute, Alexy responds that a principle, P1, can give the impression of absoluteness when there is a very large set of condi-tions in which P1 takes precedence and therefore a strong degree of certainty that

---

[62] *Republic of South Africa v Grootboom (1)* 2001 (1) SA 46 (South African Constitutional Court).
[63] Including accessibility.
[64] General Comment 3 (n 40 above).
[65] *Khosa and Mahlaule v Minister for Social Development* 2004 (6) BCLR 569 (South African Constitutional Court) para 34.
[66] ibid para 35.
[67] *Khosa and Mahlaule* (n 65 above) para 10 (italics added).

it will take precedence over other competing principles. Nevertheless, it is possible for another principle to trump P1 in particular circumstances. For example, although Article 1(1) of the German Constitution declares human dignity to be inviolable, there may be situations in which the need to protect others takes precedence, as when a convicted person is given life imprisonment because he or she could be a danger to others if released sooner.[68] The core is therefore what is left after P1 has been balanced with other principles. Alexy applies his analysis to the German constitutional law principle of a minimum core. Article 19(2) of the German Constitution states: 'In no case may the core content of a constitutional right be infringed.' The German Federal Constitutional Court calls the area protected by the rules giving precedence to P1 'the absolutely protected core area of private autonomy'. Even here, Alexy argues, the core is what is left after P1 has been balanced with other principles. Principles might always outweigh the core of other principles, even though the likelihood is so small in the case of the absolute core that one could say with almost certainty that it would not be.[69]

Applying this to the question of whether the positive duty to fulfil contains a minimum core obligation, it can be seen that there is a set of basic conditions which should take precedence in almost all situations, but which can be outweighed in very particular situations. The minimum core refers to the duty to do everything possible to optimize the basic right of survival of the most destitute and disadvantaged in society, because there is very little that can take priority over the basic right of survival. This can be explained as a failure to value the fundamental dignity of the most deprived,[70] or developed as a principle in its own right. The South African Constitutional Court itself has recognized this in the *Grootboom* case, when it held that the State was required to ensure that 'those whose needs are most urgent and whose ability to enjoy all rights therefore is most in peril, must not be ignored by the measures aimed at achieving the realisation of the right'. When these needs are not satisfied by the State, it faces a high burden of proving that it is genuinely not in a position to do so.

Is reasonableness review sufficient to deal with these issues, as the South African Constitutional Court has stated, given that the Court has built in an explicit weighting towards the most disadvantaged within that standard? According to Alexy's analysis, the minimum core is the aspect of the duty which is most difficult to trump. The State's duty to optimize the principle therefore requires this aspect of the duty to be fulfilled unless there are extremely weighty principles which justify delaying its full implementation. This is captured in part by the South African Court's decision in *Grootboom* that those who are most in need must not be ignored. However, reasonableness on its own is too

[68] Alexy (n 10 above) 65.
[69] ibid 194–196.
[70] S Liebenberg 'The Value of Human Dignity in Interpreting Socio-economic Rights' (2005) 21 South African Journal on Human Rights 1.

diffuse a standard to capture the power to override other principles which attach to a minimum core principle. As Liebenberg convincingly argues, the standard of reasonableness has the effect of placing the burden on claimants to show that the State's lack of action is unreasonable. The legal and factual complexity of proving such a claim makes it unfair on the applicants and unlikely to succeed.[71] Her solution is to argue that there should be a presumption of unreasonableness, which the State is required to rebut with compelling reasons. This proposal can be seen to be a specific application, within a litigation context, of the broader analysis presented here. The analysis favoured here also means that it is not necessary to define precise standards which must be met to fulfil the minimum core. Instead, the minimum core is defined according to the parameters of effectiveness, participation, accountability, and equality. The need for the State to justify its omissions in respect of the minimum core is then a reinforcement of the accountability parameter.

(vi) Rights and duties: the individual claim

One of the key difficulties facing a positive duties approach, particularly in respect of the duty to fulfil, is the relationship between the individual right-holder and the duty. Under a duty of restraint, it is clear that the right-holder has an immediate claim to protection from the State, and is therefore the primary beneficiary of the duty. This is true too for the duty to protect: an individual whose rights have been infringed by another individual because of the State's failure to take appropriate action has a clearly delineated claim against the State for an individualized remedy. Is this the case for the duty to fulfil? Clearly, this depends on the way in which the positive duty is formulated. In *Airey*, the right to legal aid vested in the individual led to an immediately realizable claim on her behalf. Positive duties to provide social security can lead to immediately vested rights to social security benefits. By contrast, the South African Court has held that rights to housing and health do not confer any direct right to claim immediate delivery of goods and services from the State. The individual right consists instead of the right to require the government to adopt a reasonable programme.[72] Rights protected at international level are even broader: the individual may benefit from the programme, but she has no immediate entitlement. In some contexts, the duty appears to be expressly divorced from the right. Thus, the directive principles, such as those in the Irish and Indian constitutions, establish duties on the State without creating corresponding justiciable rights.[73]

---

[71] ibid 22–23.

[72] *Grootboom* (n 59 above) paras 39–43; *Minister of Health v Treatment Action Campaign (no 2)* (2002) 5 SA 721 (South African Constitutional Court) paras 32–39 and 125.

[73] Indian Constitution (adopted 26 January 1950), Art 37; Bunreacht Na hÉireann, Art 45.

In examining the relationship of the duty to the right, it should be emphasized that it makes no sense to see the duty as existing without the right (leaving
aside the question of whether the right is judicially enforceable). The reason for
a duty to fulfil is that individuals have rights which must be fulfilled. There
would be no duty without the right. However, in deciding on the relationship of
the right-holder to the duty, it is helpful to distinguish between different sorts
of rights. The claim that the right-holder gains no immediate benefit assumes
that all rights take the form of a right to some specific object. Yet this does not
exhaust the field of rights. One can also have a right to an act. In the case of
duties of restraint, the right is to a negative act. This might be, as Alexy shows,
the right to non-obstruction: that is the right that the State should not prevent
or hinder acts, characteristics, or legal freedoms of the right-holder.[74] The right
that we are interested in here is the right to a positive act. This might be a right to
a positive factual act, such as a right to a State subsidy, which may or need not be
achieved by law. Alternatively, it may be a right to a positive normative act, such
as the legalizing of marriage or property. Among such positive acts might be the
granting to an individual of powers to take action herself in order to alter a legal
or factual situation. For example, an individual might be granted the power to
marry or to enter into contracts. It is then up to the individual to choose whether
to use that power.

This analysis casts further light on the nature of the right where there is a
positive duty to fulfil, and in particular, where the duty is one of progressive realization. The right in such a case can be understood as a right to a positive act by
the State, but the positive act may not at this stage consist in the provision of a
particular package of resources to the individual right-holder. Instead, it could
be a right to State action to create the legal or administrative norms necessary to
make such provision available. The corresponding duty is to take action to put
the framework into place and activate it. Once such action is taken, the individual's right crystallizes into an entitlement to the particular resource. The duty
is therefore not severed from the right. Instead, the proper formulation of the
right demonstrates the nature of the duty that follows it. This also makes sense of
the programmatic nature of such duties, recognizing the fact that it might take
time for the State to execute its duty, but placing an obligation on the State to
take such action with all due speed. Even in the *Airey* case, the Court gave the
State the autonomy to determine the most effective means of realizing the right of
access to courts. This could have been done by simplifying the procedure as much
as by providing legal aid. The complainant may not have had an immediate right
to legal aid, but instead a right that the State put in place administrative norms
necessary to simplify the judicial process.

At one level, this seems to provide the frustrating outcome that a person,
such as the applicant in the *Grootboom* case, has a right to be housed under the

---

[74] This paragraph is based on Alexy (n 10 above) 121–138.

Constitution, but no right to a house at any one time. This is certainly a disappointing outcome for her at that moment. But it simply underlines the fact that her right is not a right to a specific object, namely a house, but a right to action by the State to provide a system which, so far as possible given other duties and constraints, will house those who are unable to provide for themselves. It is of course possible to formulate the right as an immediate claim to a specific object. Liebenberg proposes that, to reflect the value we place on the dignity of each person, serious consideration should be given by the South African Court to grant individual remedies to successful litigants.[75] The individual remedy, however, depends on how the right and corresponding duty are defined. If the right is to an act rather than an object, then the duty is to perform the act, complying with the parameters of effectiveness, participation, accountability, and equality suggested above. This would not, however, give a remedy in the form of a specific object.

If the right is to an object, the remedy is more difficult. As a start, the content of the right would require closer definition if it referred to an object rather than an act. The right to be housed is an example. In the *Grootboom* case, the South African Constitutional Court referred to the variety of means in which a State can provide housing, ranging from access to mortgages to the provision of materials for individuals to build their own houses to shelters to permanent housing. With this comes a range of decisions as to services, location, size, and standard. This is complicated by the fact that, given that all individuals in the position of the claimant would have the same right, it might be assumed that the State should be in a position to provide housing or health to all. To establish the content of the individual claim, and therefore the remedy, would require a very different, and so far elusive standard. Thus, the frustration of the individual in having to wait for her benefit might need to be weighed against the advantages of a duty which addresses the underlying determinants necessary to provide for each individual rather than vesting in a particular object for the individual. However, even where the right is to an act rather than an object, there may be effective remedies to ensure that the duty to act is fulfilled. As will be seen later, the Indian Supreme Court has developed a highly effective remedy in the form of an interim injunction requiring the State to take particular steps towards realization of its duty. This is more than an administrative law remedy, requiring only that the State justify its actions. It requires the State to actually perform the actions.

This is not to say that there is never an immediate entitlement to a resource. The duty not to discriminate, for example, requires immediate satisfaction. However, in such a case the difficulties outlined above do not apply in the same way, since the duty is simply to extend the existing provision to those who have been excluded due to discrimination. This is demonstrated in the

---

[75] Liebenberg (n 70 above) 30.

South African case of *Khosa*, where child benefit and old-age benefit were extended to permanent residents who had previously been excluded because they were not citizens. There was no need for the Court in that case to determine the amount of benefit which should be provided; merely to extend existing provision.

An important advantage of viewing some rights as a right to an act rather than to an object is that, by moving away from the static view of a right as a 'package' of goods transferred to the beneficiary, it also leaves space to move beyond the understanding of the rights-bearer as a passive beneficiary with no say over the nature of the need or the benefit. Yet, as we have seen, the definition of need itself is a contested question.[76] Assigning values to different social or individual goods cannot be a technical matter: there must be an open and democratic discussion on this issue.[77] In addition, it avoids the problematic implications of conceptualizing social rights as a transfer of income from rich to poor, giving the impression that one citizen's benefits can only be achieved at a cost to another. Finally, it makes it possible to move beyond the static conception that rights should only be concerned with redistributing material resources or income, ignoring the social structures and institutional contexts which underlie these distributive outcomes.[78] Thus, Young argues that: 'Individuals are not primarily receivers of goods or carriers of properties, but actors with meanings and purposes who act with, against, or in relation to one another.'[79] Instead of conceiving of rights as possessions, she concludes, they should be seen in terms of relationship, 'institutionally defined rules specifying what people can do in relation to one another'.[80]

C. Conclusion

This chapter has analysed the structure of positive duties in detail. Rights and duties are frequently discussed entirely in the realm of their enforceability. This inevitably skews the discussion in the direction of justiciable rights. This chapter has attempted to understand and elaborate positive duties in a normative sense, rather than concentrating on what happens if they are violated. The aim is to understand positive human rights duties as permeating the political culture more generally, influencing decision-making in a proactive sense, and guiding behaviour, rather than only as a response to complaints that they have been violated.

---

[76] P Jones 'Universal Principles and Particular Claims: From Welfare Rights to Welfare States' in A Ware and R Goodin (eds) *Needs and Welfare* (Sage London 1990).
[77] A Sen *Development as Freedom* (OUP Oxford 1999) 78–81.
[78] IM Young *Justice and the Politics of Difference* (Princeton Paperbacks Princeton 1990) 22.
[79] ibid 28.
[80] Young (n 78 above) 25.

Habermas helpfully distinguishes between obedience to the law based on self-interest because of the fear of sanctions, and rational acceptance of the law through a belief in its validity.[81] The law, he argues, tolerates an actor's strategic action, but a norm's claim to validity binds the actor's free will.[82] Thus, the law must also make it possible for actors to internalize and commit themselves to the values contained in human rights. Having focussed on this normative aspect of positive human rights duties, it is now possible to turn to the question of justiciability. This is the focus of the next chapter.

---

[81] Habermas (n 23 above) 198.   [82] ibid para 1.3.1.

4

Justiciability and the Role of Courts

A. Introduction

Acknowledging that positive duties necessarily flow from human rights does not
in itself mean that they should be enforced by courts. Indeed, the role of courts
in adjudicating human rights is perhaps the most controversial aspect of modern
human rights jurisprudence. This is particularly so for positive duties. As a start,
duties to act are seen as entailing a number of choices, which courts must evaluate and rank. Such a task arguably belongs with political decision-makers. By
contrast, duties of restraint do not require judges to make value judgments,
simply to restrain the State from acting. As well as overstepping the bounds
of legitimacy, positive duties stretch the competence of the courts. While a
restraint operates immediately and once and for all, positive duties are continuing and require ongoing monitoring. This is said to be beyond the institutional
capabilities of a court. Furthermore, duties of restraint are said to be cost-free,
whereas positive duties entail a level of resource commitment which judges have
neither the legitimacy nor the competence to control. The result is that while the
justiciability of duties of restraint is generally accepted in practice (although still
controversial in theory), positive duties are considered quintessentially political.
As the Committee on Socio-economic Rights ruefully remarked: 'In relation to
civil and political rights, it is generally taken for granted that judicial remedies
for violations are essential. Regrettably, the contrary presumption is frequently
made in relation to socio-economic rights.'[1]

  This chapter begins by examining the ways in which various jurisdictions have
attempted to distinguish between positive and negative duties. This indicates clearly
that the lines of demarcation are both undemocratic and incoherent. The chapter
then moves on to address the objections to positive duties head-on. It is argued
that justiciability is justified to the extent that courts can contribute to strengthening democracy through human rights. In the light of this analysis, the third section constructs a democratic role for the courts in respect of positive human rights
duties. The final section tests these arguments by assessing South African case law.

---

[1] Committee on Economic, Social and Cultural Rights (CESCR), General Comment 9, The
domestic application of the Covenant (Nineteenth session 1998) para 10.

B. Drawing the Boundary

There has been a long tradition of drawing the boundary of justiciability at the territorial limit of duties of restraint. This can be seen both in constitutional texts and in judicial interpretation. One way of creating bright-line distinctions is to differentiate between civil and political rights and socio-economic rights, on the assumption that the former give rise to justiciable duties of restraint, while the latter are associated with non-justiciable positive duties. Thus, many jurisdictions simply exclude socio-economic rights from a justiciable Bill of Rights. The US, Canada, the UK and the ECHR are good examples of this approach.

An alternative approach expressly distinguishes duties of restraint and positive duties on the basis of justiciability. Both the Irish and Indian constitutions differentiate between justiciable rights and non-justiciable 'directive principles'. Part III of the Indian Constitution, entitled 'Fundamental Rights', contains justiciable negative rights. Part IV, by contrast, contains directive principles of social policy, which, although they aim to be 'fundamental in the governance of the country' are expressly non-justiciable. Article 37 states that 'it shall be the duty of the State to apply these principles in making laws', but that the principles 'shall not be enforced by any court'.[2] Similarly, the Irish Constitution provides for directive principles of social policy which are 'intended for the general guidance' of the legislature;[3] and 'shall not be cognisable by any Court under any of the provisions of this Constitution'. This approach was also adopted in the late stages of the drafting of the EU Charter of Fundamental Rights. The original drafters of the Charter were committed to removing artificial barriers by unifying civil and political with socio-economic rights within the document itself. Nevertheless, opponents of justiciable positive duties succeeded in including a late amendment which distinguished between judicially enforceable rights, and 'principles' to be implemented by legislative and executive acts. The Charter therefore states that principles 'shall be judicially cognisable only in the interpretation of such acts and in ruling on their legality'.[4]

These textual demarcations need not conclusively exclude positive duties, since civil and political rights are fully capable of giving rise to positive duties. In practice, then, the role of boundary drawing falls to the courts. Opponents of justiciability would expect that judges would be only too ready to seize power from the legislature. In reality, however, it is judges themselves who are quick to exclude

---

[2] Indian Constitution (adopted 26 January 1950), Article 37.
[3] Bunreacht Na hÉireann, Article 45.
[4] EU Charter of Fundamental Rights, Article 52(5). See further MP Maduro 'The Double Constitutional Life of the Charter of Fundamental Rights of the European Union' in T Hervey and J Kenner (eds) *Economic and Social Rights under the EU Charter of Fundamental Rights* (Hart Oxford 2003); S Fredman 'Transformation or Dilution: Fundamental Rights in the EU Social Space' [2006] 12 European Law Journal 41–60.

positive duties from their remit. The reasons given by judges mirror the general concerns about legitimacy sketched above. Possibly the most forceful exponent of this view has been the US Supreme Court. In *Deshaney*,[5] a child claimed that the State had not taken appropriate steps to protect him against abuse by his father. He relied on the Due Process Clause of the Fourteenth Amendment, which states: 'No State shall... deprive any person of life, liberty or property without due process of law.' The Court rejected the argument that this gave rise to a positive duty on the State to protect individuals against other individuals. Giving the opinion of the Court, Rehnquist J stated emphatically:

Nothing in the language of the Due Process Clause itself requires the State to protect the life, liberty, and property of its citizens against invasion by private actors. The Clause is phrased as a limitation on the State's power to act, not as a guarantee of certain minimal levels of safety and security. It forbids the State itself to deprive individuals of life, liberty, or property without 'due process of law,' but its language cannot fairly be extended to impose an affirmative obligation on the State to ensure that those interests do not come to harm through other means. Nor does history support such an expansive reading of the constitutional text.[6]

The reason for this is primarily the view that positive duties are appropriate only for political resolution. It would be anti-democratic for unelected, unaccountable judges to impose positive duties on elected legislators. Thus, Rehnquist J continued:

The people of Wisconsin may well prefer a system of liability which would place upon the State and its officials the responsibility for failure to act in situations such as the present one. They may create such a system, if they do not have it already, by changing the tort law of the State in accordance with the regular lawmaking process. But they should not have it thrust upon them by this Court's expansion of the Due Process Clause of the Fourteenth Amendment.

UK courts have similarly emphasized the democratic objection to justiciable positive duties. Until recently, this has been done in human rights litigation by attempting to delineate separate spheres of decision-making for elected representatives and for judges.[7] In a well-known dictum, Lord Hope asserted in the House of Lords that courts should recognize 'an area of judgment within which the judiciary will defer, on democratic grounds, to the considered opinion of the elected body'.[8] Key to the delineation of the separate spheres is the judicial attempt to

---

[5] *DeShaney v Winnebago County Department of Social Services* 1009 S Ct 998 (1989) (US Supreme Court).

[6] ibid 195.

[7] See also M Hunt 'Why Public Law Needs "Due Deference"' in N Bamforth and P Leyland (eds) *Public Law in a Multi-layered Constitution* (Hart Oxford 2003). This section is taken from S Fredman 'From Deference to Democracy: the Role of Equality under the Human Rights Act 1998' (2006) 122 Law Quarterly Review 53–81.

[8] *R v Director of Public Prosecutions, ex parte Kebilene* [2000] 2 AC 326 (HL) 380–381.

distinguish between the political and the legal: 'The more purely political (in a broad or narrow sense) a question is, the more appropriate it will be for political resolution...Conversely, the greater the legal content of any issue, the greater the potential role of the court.'[9]

Political decisions in turn are defined as those which require difficult choices between the interests of the individual and the needs of society:

Those conducting the business of democratic government have to make legislative choices which...are very much a matter for them, particularly when (as is often the case) the interests of one individual or group have to be balanced against those of another individual or group or the interests of the community as a whole.[10]

This is particularly true in respect of decisions on which there is room for conflicting views,[11] such as 'matters of social or economic policy, where opinions may reasonably differ in a democratic society and where choices on behalf of the country as a whole are properly left to government and to the legislature'.[12] Planning and housing policy have been two areas in which the courts have stressed 'the obvious unsuitability of the courts' to make decisions which 'have acute social, economic and environmental implications'.[13] Thus, in the housing case of *Poplar* Lord Woolf stated: 'The economic and other implications of any policy in this area are extremely complex and far-reaching. This is an area where, in our judgment, the courts must treat the decisions of Parliament as to what is in the public interest with particular deference.'[14] By contrast, courts consider that they have exclusive competence to determine prison sentences. As Lord Steyn put it in *Anderson*: 'In our system of law the sentencing of persons convicted of crimes is classically regarded as a judicial rather than executive task.'[15]

In defending this demarcation, UK judges have argued that the indeterminacy of positive duties makes them more suitable for the political than the judicial process. On this view, where there are no predefined legal standards, and opinions might reasonably differ on the outcome, decisions can only be made by weighing up different interests according to political criteria. Judges have no legitimate means to make such decisions: they can only be taken by those who must be responsive to the range of affected interest groups, and face the consequences of their decisions through their accountability to the electorate. Thus, stated Lord Nolan in *Alconbury*: 'To substitute for the Secretary of State an independent and

[9] *A v Secretary of State for the Home Department* [2004] UKHL 56, [2005] 2 WLR 87 (HL) [29].
[10] ibid [38].
[11] *Poplar Housing and Regeneration Community Association Ltd v Donoghue* [2001] EWCA Civ 595, [2002] QB 48 [71].
[12] *A* (n 9 above) [108].
[13] *R (Alconbury Developments Ltd and Others) v Secretary of State for the Environment, Transport and the Regions* [2003] 2 AC 295 (HL) [60].
[14] *Poplar* (n 11 above) [71].
[15] *R (Anderson) v Secretary of State for the Home Department* [2002] UKHL 46, [2003] 1 AC 837 [39].

impartial body with no central electoral accountability would not only be a recipe for chaos: it would be profoundly undemocratic.'[16]

Judges have also justified separate spheres on the grounds of 'relative institutional competence'.[17] On this view, judges are not competent to make decisions where the facts are not accessible to the courts, either because, like national security, they need to be kept secret, or because, like socio-economic policy, they are wide-ranging and polycentric. The bipolar, reactive, dispute-based nature of judicial processes means that judges cannot achieve the wide lens necessary to make polycentric decisions. Thus, in *Bellinger*,[18] the validity of a marriage where the wife was a transsexual woman who had been born a man, was said to be a decision 'pre-eminently for Parliament'. According to Lord Nichols, the case 'raises issues whose solution calls for extensive enquiry and the widest public consultation and discussion. Questions of social policy and administrative feasibility arise at several points, and their interaction has to be evaluated and balanced. The issues are altogether ill-suited for determination by courts and court procedures.'[19] Judges only see the facts of the case before them and so cannot cater for the many different issues that need to be determined.[20]

(i) Distorting democracy: privileging duties of restraint

Although these arguments appear plausible on the surface, the underlying assumption that duties of restraint can and should be protected while positive duties should not is highly problematic. Most serious is its counter-productive impact on the very democracy it seeks to protect. This is because courts can use their jurisdiction over duties of restraint to trump democratic decisions in the arena of positive duties, including welfare policies and social provision. Litigants relying on civil and political rights can thereby force governments to retrench on social provision. A good example is the role of the US Supreme Court in striking down social legislation during the New Deal. In *Lochner v New York*,[21] State legislation limiting bakers' hours of work to a maximum of 60 per week was struck down as an interference with freedom of contract. Peckham J, giving the judgment of the Court, declared:

The general right to make a contract in relation to his business is part of the liberty of the individual protected by the 14th Amendment of the Federal Constitution. Under that provision, no state can deprive any person of life, liberty, or property without due

---

[16] *Alconbury* (n 13 above) [60].
[17] *A* (n 9 above) [29].
[18] *Bellinger v Bellinger* [2003] UKHL 21, [2003] 2 AC 467.
[19] ibid at [36].
[20] *Bellinger* (n 18 above) [39].
[21] *Lochner v New York* 198 US 45, 25 S Ct 539 (1905) (United States Supreme Court).

process of law. The right to purchase or to sell labour is part of the liberty protected by this amendment, unless there are circumstances which exclude the right.[22]

As Holmes J recognized in his dissenting opinion, this seriously undermines the democratic decisions of State legislatures to pursue their positive duties, particularly, the duty to care for the lives, health, and well-being of their subjects: 'The word "liberty", in the 14th Amendment, is perverted when it is held to prevent the natural outcome of a dominant opinion.'[23]

The extent to which privileging duties of restraint can undermine a State's attempts to fulfil its positive duties was strikingly illustrated in recent Canadian litigation. In order to sustain comprehensive public health provision, Quebec legislation prohibited private health insurance. In *Chaoulli*, a doctor and a patient claimed that this infringed the right to security of the person because it prevented them from accessing private health care and subjected them to long waiting lists for publicly funded health care. This raised starkly the potential conflict between the State's positive duty to provide publicly funded health care and its duty not to interfere with freedom of contract. The Court upheld the claim. Bastarache J for the majority characterized the claim in terms of whether the State should be restrained from interfering with individual liberty: 'In essence, the question is whether Quebeckers who are prepared to spend money to get access to health care that is, in practice, not accessible in the public sector because of waiting lists may be validly prevented from doing so by the state.'[24]

What was missing from this analysis was any robust recognition of the positive duties to make provision for all Canadian citizens. According to the trial judge, the purpose of the prohibition on private insurance was 'to promote the overall health of all Quebeckers without discrimination based on economic circumstances. In short, they constitute a government action whose purpose is to promote the well-being of all the people of the province.'[25] For the Supreme Court, however, this was no more than a government policy, which had to be justified against the high standard provided by section 1 of the Charter. This, the Court held, had not been discharged. McLachlin CJ stressed that 'the Charter does not confer a freestanding constitutional right to health care. However, where the government puts in place a scheme to provide health care, that scheme must comply with the Charter.'[26]

If the duty to provide for the health of all without discrimination had been regarded as a human right duty in its own right, the weight given to it by the Court would have been of an entirely different order. As a Canadian human rights lawyer commented, 'critics of the idea of using courts to promote social

---

[22] ibid 52.
[23] *Lochner* (n 21 above) 65.
[24] *Chaoulli v Quebec (Attorney General)* (2005) SCC 35 (Supreme Court of Canada) para 4.
[25] Cited in *Chaoulli* (n 24 above) para 241.
[26] ibid para 104.

and economic justice will see the *Chaoulli* decision as our "just deserts" for being foolish enough to encourage an increasingly neo-liberal Supreme Court, with little sympathy evidenced for the plight of the poor, to adjudicate rights in the field of complex issues such as health care delivery'. However, he continues, 'the judgment of the majority in *Chaoulli* was not the result of a court stepping into the field of social rights, but rather, of a court refusing to do so'.[27] In either case, it can be seen that protection of negative duties without positive duties skews the judicial approach in favour of the former whenever there is a clash.[28]

(ii) A difficult distinction

As well as privileging duties of restraint over positive duties, the attempt to demarcate justiciable duties of restraint from non-justiciable duties is problematic because it assumes that the duties are easily disentangled. It has been demonstrated in previous chapters that all rights, whether civil and political or socio-economic, give rise to a range of duties, both positive and negative. Attempting to draw a bright line between them leads judges to overlook one or other dimension. The same judges who set themselves against implying positive duties in the field of housing and social policy unhesitatingly require State action in respect of the provision of a fair trial. Thus, the British House of Lords has held that the right to a fair trial under Article 6 of the ECHR is breached if a criminal charge is not determined at a hearing within a reasonable time. Crucially, this is both a positive and a negative duty: the right was breached whether by the action of a public authority or its failure to act.[29] The courts had no hesitation in expecting that necessary resources be found to fulfil this duty. Conversely, courts may characterize a right as non-justiciable because it seems to give rise to a positive duty, whereas in fact the point at issue concerns only a duty of restraint. This can be illustrated by a recent decision of the British Court of Appeal, in which social housing tenants argued that their right to respect for their home under Article 8 of the ECHR was breached by the statutory regime,[30] which obliged courts to issue a possession order without examining the reasons.[31] Lord Woolf acknowledged that the applicants' Article 8(1) right had been breached. Nevertheless, he held:

The court has to pay considerable attention to the fact that Parliament intended ... to give preference to the needs of those dependent on social housing as a whole over those in the

---

[27] B Porter 'A Right to Health Care in Canada—Only if You Can Pay for It' [2005] 6 Economic and Social Rights Review.

[28] S Fredman 'Substantive Equality and the Positive Duty to Provide' [2005] 21 South African Journal of Human Rights 163–190, 67–68.

[29] *Attorney-General's Reference (No 2 of 2001)* [2004] 1 Cr App R 25 (HL).

[30] Housing Act 1988, s 21(4).

[31] *Poplar Housing and Regeneration Community Association Ltd v Donoghue* [2002] QB 48 (CA).

position of the defendant... The Human Rights Act 1998 does not require the courts to disregard the decisions of Parliament in relation to situations of this sort.[32]

In fact, the applicants were not claiming a breach of the positive duty to provide housing, but only of the duty of restraint on the State from evicting tenants from their homes without scrutiny of the reasons.

The difficulty in disentangling positive from negative duties suggests that a court's decision to endorse or ignore positive duties is based on their background understanding of freedom rather than on the text of the human right at issue. This can be seen by considering the wording of the Canadian right to security at issue in *Chaoulli*. Section 7 of the Canadian Charter states: 'Everyone has the right to life, liberty and security of the person and the right not to be deprived thereof except in accordance with the principles of fundamental justice.' Although the Court in *Chaoulli* construed this as giving rise to a negative duty only, Arbour J pointed out in her dissenting opinion in *Gosselin*, that the duty of restraint only appears in the second half of the formulation. The first is a free-standing right, which must be secured by the State.[33] It is therefore open to a court to interpret the right as giving rise to both positive and negative duties. It is only because of a conception of freedom as non-intervention that a Court would choose to endorse only negative duties. This is even more clearly demonstrated by considering the approach of the European Court of Human Rights. In a provision very similarly worded to the Canadian Charter, Article 2 of the ECHR provides: 'Everyone's right to life shall be protected by law. No one shall be deprived of his life intentionally save in the execution of a sentence of a court following his conviction of a crime for which this penalty is provided by law.' In the *Osman* case, the Court held that this enjoins the State not only to refrain from the intentional and unlawful taking of life, but also to take appropriate steps to safeguard the lives of those within its jurisdiction.[34] Particularly interesting is the decision of the UK House of Lords that positive duties can arise from Article 3 of the ECHR, which provides: 'No one shall be subjected to torture or to inhuman or degrading treatment or punishment.' In *Limbuela*,[35] it was held that the State had breached this right in relation to destitute asylum seekers because it failed to provide them with either social security or the right to seek paid employment. This was because the State was responsible for the legal system which had this effect. On this line of reasoning, even the Due Process clause in the US Bill of Rights should be construed as giving rise to positive duties. It is true that the latter refers only to the State's responsibility not to deprive any person of life. But it is only on a very narrow understanding of causation that it could be argued that the State's role in

---

[32] ibid 69.

[33] *Gosselin v Quebec* 2002 [SCC] 84 (Canadian Supreme Court) paras 338–358.

[34] *Osman v United Kingdom* (2000) 29 EHRR 245 (ECHR) para 151.

[35] *R (on the application of Limbuela) v Secretary of State for the Home Department* [2005] UKHL 66, [2006] 1 AC 396 (HL).

society is limited to its actual actions, and does not extend to the way it decides to configure its legal and social powers. A decision to structure the legal framework in such a way as not to provide protection for the right to life is, as was acknowledged in *Limbuela*, itself a positive action.

C. Strengthening Democracy through Justiciability

Attempts to distinguish between duties of restraint and positive duties are therefore both undemocratic and incoherent. This does not in itself mean that positive duties should be justiciable. It could be argued that coherence and logic are achieved by removing all human rights from the reach of judges rather than adding positive duties. This part addresses the broader argument against justiciability, and particularly the democratic argument. It does so by challenging the all-or-nothing character of that argument. Many opponents of justiciability assume that justiciability entails giving courts an overriding veto power against legislation to which popular assent has been given. However, it was established in Chapter 2 that popular assent is at best tenuous in modern democracies. Instead, a major role of positive human rights duties is to strengthen democracy. This suggests that justiciability may be appropriate to the extent that it can be harnessed to the achievement of these aims. Instead of re-ploughing the well-worked terrain which ranges justiciability against non-justiciability, the real challenge is to formulate a democratically justifiable role for the courts. Courts need not have non-revisable powers; nor are they necessarily bound to a procedure which is adversarial, costly, slow, and unable to deal with polycentric questions. As the experience in India shows, there is no reason why the institutional structure of courts should remain fixed. This part deals with legitimacy issues, while the next chapter explores the Indian experience of changing the structure of the court.

(i) Arguments from democracy: refashioning justiciability

The first challenge in shaping a role for the courts in respect of positive duties is to demonstrate that such a role can be legitimate. This in turn requires facing up to democratic objections. Perhaps the most cogent of such objections is that put forward by Jeremy Waldron. For Waldron, the most fundamental of rights is the right to participate on equal terms in social decisions. This right should not be confined to interstitial matters of social and economic policy, but should essentially concern issues of high principle such as those addressed by human rights.[36] Giving judges the power to decide issues of high principle, such as the content of human rights, entails a profound disrespect for people in their democratic and representative capacities. Behind such a power is the assumption that any

---

[36] J Waldron *Law and Disagreement* (OUP Oxford 1999) 213.

conception 'concocted by elected legislators next year or in ten years' time is so likely to be wrong-headed or ill-motivated that [the judge's] conception should be elevated immediately beyond the reach of ordinary legislative revision'.[37] To the contrary, Waldron maintains, the reasons why we think of individuals as bearers of rights are the very reasons why we should trust them as the bearers of political responsibilities.[38]

Waldron's approach is based on two questionable assumptions. The first is that justiciability means that judges have the last word on the matter. This need not be the case. It is possible for judges to exercise a meaningful role without having the last word. The second is that the right of participation is alive and well in the political system. This is based on both a simplistic understanding of democracy and an idealistic vision of the nature of participation. It is argued here that re-examining both these premises makes it possible to fashion a role for judges which augments and reinforces democratic participation rather than undermining it.

The first assumption, that justiciability gives judges a non-revisable power, generalizes from the US constitutional model,[39] according to which the Supreme Court can strike down decisions of the legislature on the basis of an interpretation of a broad and open-textured document formulated centuries earlier. However, positive duties can be justiciable in a meaningful way without judges having the last word. The British Human Rights Act 1998 (HRA 1998) is the leading example. Under this legislation, judges do not have the power to override legislation. Instead, judges faced with a successful human rights challenge to legislation can do one of two things. They can interpret the legislation so far as possible to comply with the courts' understanding of the right at issue,[40] in which case the amended legislation may be repealed or further amended by Parliaments. Alternatively, they can issue a declaration of incompatibility.[41] Such a declaration does not itself alter the law, but gives a powerful signal to the legislature that the law ought to be altered.

Thus, the democratic dilemma under the HRA 1998 is different from that faced by judges with the power to strike down legislation and therefore to remove issues entirely from the political process. Instead, a key to resolving the dilemma for UK courts is to see adjudication as feeding into the political process. By making a declaration of incompatibility, the courts can reopen the political debate, as well as enriching it by the insights uniquely generated through the process of judicial deliberation. In this sense, as Lord Scott recognized,[42] the import of the declaration of incompatibility is political not legal. There are those who have argued that legislatures would find it so difficult to gainsay the court that this amounts to a power of veto. However, this misunderstands the difference

---

[37] ibid 222.
[38] Waldron (n 36 above) 251.
[39] ibid 213.
[40] HRA 1998, s 3.
[41] HRA 1998, s 4.
[42] *A* (n 9 above) [143].

between legally binding decisions, and those which enter the political process as a factor, albeit weighty, which legislators consider. The HRA 1998 operates as an input into the political process, not as a point of closure. This expands rather than contracts democratic participation.

Even where judges do in principle have the power to strike down legislation, this does not generally mean, as Waldron suggests, that the decision is permanent and non-revisable. Constitutional courts have acknowledged that constitutions contain open-textured principles whose interpretation remains open to further discussion. Bills of rights are frequently referred to as a 'living tree', where changing social norms and values infuse judicial interpretation in order to reinvigorate constitutional texts. Similarly, it is well known that dissenting judgments may in time convince the majority. In the case of positive duties, this is particularly pronounced, since they are programmatic and forward moving and judicial input even at its strongest must incorporate elements of partnership and joint management. In any event, as we have seen, judges, conscious of their position relative to accountable decision-makers, have often been quick to carve out areas of autonomy for decision-makers. In particular, concepts such as 'reasonableness' permit the ongoing interaction between judges and elected officials even in a binding constitution. Nor are all constitutions as difficult to amend as that of the US Constitution. The Indian Constitution was amended by Parliament after a series of early cases in which it struck down social legislation in the name of the right to property.[43] Although the Court reasserted jurisdiction so that the 'basic structure' of the Constitution could not be amended, the possibility of legislative override nevertheless acted as a constraint on the Court.[44]

The second dimension of the argument against justiciability is that it undercuts the basic premise of democracy, namely that all important decisions should be settled by the people themselves. Waldron maintains that everyone has sufficient deliberative potential to be trusted with final decision-making power. However, as was argued in Chapter 2, there is little basis for asserting that the people themselves actually do make important decisions. Decision-making is in practice skewed towards those with power in society, and even where majorities do make decisions, there is a risk that they will override the rights of minorities. Opponents of justiciability argue that if the political system is defective in the extent to which ordinary people participate, the answer is to improve the political system rather than taking away more power from the people and giving it to the courts. However, this is a false juxtaposition. It has already been established that human rights and particularly positive human rights duties are essential to protect the basics of democracy, including the socio-economic conditions necessary to ensure substantive equality in the right to vote.

---

[43] *State of Madras v Champakam Dorairajan* AIR 1951 SC 226 (Indian Supreme Court).
[44] *Golaknath v State of Punjab* AIR 1967 SC 1643 (Indian Supreme Court); *Kesavananda Bharati v State of Kerala* (1973) 4 SCC 225 (Indian Supreme Court).

(ii) Justiciability: a democratic role?

Is it therefore possible to create a democratic role for courts in adjudicating positive human rights duties? In Chapter 2, it was argued that there are three key values behind the democratic ideal: accountability, participation, and equality. The role of the courts is therefore legitimate to the extent that they can fulfil an auxiliary role in each of these respects.

Accountability

Accountability means that representatives can be removed from power by the electorate and therefore are required to be responsive to the wishes of the majority. It also means that elected representatives have the duty to explain and justify their actions to the electorate on the basis of arguments which are acceptable to all. It is through enforcing the latter duty that courts can play a powerful role in enforcing positive duties without undermining democracy. Courts do not prescribe to elected representatives exactly what decisions should be taken, but instead require them to justify why those decisions have been made in the light of other competing principles. Requiring decision-makers to justify their decisions publicly exposes them both to political scrutiny in case of abuse and to more general public debate. Dyzenhaus argues that this role is inherently democratic: 'What justifies all public power is the ability of its incumbents to offer adequate reasons for the decisions which affect those subject to them... The courts' special role is as an ultimate enforcement mechanism for such justification.'[45]

This is appropriate for both duties of restraint and positive duties, but the number and complexity of competing principles is often greater in the context of positive duties. This is because positive duties require action to be taken in a context where several choices might be available. Taking action in one direction might foreclose other policy choices; it may require distributive decisions; and it may necessitate removing resources from some to give to others. In addition, because the steps have yet to be taken, decisions are based on prognosis or the ability to judge the future. This is particularly true when positive duties are programmatic, in the sense that the duty requires the State to 'roll out' its programme progressively over time. Thus, although courts might regard such decisions as too polycentric for judges to handle, in fact, in the context of human rights, their very complexity might make it even more important to reinforce the duty of explanation. The court's role is not to make the decision in the place of the decision-maker, but to require the decision-maker to give an open account of why a duty has not been fulfilled or has been fulfilled in one way rather than another.

This suggests, however, that it is sufficient to require politicians or the executive to justify their policies or actions. But should the fact of explanation be sufficient,

---

[45] D Dyzenhaus 'The Politics of Deference: Judicial Review and Democracy' in M Taggart (ed) *The Province of Administrative Law* (Hart Oxford 1997) 305.

leaving it to the political process to react, or should judges set the parameters for what counts as justification? The former approach might be thought to be the best way of preventing judges from entrenching on political decisions. Its chief effect is a demand for transparency. On the face of it, this absolves judges of the need to make value judgments; the principle being that reasons, once in the public domain, are subject to political rather than judicial scrutiny. The only constraint on the nature of the decision to be offered is the politicians' own sensitivity to their perception of public opinion. On the other hand, this risks depriving positive duties of any legally normative value, at least so far as justiciability is concerned.

To resolve this dilemma, it is crucial to recall that not all explanations will suffice to fulfil the criterion of accountability in a human rights context. The function of justiciability is not just to obtain an explanation, but to require decision-makers to provide an account of whether they have complied with a positive human rights duty and if not, why not. There are therefore predetermined grooves within which reasons must fall in order to be an adequate account. This is most easily understood by reverting to Alexy's notion of competing prima facie principles. For Alexy, the difference between a binding and a non-binding principle lies in whether acceptable reasons can be adduced for non-satisfaction of a prima facie duty. Such reasons must take the form of relevant competing principles. On the one hand are the prima facie duties to fulfil the right itself, as well as the principle of factual (as against merely formal) freedom; on the other are the opposing principles of separation of powers, legislative and executive competence, and the social and legal rights of others.[46] If no such reasons are given, the prima facie duty becomes definitive. The question the Court asks in these circumstances is not so much whether the duty has been satisfied, but, once competing principles have been taken into account, how much of the duty becomes definitive and whether that part has been satisfied.

What remains open, however, is whether it is enough simply to cite a competing principle (such as the separation of powers) or whether it is necessary to show that that principle has at least more than trivial weight when compared with the non-satisfaction of the prima facie duty. For the purposes of accountability, the judicial task is to require an open explanation in terms of competing prima facie principles, rather than to substitute their opinion on the relative weights to be given to different principles. On the other hand, the prima facie duty that arises from a right has significant weight by virtue of being a human right. It cannot therefore be displaced by trivial principles. This makes it clear that accountability is only a part of a meaningful judicial role. While it may be possible for judges to remain neutral as between competing principles outside of a human rights context, to regard the weight to be given to human rights principles as no different from other public policy principles would be to denude them of their intrinsic

⁴⁶ R Alexy *A Theory of Constitutional Rights* (OUP Oxford 2004) 348.

power as human rights. It is therefore necessary to go beyond accountability and consider what other democratic values judges should rely on as a yardstick for testing the justification offered. This brings us to the second and third values mentioned above: participation and equality. The next section considers participation, primarily in the form of deliberative democracy.

Participation through deliberation

In order to fashion a legitimate role for the courts, it is necessary to find a way of enhancing rather than undermining democratic participation. It was seen in Chapter 2 that participation can either take the form of bargaining on the basis of interests, or of deliberative democracy. While interest group bargaining is an inevitable component of democracy, the possibility of deliberation stands out as an alternative which can transcend inequalities in bargaining power. It will be recalled that deliberative democracy requires parties to come into the process prepared to produce reasons for their opinions which can convince others, but also prepared to be convinced themselves. In addition, instead of taking preferences as given, deliberative democracy is capable of influencing preference formation itself. Parties to the process can become aware of the extent to which they may have adapted their preferences to their limited circumstances, or have been influenced by powerful forces in society, and a wider range of perspectives may be opened up. An aim of democracy is therefore to increase the scope for deliberation. Is it possible to argue that courts, suitably adapted, can perfect the process of democracy by steering decision-making away from interest bargaining towards value-oriented deliberation or functioning as a forum for deliberation?

Courts display some central features of the deliberative process. The most important is that rights-based claims do not depend for their success on economic, social, political, or collective power, as in interest bargaining, but on the ability of the parties to convince the court of the soundness of their claim. Judges are required to come to the process open to the possibility of being persuaded by one side or the other, and the outcome is often a synthesis of the arguments of both sides. This can augment deliberative democracy in two ways. The court can function as a deliberative forum in its own right. This is not necessarily self-contained: the arguments of the parties, as well as both majority and dissenting judgments feed into the wider deliberative process. The second is to attempt to steer legislative and executive decision-making away from interest bargaining and towards deliberation. This means that decision-makers must do more than account for their decisions. In addition, they must show that their decisions have been reached in a deliberative manner. By requiring decision-makers to lay out their reasons and the process of reaching the decisions, courts constitute an incentive on decision-makers to make decisions in a deliberative way even outside of the courtroom.

There are of course important points of divergence between a court and the ideal deliberative forum. Three such points are particularly salient. The first is the role of the rights which are at the basis of the dispute. One influential stream of thinking on deliberative democracy argues that the process should be impartial. Any values are acceptable provided they can be supported by reasons which all those participating are able to accept. The existence of a constitutional right might be thought to breach this principle: it introduces a pre-established value, and deliberation can be concerned only with its meaning rather than its validity. However, as was argued in Chapter 1, impartiality is an impossible ideal. Within a deliberative context, absence of any predetermined values can lead to an impasse. If all viewpoints must be other-regarding as well as self-regarding, and the only criterion for choice between viewpoints is that the reasons offered are capable of convincing everyone, there may well remain intractable differences of opinion with no clear way forward. Sunstein also demonstrates that deliberation among participants who are too like-minded can simply lead to a reinforcement of a particular, possibly extreme or one-sided view. Human rights offer a way out of the impasse, since the values underpinning them have already been the product of an earlier broadly deliberative process. The deliberation taking place in court constitutes a further elaboration based on some pre-existing consensus.

Waldron does not accept that constitutional human rights can perform this role. Instead, he argues that having to refer to a legal document distorts the process, because deliberation must be framed in terms of the legal concepts therein. Drawing on the US experience, he points to the abortion debate as an example. Since the US constitution does not refer to abortion, deliberation in court has focussed on what he considers tangential issues, such as the right to privacy or freedom from intrusion, which emerge from a scrap of paper agreed three centuries before. However, as has been argued above, the process of determining human rights values is an ongoing one and could not in any event be contained within a rigid view of a human rights text. The text anchors rather than concludes the discussion. It sets out prima facie principles whose meaning and weight need to be continually elaborated upon. There is no reason why this should not take place in a plurality of different fora, including that of the court.

A second point of divergence concerns the litigants themselves. Litigation arguably derails rather than augments democracy, since it gives a second vote to the litigant in matters already dealt with through the ballot box. However, there is no reason why the individual's only opportunity to participate in political decision-making should be through the ballot box. Where a person is actually affected by a decision, it makes full democratic sense to allow her to participate in the process of decision-making both in respect of the particulars of her own situation and by contributing to the choice of values guiding the decision-maker.[47]

---

[47] G Cartier 'The Baker Effect: A New Interface between the Canadian Charter of Rights and Freedoms and Administrative Law' in D Dyzenhaus (ed) *The Unity of Public Law* (Hart Oxford 2004) 83.

More problematic is the objection that a courtroom, far from enhancing democratic participation, is an arena in which elites are able to augment their already powerful position. Litigation is sufficiently expensive, protracted, and framed in mystifying language, to make it inaccessible to most people. Thus, to the extent that litigation permits the litigants to participate in the political process, it does so in a wholly unrepresentative manner, privileging those with the resources and energy to pursue their grievance. The current structure of many courts makes this a real criticism. However, it is not a necessary feature of justiciability. If courts are going to be taken seriously as deliberative fora, then accessibility and equality within the courtroom must be a priority. Legal aid, demystifying language, and a simpler and more accessible procedure and tone are all possible. It is only by giving an opportunity to those who cannot participate fully in the democratic process that litigation supplements democracy; not by giving a further platform to those already well represented in that process. As will be seen below, a major contribution of the Indian courts has been to demonstrate ways in which courts can be opened up to the most disadvantaged in society.

On the other hand, it should not be thought that the political process provides a more accessible or equal alternative. The ability of elites to manipulate and dominate is not confined to the courtroom. The political process, particularly where it involves interest bargaining, is highly vulnerable to such domination. In this respect, justiciable positive rights are capable of correcting rather than reinforcing inequality. A key aim of positive duties is to ensure that individuals are able actually to exercise their rights and to remedy inequalities within the political process. This is a function which cannot be carried out within the political process itself.

A third divergence consists in the adversarial process. At one level, this appears to be the opposite of a deliberative framework. Each side appears before the court in an entirely defensive or accusative mode, aiming to persuade the court from a rigid position. This is true for ordinary civil or criminal disputes. Human rights disputes can, however, be fashioned in a way which transcends the bipolar nature of common law procedure. In particular, rules of standing and intervention can be adapted so that a wider range of perspectives is permitted to enter into the debate. This also has the advantage of countering one of the acknowledged weaknesses of some models of deliberative democracy, namely the assumption that all participants share the same ways of articulating and perceiving reality. Opening up the procedure to a wide variety of interested groups makes it possible to ensure that a range of perspectives is incorporated. This also clarifies the role of parties to proceedings in cases of positive duties where there is no immediate benefit to the right-holder. Where a right is programmatic and future oriented, a successful case would only yield a duty to carry out an approved plan, which may not provide an immediate tangible benefit to the winning party. Instead of a right-holder making a realizable claim to an individual benefit, the role of participants is to bring to the process a particular deliberative solution to the problem. From a republican perspective, public interest litigation of this sort can be characterized as a part of civic participation and an aspect of civic virtue.

It is still possible that the process of litigation remains sufficiently combative to prevent participants from being open to revising their own positions as a result of participating in the process. Even in such cases, it is possible to defend the deliberative function by looking at the process as a whole. The overall result of the process is for judges to deliberate on the basis of well-informed and reasonably supported arguments.[48] What feeds back into the public arena then, is a record of a deliberative process which others can take forward.

This brings us to the most difficult aspect of reconciling human rights litigation with the deliberative model. This is the role of the judges. The aim of the deliberative process, if it is to be democratic, is for the participants themselves to have the discussion, and revise their positions or convince others to do so. It is not to surrender their decision-making power to judges but to contribute to the deliberative process itself. This problem can be addressed by emphasizing that the role of the courts is to insist on proper deliberation within the political process. Thus, a central function of justiciable positive duties is the requirement that the State explain and justify to the court, and therefore to the litigants and the public more generally, the grounds of its decisions and the reason for the selection of particular means. A proper explanation by the State cannot be based on particular private interests, but instead requires reasons which can be publicly advocated. In other words, one of the aims of judicial intervention is to rejuvenate the deliberative process.[49] For Habermas, this need not amount to a court overstepping the grounds of legitimation by substituting for the democratic process. Instead, 'the source of legitimacy includes, on the one hand, the communicative presuppositions that allow the best arguments to come into play in various forms of deliberation and, on the other, procedures that secure fair bargaining conditions'.[50]

However, the deliberative process does not mean that decisions can never be made. As Habermas argues, there is a need to reach a point of closure under pressure of time, both for the parties before the court and in creating settled expectations by which others, including State bodies, can organize their decisions and actions. How then can the paradox be resolved between the ongoing deliberative debate, which requires revisability of judicial decisions, and the dispute before the court, which requires closure in decision-making? Clearly, judges should not have the last word on the meaning of human rights values, nor should they be fossilized by non-revisable decisions. However, courts need to be in a position to enforce the decision in the case before them, as well as creating settled expectations and consistent standards. The way forward is to

---

[48] For a similar argument, see J Habermas *Between Facts and Norms* (Polity Press 1997) 231.
[49] C Sunstein 'Interest Groups in American Public Law' (1985) 38 Stanford Law Review 29 at 58.
[50] Habermas (above n 48) 278–279.

regard courts' decisions as binding for the issue before them, but revisable in the long-term through the dynamic forum of deliberative democracy. At the point of decision-making, the duty is fixed, and the State is required to take action or is absolved from action, as the case may be. But on the broader scale, the decision remains part of a process of continuing revisability, whether through Parliament, case law or public discourse. This does not differ from the court's role in common law disputes in general. Here too, the court's decision can be revised by Parliament, but the change in the law cannot reverse the effect on the particular parties. Similarly, the court itself can, as part of the deliberative process, revise its views. But here the principle of stability requires change to be incremental, so that State officials and private individuals can order their lives according to reasonably settled rules. This is the basis of the rule of precedent, which restrains the extent to which courts revise their own decisions.

Equality and the representation reinforcing theory

The third potential role for justiciable positive duties is to address the inequalities in influence and voice in modern representative democracy. When minorities are excluded from the political process, or their voice is systematically silenced, representative democracy is not functioning properly. Arguably then, the democratic role of the judiciary is to remedy this deficit, and it is this which gives the judicial function its legitimacy. This approach originates in the famous *Carolene Products* case in which the Supreme Court of the United States noted that judges should scrutinize particularly carefully laws which, inter alia, restricted 'those political processes which can ordinarily be expected to bring about repeal of undesirable legislation'; laws 'directed at particular religious ... or national ... or racial minorities'; or laws reflecting 'prejudice against discrete and insular minorities'.[51] Taking his cue from the *Caroline Products* case, John Hart Ely has argued that the function of judicial review should be 'representation-reinforcing'. In this way, courts can be harnessed to buttress democracy without overstepping their legitimate bounds.

Ely's theory is particularly apposite for the interest-bargaining aspect of democracy. He recognizes that, left to its own devices, interest group bargaining favours the powerful, so that some groups are permanently excluded from the possibility of sharing power. This constitutes a serious malfunction in the process of democracy. In his words, this occurs when:

(1) the ins are choking off the channels of political change to ensure that they will stay in and the outs will stay out or (2) though no-one is actually denied a voice or a vote, representatives beholden to an effective majority are systematically disadvantaging some minority out of simple hostility or a prejudiced refusal to recognize commonalities of

---

[51] *United States v Carolene Products Co* 304 US 144, 152 n 4 (US Supreme Court).

interest and thereby denying that minority the protection afforded other groups by a representative system.[52]

It is here that judicial review comes into its own. Judicial review can make it possible for representative democracy to function properly by creating procedural means to free up the process of representation, and make sure that all are in fact accorded equal regard and respect.

The representation reinforcing theory is valuable in that it sees justiciable human rights as enhancing democracy rather than detracting from it. However, in the form Ely presents it, it is subject to several serious drawbacks. As a start, it is limited by his assumption that judicial review is only legitimate if it is value neutral or impartial. For Ely, it remains fundamental to representative democracy that 'value determinations are to be made by our elected representatives, and if in fact most of us disapprove, we can vote them out of office'. This leads him to argue that the representation-reinforcing function is only a procedural rather than a substantive one. Judicial review should be aimed at freeing up the process of representation, but not at dictating any particular outcome, since the latter would constitute an illegitimate usurpation of the function of democratic decision-makers. This is particularly so in respect of distributive justice. Ely argues that the only concern of judicial review in the context of distributive justice should be to ensure that the procedure whereby benefits and burdens are distributed is fully representative. The actual distribution should remain with the political process. 'Benefits—goods, rights, exemptions or whatever—that are not essential to political participation or explicitly guaranteed by the language of the constitution, ... we can call constitutionally gratuitous—though obviously they may be terribly important—and malfunction in their distribution can intelligibly inhere only in the process that effected it.'[53]

This distinction between procedure and outcome is, however, impossible to sustain. As was seen in Chapter 1, the possibility of effective participation in politics and society more generally depends on access to resources. If judicial review is to play a genuine role in reinforcing representation, the distribution of benefits must be seen as essential to political participation and not constitutionally gratuitous. This demonstrates that for judicial review to be legitimate in a democratic sense, it is neither possible nor necessary to sterilize its role of all evaluative content. Human rights represent a value pre-commitment to which society as a whole is bound; and judicial review should reflect that. Indeed, democracy itself is one of the values to which human rights are committed. This does not, of course, mean that all values are legitimate for judicial determination. It is only those specific values which promote democracy that are within the range of judicial legitimacy.

[52] JH Ely *Democracy and Distrust: A Theory of Judicial Review* (Harvard University Press 1980) 103.
[53] ibid 136.

Ely's theory is also limited by the model of pluralism on which it is based. In order to distinguish between minorities who are systematically excluded and those who are simply the transient losers in any majority voting system, Ely argues that the representation-reinforcing function of judicial review is specifically aimed at 'discrete and insular minorities'. Drawing on *Carolene Products*,[54] Ely argues that it is 'discrete and insular minorities', who are thus 'barred from the pluralist's bazaar...for reasons that are in some sense discreditable'[55] and to 'whose needs and wishes elected officials have no apparent interest in attending'.[56] This assumes that all groups are able to organize around common interests and thereby achieve an effective bargaining position. Deficiencies in representation are also characterized as group based. However, as Ackermann shows, those who are in fact least likely to succeed in the 'pluralists' bazaar' are those who are neither discrete nor insular. It is precisely because they are diffuse that certain groups find it difficult or impossible to organize themselves sufficiently to compete. Those who have the least access to resources are possibly the most diffuse, and it is they who should have the greatest claim to judicial concern with the fairness of the political process.[57] As Ackerman concludes, once the focus on interest groups is undermined, it becomes evident that it is not truly possible to 'perfect the pluralist process of democracy'.[58]

Nor is Ely's theory capable of taking us beyond the pluralist characterization of democracy, namely, that it consists of no more than interest bargaining. Interest bargaining is clearly an important part of decision-making in a democracy; but if it is the only form of coordination, then those without factual power will never have their interests given appropriate weight. In addition, the characterization of decision-making as entirely interest governed gives no weight to the collective values or aspirations which transcend interest group accommodation. Nor is there a principled yardstick by which judges can correct the imbalance in interest bargaining, since by definition it depends on the power of the parties. Instead, if there is to be a real commitment to equality in decision-making, justiciable duties must be based on substantive values, principles which 'pluralist politicians are simply not allowed to bargain over'.[59]

Representation-reinforcing theories are also ambiguous as to how exclusion from democratic decision-making should be addressed. Should minorities be given a voice or should they be allowed to win the argument? The first option requires the majority to take excluded groups' interests into account ('virtual representation' in Ely's sense). But this could mean no more than that the

---

[54] *United States v Carolene Products Co* 304 US 144, 152 n 4 (US Supreme Court).
[55] Ely (n 52 above) 152.
[56] ibid 151.
[57] B Ackerman 'Beyond Carolene Products' [1985] 98 Harvard Law Review 713 at 718.
[58] ibid 741.
[59] Ackermann (n 57 above) 741.

majority, having considered minority interests, reaches the same decision. The second option in effect permits the judiciary to withdraw the issue wholly from democratic decision-making.[60] But this risks subverting democracy.

Nevertheless, the representation-reinforcing approach is an essential element in the potential of the courts to contribute to democracy. The difficulties with Ely's approach can be avoided in two ways. The first is to move beyond the attempt at neutrality inherent in his focus on procedure. Instead, it is necessary openly to endorse the substantive value of equality in protecting minorities. As Baroness Hale has emphasized in the British House of Lords: 'It is a purpose of all human rights instruments to secure the protection of the essential rights of members of minority groups, even when they are unpopular with the majority. Democracy values everyone equally even if the majority does not'.[61] Equality also serves democracy generally: in the famous words of Justice Jackson of the US Supreme Court:

There is no more effective practical guaranty against arbitrary and unreasonable government than to require that the principles of law which officials would impose upon a minority must be imposed generally. Conversely, nothing opens the door to arbitrary action so effectively as to allow those officials to pick and choose only a few to whom they will apply legislation and thus to escape the political retribution that might be visited upon them if larger numbers were affected. Courts can take no better measure to assure that laws will be just than to require that laws be equal in operation.[62]

The second is to move beyond his attempt to perfect the pluralist approach to a recognition that interest bargaining will always reflect inequalities of power. Pluralist democracy characterizes the political process as one in which groups vie for power to further their own interests, with the majority principle playing an indispensable role in determining whose interests count.[63] Instead, the role of the court, as argued above, is to augment deliberative democracy. While interest groups will always be unequal, deliberative democracy should foster equality of participation. But this too requires intervention. Not all participants will have the same level of articulacy, nor the same skills in expressing a perspective and convincing others. Not all will even find their way into the deliberative forum. Courts in human rights litigation can only play a legitimate role if they make it possible for even the weakest voice to be heard and give equal persuasive power to all. Thus, Michelman has argued that the Constitutional Court should 'reach

---

[60] WN Eskridge 'Pluralism and Distrust: How Courts Can Support Democracy by Lowering the Stakes of Politics' [2005] 114 Yale Law Journal 101–149.

[61] *Ghaidan v Godin-Mendoza* [2004] UKHL 30, [2004] 2 AC 557 (HL) at [132] and see also *A* (n 9 above) at [108], [237]; and *West Virginia State Board of Education v Barnette* 319 US 624 (1943), para 3.

[62] *Railway Express Agency Inc v New York* 336 US 106 (United States Supreme Court) at 112–113.

[63] D Held *Models of Democracy* (Polity 1987) 186–220.

for the inclusion of hitherto excluded voices of emergently self-conscious social groups'.[64]

Placing litigation in a deliberative context also resolves the problem of the weight to be given to a minority group. A judicial decision should not necessarily give a veto power to a minority. But neither is it sufficient merely to require due consideration of the interests of the weaker group. Instead, the aim of judicial review is to enable excluded groups to play an equal part in the deliberative process, through taking minority arguments as seriously as majority perspectives and coming to a deliberative resolution based on the power to convince rather than the power to overwhelm. This fundamentally changes the political, if not the legal, power of the litigants. As will be seen in the following chapter, the Indian courts have deliberately taken the view that the function of the court is to give a voice to the most disadvantaged. It is in this context that the representation-reinforcing theory comes into its own.

D. Adjudicating Positive Duties

To what extent can courts be said to be approaching their jurisdiction in the light of the democratic principles set out above? This section will focus on the socio-economic rights jurisprudence of the South African court, because of its express jurisdiction, its sensitivity to the democratic issues, and the pioneering manner in which it has developed its jurisprudence.

The South African Constitution is unique in expressly recognizing that all rights give rise to a range of duties. Section 7 of the South African Constitution provides that: 'The state must respect, protect, promote and fulfil the rights in the Bill of Rights.' This has the striking result that even traditional civil and political rights such as the right to life give rise to positive duties. Moreover, these duties are not subject to the constraints of progressive realization or available resources. There is also a group of socio-economic rights which give rise to an immediate duty and are not expressly subject to resource constraints. Particularly important among these are the rights of children to family, parental, or appropriate alternative care, and to basic nutrition, shelter, basic health care services, and social services.[65] Similarly immediate and not subject to resources are the rights to emergency medical treatment;[66] and to basic education.[67] Finally, there is the right of detained persons to adequate accommodation, nutrition, reading material, and medical treatment.[68]

---

[64] FI Michelman 'Law's Republic' [1988] 97 Yale Law Journal 1493 at 1529.
[65] South African Constitution, s 28(1).
[66] South African Constitution, s 27(3): No one may be refused emergency medical treatment.
[67] South African Constitution, s 29(1)(a).
[68] South African Constitution, s 35(2)(e).

But most important for our purposes are the rights which give rise to qualified duties. These are the major socio-economic rights in sections 26 and 27.
According to section 26(1): 'Everyone has the right to have access to adequate
housing.' Section 27(1) provides:

Everyone has the right to have access to–
   (a) health care services, including reproductive health care;
   (b) sufficient food and water; and
   (c) social security, including, if they are unable to support themselves and their
        dependants, appropriate social assistance.

In respect of each of these rights, a second paragraph expressly sets out the nature
of the duty, namely to 'take reasonable legislative and other measures, within its
available resources, to achieve the progressive realisation of this right'. In addition,
section 25(5) provides: 'The state must take reasonable legislative and other measures, within its available resources, to foster conditions which enable citizens to
gain access to land on an equitable basis.'

   In adjudicating on these duties, the Court has been acutely aware of its
position relative to the newly democratic State. While its mandate to adjudicate
on positive duties is more explicit than most courts, its political positioning has
had an important impact on its self-perception. Specially constituted to constitute a complete break with the abuses of the past, the Court at its inception was
composed of judges who were committed to the transformational agenda. It is
wrong, however, to assume that these are necessarily the ingredients of an activist
court. While strongly committed to the ideals and values in the Constitution,
the Court has been sensitive to the enormity of the task facing the government in
reversing the evils of apartheid. In addition, the commitment to a new democracy suggests that the Court has viewed the elected government, rather than
itself, as the primary agent for realizing the transformative project embodied in
the new constitution.

   The vehicle within which it has attempted to shape a role for itself is through
the concept of reasonableness found in the express duty on the State to 'take
reasonable legislative and other measures' in sections 26(2) and 27(2). Even cases
which have been brought under the provisions requiring immediate fulfilment,
such as the rights to emergency health care or shelter for children, have been
deflected to the programmatic provisions, permitting the Court to utilize the
reasonableness concept. Thus, the first major case, *Soobramoney*, was litigated on
the basis of the right to life and the right to emergency health care, both of which
would give rise to an immediate duty on the state to fulfil the right. Instead, the
court preferred to deal with the case under the right to access to health care in
section 27(1), triggering the reasonableness criterion in section 27(2). Similarly,
in *Grootboom*, the litigants framed their case in part as a breach of the immediate
duty to fulfil the rights of children to shelter. They succeeded at first instance.
Again, the Constitutional Court refused to go down this road, emphasizing the

distributive nature of positive duties to fulfil, which meant that any particular person's entitlement needed to be weighed against others. Here too, the Court preferred to use the right to access to housing in section 26(1) so that it could determine the case according to the reasonableness criterion in section 26(2). In both cases, the reasonableness standard was thought to better accommodate the balance between judicial and executive power.

Reasonableness has been criticized as establishing an overly deferent approach, along the lines of administrative law review. However, the court has made it clear that the standard of reasonableness is a higher standard than rationality.[69] What is of interest here is whether it has succeeded in developing reasonableness in a way which furthers the democratic values of accountability, equality, and deliberative democracy. Also of key importance in shaping a democratic role is the nature of the remedy provided. Can the Court use its remedial powers to trigger deliberative decision-making in which participants have an equal voice, thus avoiding the pitfalls both of a mandatory remedy which stifles democracy, and a deferent approach which fails to improve democracy? A further complexity concerns the relationship between the right-holder and the duty. On the one hand, the right-holder's role might be conceived of in terms of activating democracy, rather than gaining a concrete personal benefit. On the other hand, this might be thought to reduce the right to a mere policy prescription. As argued earlier, this dilemma can be addressed by characterizing the right-holder as having the right to an act rather than an object. Can the reasonableness concept as developed by the South African court address these complexities?

The Constitutional Court's first opportunity to express its view of the socio-economic rights provisions took place during the 'certification' process, which gave it the unusual role of certifying the constitution's compliance with the basic constitutional principles agreed during the constitution building process. In rejecting the challenge mounted against the justiciability of socio-economic rights, it is notable that the Court focussed on duties of restraint. Positive duties were not alluded to except in the sense that the Court was undaunted by the possibility of adjudicating on issues with budgetary implications. 'The fact that socio-economic rights will almost inevitably give rise to [budgetary] implications does not seem to us to be a bar to their justiciability. At the very minimum, socio-economic rights can be negatively protected from improper invasion.'[70] Thus, its role in respect of positive duties was left wide open.

In the first major case, *Soobramoney*,[71] the applicant, who suffered from heart disease and renal failure, claimed that his right to life and to emergency health

[69] *Bel Porto School Governing Body and Others v Premier, Western Cape and Another* 2002 (3) SA 265 (CC), 2002 (9) BCLR 891 (CC) at para 46.

[70] *Ex Parte Chairperson of the Constitutional Assembly: In re Certification of the Constitution of the Republic of South Africa* 1996 (4) SA 744 (CC) (South African Constitutional Court).

[71] *Soobramoney v Minister of Health, Kwa-Zulu-Natal* 1998 (1) SA 765 (CC) (South African Constitutional Court).

treatment had been breached when he was refused life-prolonging renal dialysis. The hospital authority argued that given the shortage of dialysis machines, there was a need to ration their availability, and this had been done by offering dialysis only to patients who did not suffer from heart disease. The judgment focusses on obtaining an explanation of the reasons for the refusal of treatment to the patient rather than casting judgement on the worth of those reasons. It was held that the rationing decision had been made on clear and transparent criteria which were consistently applied and reflected the need to harmonize the conflicting pulls of shortage of resources and high levels of demand. Chaskalson CJ stated that the local administration:

> . . . has to make decisions about the funding that should be made available for health care and how such funds should be spent. These choices involve difficult decisions to be taken at the political level in fixing the health budget, and at the functional level in deciding upon the priorities to be met. A court will be slow to interfere with rational decisions taken in good faith by the political organs and medical authorities whose responsibility it is to deal with such matters.[72]

It is arguable that even on a more searching standard of review, the same decision would have been reached in the *Soobramoney* case. However, by framing the standard as one of rationality rather than the fuller concept of reasonableness, the Court is applying a standard which is appropriate for judicial review of executive policies but does not give enough weight to human rights and their associated duties. The legacy of *Soobramoney* has therefore been rightly criticized as requiring so little beyond transparency as to lose the thrust of a human rights duty at all. At most, the case could be read as endorsing the accountability parameter; but the equality and deliberative dimensions are missing. In particular, the Court was reluctant to address the fact that it was the claimant's poverty that prevented him accessing the health care that was readily available in the private sector.

The second case, *Grootboom*,[73] developed a more substantive notion of reasonableness, focussing not just on accountability but also on the value of equality.[74] The case concerned a group of people who had been living in intolerable conditions in a squatter settlement near Cape Town. Having been on the waiting list for low-cost housing for seven years, they moved onto private land. Yakoob J described their plight thus:

> At the beginning of the cold, windy and rainy Cape winter, the respondents were forcibly evicted at the municipality's expense. This was done prematurely and inhumanely: reminiscent of apartheid-style evictions. The respondents' homes were bulldozed and burnt and their possessions destroyed. Many of the residents who were not there could

---

[72] ibid at para 29 per Chaskalson CJ.

[73] *Republic of South Africa v Grootboom (1)* 2001 (1) SA 46 (South African Constitutional Court).

[74] See also *Bel Porto School Governing Body and Others v Premier, Western Cape and Another* 2002 (3) SA 265 (CC); 2002 (9) BCLR 891 (CC) at para 46.

not even salvage their personal belongings... The respondents went and sheltered on the Wallacedene sports field under such temporary structures as they could muster. Within a week the winter rains started and the plastic sheeting they had erected afforded scant protection.[75]

They took proceedings in court demanding that the municipality meet its constitutional obligations and provide temporary accommodation.

Notably, the Court does not see positive human rights duties as opposed to democracy, but stresses their inter-dependence. Yakoob J's judgment reiterates the importance of positive duties in realizing all the rights in the constitution.[76] 'A society must seek to ensure that the basic necessities of life are provided to all if it is to be a society based on human dignity, freedom and equality.'[77] At the same time, he avoids pitting the views of the Court against those of elected representatives by emphasizing the considerable space left within the concept of reasonableness for policy-makers' autonomy. While the programme must be capable of facilitating the realization of the right:

... the precise contours and content of the measures to be adopted are primarily a matter for the legislature and the executive... A court considering reasonableness will not enquire whether other more desirable or favourable measures could have been adopted, or whether public money could have been better spent... It is necessary to recognise that a wide range of possible measures could be adopted by the state to meet its obligations. Many of these would meet the requirement of reasonableness...[78]

This understanding of reasonableness incorporates more than the accountability parameter found in *Soobramoney*. In addition, it emphasizes the parameter of equality. Those who are most disadvantaged and who are most likely to lose out in the politics of interest bargaining are exactly those who should gain a voice in the deliberative forum represented by the court. Thus:

... a programme that excludes a significant segment of society cannot be said to be reasonable... Those whose needs are the most urgent and whose ability to enjoy all rights is most in peril, must not be ignored by the measures aimed at achieving the realisation of the right... the Constitution requires that everyone must be treated with care and concern.[79]

The national programme gave priority to the development of permanent housing, but made no interim provision for families in desperate need. Given the severe backlog in provision of permanent housing, the reality was that the most desperate would be left indefinitely without any form of assistance. The Court therefore concluded that the nationwide programme breached the obligations imposed on

---

[75] *Republic of South Africa v Grootboom (1)* 2001 (1) SA 46 (South African Constitutional Court).

[76] ibid para 23.

[77] *Grootboom* (n 75 above) para 44.

[78] ibid para 41.

[79] *Grootboom* (n 75 above) para 43–44.

national government to the extent that it failed to provide for relief for those in desperate need. This also meant a budgetary allocation. Again this was defined in terms of reasonableness: provided a reasonable part of the national housing budget was devoted to those in desperate need, the precise allocation was for national government to decide in the first instance.[80]

The deliberative dimension is more evident in the *TAC*[81] case, possibly because of the central role played by the activist group Treatment Action Campaign, which sees litigation as an element of a wider strategy of lobbying, education, grass-roots mobilization, and citizen action. The Mbeke government had for many years refused to take effective measures to combat the AIDS pandemic that has been devastating the country. The result was that despite the proven efficacy of nevirapine in diminishing the risks of mother-to-child transmission of the virus, the government refused to permit the drug to be administered in State hospitals outside of a handful of 'pilot schemes'. The policy was challenged as constituting a breach of the duty to fulfil the right of access to health care services. Notably, there was no difficulty in finding resources as sufficient quantities of the drug had been offered free for three to five years by the manufacturer. The Court upheld the challenge.

All three of the parameters above are evident. The first is accountability. As the judgment notes: 'In our country the issue of HIV/AIDS has for some time been fraught with an unusual degree of political, ideological and emotional contention.'[82] By requiring the government to prove that its concerns over the safety of nevirapine were based in evidence, the court introduced a strong requirement of accountability and transparency. It was not enough simply to produce reasons; they were also required to be reasonable. In this light, it was clear that the reasons put forward were lightweight relative to the enormous costs in human lives that the refusal entailed. But the judgment goes further than accountability, introducing a deliberative element into decision-making. This is because the government was required to explain its policies in a way which could convince others of their reasonableness, and on terms which were free of ideological or self-interested perspectives. Those who had previously had no voice in democratic decision-making were able to introduce their own perspectives, so that the Court could create synthesis of both. The equality parameter is also evident, in that the chief victims of the policy were the poor who could not afford to buy the drug privately.

It is when it comes to the remedy that the deliberative model faces more challenges. On the one hand, the democratic imperative suggests that courts should not impose solutions; but should instead act as a catalyst for democratic

---

[80] ibid para 66.

[81] *Minister of Health v Treatment Action Campaign (no 2)* (2002) 5 SA 721 (CC) (South African Constitutional Court) (henceforth *TAC*).

[82] ibid para 20.

initiatives. On the other hand, positive duties would be of no value if they did not make it necessary to take action to fulfil the duty. The closure of the discussion through a mandatory order by the court might be seen to be an undemocratic intrusion by the court into the business of elected representatives. But this misunderstands the nature of deliberative democracy. Deliberative democracy does not only require that deliberation takes place. It also necessitates action on the results of deliberation. There is no value to the deliberative process if one party, in this case, the government, is free to carry on acting on the basis of its pre-deliberative stance. At the same time, deliberation should continue at a different level, that of finding the most effective ways of fulfilling the duty. Participation remains essential to ensure that solutions are appropriate and take into account the perspectives of both decision-makers and those affected. It is also essential for compliance.

The South African Court has been cautious in developing such deliberative remedies. A potential solution is through the declaratory remedy, since it feeds into the political process rather than imposing the will of the court. It was the preferred remedy in *Grootboom*, where the Court issued a declaration which required the State to make reasonable provision within its available resources for people in the Cape Metropolitan area with no access to land, no roof over their heads, and who were living in intolerable conditions or crisis situations. The State was required to devise and implement a coherent, coordinated programme designed to meet its obligations.

However, this solution leaves too much to the goodwill of the government, both because there is no inbuilt mechanism to prevent the government from reverting to its pre-deliberative stance, and because it pays too little attention to building a deliberative and participative element into the remedial structure itself. Without any requirement that the government incorporate stakeholders both in problem solving and in monitoring of implementation, and without any ongoing supervision by the court to ensure that a deliberative and participative process in fact occurs, the remedy gives too little normative steer. Not surprisingly, then, little was done. By 2002, the waiting list for housing in the Cape Town area was ten years, and the municipality had still not made special provision for truly desperate or homeless people.

The absence of deliberative content to the remedy was aggravated by the lack of attention to the individual rights-holder. It was stressed in *Grootboom* that the remedy did not entitle the respondents to claim shelter or housing immediately upon demand. But because it did not ensure that the respondents and other affected people had a continuing role in the process of provision of housing, they were left with little content to their rights.

More progress was made towards achieving a synthesis of deliberative and mandatory remedies in the *TAC* case, possibly because State inaction in that case was primarily motivated by political rather than resource-based considerations.

The State argued that the appropriate remedy was a declaration, leaving the 'government free to pay heed to the declaration made and to adapt its policies in so far as this may be necessary to bring them into conformity with the court's judgment'.[83] This was emphatically rejected by the Court, on the grounds that a clear breach of the Constitution required an effective remedy. This opened up the possibility of the Court taking on a more direct supervisory role by issuing a structural interdict, which would require the State to report regularly to the Court on its progress in implementing the order. Lower courts in South Africa have begun to use remedies of this sort, as had the High Court in *TAC* itself. However, although it was not against the use of a structural interdict where appropriate, the Constitutional Court took the view that such an interdict was unnecessary in this case because the government had always respected and executed orders of the Court and there was no reason to believe that it would not do so on this occasion. Instead, it issued a mandatory order, without the supervisory content. The order required the State to lift the restrictions on nevirapine and to facilitate its use, as well as making provision for counsellors and taking reasonable measures to extend testing and counselling throughout the public sector. Notably, the government was ordered to implement the order without delay.

Although framed in mandatory terms, the remedy leaves open the possibility of further deliberation. This is done firstly by requiring all relevant bodies to produce a public plan for fulfilling their duties,[84] and secondly by building in an element of flexibility, so that ongoing decision-making can take place.

A factor that needs to be kept in mind is that policy is and should be flexible. It may be changed at any time and the executive is always free to change policies where it considers it appropriate to do so. The only constraint is that policies must be consistent with the Constitution and the law. Court orders concerning policy choices made by the executive should therefore not be formulated in ways that preclude the executive from making such legitimate choices.[85]

The Court does not, however, go far enough in ensuring that this flexibility is more than a unilateral discretion for government. This would require closer attention to the role of transparency, accountability, and genuine participation. Roach and Budlender suggest that one way of achieving this is to require the government to formulate its own plan and make it available to the public or file it with the Court, together with timetables for achievement.[86] This not only improves accountability but ensures the deliberative process is continued by giving the applicant and other stakeholders the opportunity to make representations to the

---

[83] *TAC* (n 81 above) para 96.
[84] ibid para 123.
[85] *TAC* (n 81 above) para 114.
[86] G Budlender and K Roach 'Mandatory Relief and Supervisory Jurisdiction: When is it Appropriate, Just and Equitable?' [2005] 122 South African Law Journal 325–351.

Court or to raise concerns in the political process and civil society. One potential illustration of this approach was that of the Cape Town High Court in 2002, where squatters, faced with eviction charges, counter-claimed that the municipality had breached its positive duty under *Grootboom*. The Court ordered the City to comply with its obligations and required the City to produce a report within four months stating what steps it had taken to comply with its legal obligations as declared in the Order, what future steps it would take in that regard, and when they would be taken.[87]

A further possibility is to require deliberation to take place in order to formulate the plan in the first place. The Court's order would consist of an instruction to the parties to discuss possible solutions. The temptation to revert to interest bargaining, with government exercising overwhelming power, would be avoided by ensuring that all parties have an equal voice and that deliberation takes place within the structure of the rights in question. Some glimmering of such an approach is evident in the *Port Elizabeth Municipality*[88] case, where the Court strongly endorsed the need for proper discussion and, where appropriate, mediation as a way to resolve these conflicts.[89] But perhaps the most interesting step towards a genuinely deliberative mandatory remedy was taken in the very recent *Rand Properties* case. In this case, occupiers of dilapidated buildings in central Johannesburg challenged the City's attempts to evict them on the grounds of health and safety. The occupiers argued that the City had a positive duty to provide appropriate alternative housing. In an interim order issued on 30 August 2007,[90] the Court required the parties to 'engage with each other meaningfully . . . and in the light of the values of the Constitution, the constitutional and statutory duties of the municipality and the duties of citizens concerned' to resolve the dispute. It also required the parties to engage with each other in an effort to alleviate the plight of the applicants in the buildings concerned 'by making the buildings as safe and conducive to health as is reasonably practicable'.[91] The parties were given about four weeks to report on the results of the engagement, and account would be taken of the results in the preparation of the judgment. The outcome is an important demonstration of the ways in which a Court can trigger deliberative decision-making in the shadow of the law. By means of the interim order, the Court created a deliberative space in which the occupiers, a group with minimal political or social influence, were given a real voice in the decision-making process. The resulting agreement protected the occupiers against immediate eviction

---

[87] *Rudolph v City of Cape Town* reported by A Mahomed 'Grootboom and Its Impact on Evictions' [2003] ESR Review 4.3.

[88] *Port Elizabeth Municipality v Various Occupiers* 2005 (1) SA 217 (CC) (South African Constitutional Court).

[89] ibid para 43 at 240E.

[90] *Occupiers of 51 Olivia Road v City of Johannesburg* Case No CCT 24/07 Interim Order dated 30 August 2007.

[91] I am indebted to Geoff Budlender for referring me to this order and for his helpful insights on it.

and required the city authorities to take interim measures to improve the safety of the building. At the same time, the city authorities were required to make available suitable alternative temporary accommodation pending the provision of suitable permanent accommodation. For all these measures, the city authorities undertook to consult closely with the occupiers. The result is to enable the court to issue a mandatory remedy without stepping on the toes of democratic decision-makers as well as incorporating those affected so that they can monitor the remedy.[92] There remains the question of whether the court retains a role in ensuring that the outcome reflects not just the deliberative criteria, but the essence of the right itself. As argued above, deliberation cannot take place at large, but in order to find an appropriate way of fulfilling the right. Those participating in deliberation, particularly the State, must do so in the knowledge that the result will not be acceptable to the court unless it can be justified as a convincing means of fulfilling the right. The court therefore retains a vital role in ensuring that the deliberative outcome is justifiable in this sense.

Nevertheless, the extent to which the South African Court can take the deliberative function forward remains limited by its reluctance to stray too far from the traditional judicial function. This is manifested in its continuing adherence to the adversarial process. There is in principle scope for the Court to have developed an innovative process. Standing rules are very wide, permitting anyone acting in the public interest to bring an action.[93] This has made it possible to build on the dynamic tradition of public interest litigation which had already taken root as an aspect of the resistance to apartheid. However, in most other respects, the adversarial procedure remains unchanged. Applications must be initiated by the litigants, with the Court taking the role of a passive adjudicator. Although there is provision for direct access by litigants, the Court has established a set of criteria for admission which are so narrow as to make direct access impossible in practice.[94] The process remains essentially combative rather than cooperative, with State respondents frequently defending their position at all costs, including the use of obstructive procedural strategies. The result is that litigation is slow, expensive, and extremely taxing on the applicants. Its reluctance to issue supervisory orders is a direct result of its view that the Court should wait for litigants to come to it, rather than that it should initiate proceedings. Even in the clear knowledge that its declaratory remedy in *Grootboom* was not being implemented, the Court has not been inclined to initiate further responses, preferring to wait for disgruntled applicants to move the Court for further remedies. This puts great pressure on disadvantaged applicants to implement their own orders. Irene Grootboom for one has reportedly disappeared, and is in any event highly unlikely to be in a position to initiate further proceedings.

[92]   I am grateful to Geoff Budlender for his insights on this case.
[93]   South African Constitution, s 39.
[94]   J Dugard 'Court of First Instance? Towards a Pro-poor Jurisdiction for the South African Constitutional Court' (2006) 22 South African Journal of Human Rights 261.

These constraints have combined to produce a picture of a court at the very periphery of implementation of positive human rights duties. Only a handful of cases on socio-economic rights have in fact reached the Court, and all have been adjudicated cautiously. Constitutional Court judges are known to have suggested extra-judicially that more positive duties cases should be initiated and sent their way, but the constraints outlined above have clearly militated against such actions forthcoming. Public interest litigants take many months and even years to prepare their cases, and then must make their way laboriously through the lower courts before reaching the Constitutional Court. Attorneys report that the sheer paperwork in such a case could amount to up to half a million pages with the attendant expense. On the substance of a case, leading barristers frequently advise great caution in instigating litigation, concerned that the most to be expected from the Court is a polite prodding of the State into action.

This suggests that more attention needs to be paid to alternatives to the adversarial structure of courts in triggering the appropriate response. It is here that the Indian Court has struck out in an entirely new direction, as will be seen in Chapter 5. To this need to be added non-judicial methods of compliance, which are the subject of Chapter 6. It will be argued that a synergistic approach, drawing on a variety of different strategies, is the way forward.

E. Conclusion

It has been argued in this chapter that it is possible to structure adjudication of positive human rights duties in a way which strengthens rather than detracts from democracy. By subjecting State action or inaction to scrutiny against the yardsticks of accountability, equality, and deliberative democracy, courts can reach decisions which, far from insulating an issue from further political debate, instead form a crucial part of that debate. This does not mean, however, that judges should mimic political decision-making. Deliberative decision-making based on human rights values and principles, on the instigation of litigants who contribute to the shape and content of the debate, is a unique judicial contribution. However, to fully achieve a democratic role for the court, it is necessary to adjust its institutional structure. This has been achieved in a remarkable way by the Indian Court. The risks and benefits are examined in the next chapter, which is a detailed examination of the Indian developments.

5

Restructuring the Courts: Public Interest Litigation in the Indian Courts[1]

A. Introduction

Even if courts can play a legitimate role in reinforcing democracy through adjudicating positive human rights duties, they remain limited by their institutional structure, and particularly, the adversarial, passive, and retrospective nature of the litigation process. However, there is no reason why the process itself cannot be adapted to respond to the needs of positive duties litigation. The most sophisticated set of such adaptations has been undertaken by the Indian Supreme Court, through the development of a wide-ranging public interest litigation process.[2] By recognizing the inherent inequalities in the adversarial court system, the Court has adapted its processes so that the voices of the poor and disadvantaged can be heard. This entails a series of radical adaptations: widening standing to anyone litigating in the public interest; instituting court-initiated fact finding; issuing mandatory orders which give the Court ongoing supervisory powers, and monitoring the implementation of those orders. The result has been a transformation of the role of the Court in protecting and promoting the actual enjoyment of human rights, particularly the right to life.

However, this role has also been highly controversial. Some argue that public interest litigation (PIL) has opened up the possibility of an inclusive deliberative democracy. Others point to the Court as a site of betrayal and compromise, where instead of promoting equality, the Court has replicated structures of power already existing in society. Similarly, there are many who see the Court as energizing the political process, triggering action where apathy previously ranged.

---

[1] This piece has been inspired and greatly assisted by Additional Solicitor General Gopal Subramanium; and Justice M Lokur, Justice S Muralidhar, Colin Gonsalves, Professor Kamala Sankaran, Professor U Baxi, Indira Jaising, Jaina Kothari, Sudhir Krishnaswamy, Professor M Mohanti, Justice Bannurmath, Laila Ollapally, and Tarunabh Khaitan, who generously shared their thoughts and experience with me. The errors are all my own.

[2] See generally A Desai and S Muralidhar 'Public Interest Litigation: Potential and Problems' in B Kirpal (ed) *Supreme but not Infallible: Essays in Honour of the Supreme Court of India* (OUP New Delhi 2000); P Singh 'Promises and Perils of Public Interest Litigation in Protecting the Rights of the Poor and the Oppressed' (2005) 27 Delhi Law Review 8–25, C Gonsalves 'Economic Rights and the Indian Supreme Court' unpublished paper.

Others consider that the courts have encroached on executive power, leading to paralysis and a sapping of initiative.

This controversy masks a more fundamental question, namely what function the Court should be serving. Its achievements can only fairly be mapped against an underlying paradigm of what can and should be expected of it. Ultimately, courts cannot supplant either political activism or the legislative process. Nor can courts make good the failings of executive government, whether the latter are due to incompetence, lack of resources, or lack of political will. What courts can do, however, is to act as a catalyst for the democratic pressures which ultimately make recalcitrant or incompetent governments act. A democratic role for the court entails enhancing accountability, facilitating deliberative democracy, and promoting equality. Accountability is enhanced by enabling ordinary people to require governments to come to court and explain and justify their actions or inactivity. Deliberative democracy is facilitated when courts encourage governments to listen and interact with civil society. And equality is promoted by ensuring that those whose voices are drowned in the political melee are given full and equal participation rights. This applies too to judicial remedies. Energizing the political process, rather than substituting for it, requires the court to act as a facilitator, promoting the creation of structures which can themselves produce outcomes. This too requires a participative ethic, ensuring that those who are most affected by an order have a central role in shaping and policing it.

The ideal behind the PIL is to construct the court as a vehicle for social conversation between co-equal citizens. Instead of interest-bargaining, where success depends on economic or political power, the judicial process requires decision-making based on a dynamic interplay between the different perspectives brought together in the social conversation. Can PIL achieve this? As will become clear below, the record is mixed. Many believe that the record of the Court shows that the space for 'conversation' has long disappeared and instead the judiciary has become a powerful but unaccountable force of its own. Others argue that even if the Court does not always meet the ideal, and sometimes spectacularly misses it, there is nevertheless an ongoing and dynamic set of potentialities which need to be developed.

This chapter explores in detail the institutional innovations of the Indian Supreme Court. It is written with the diffidence of an outsider, whose approach is inevitably framed by comparative experience. In the light of that experience, the achievements of the Court are indeed radical and unparalleled. At the same time, comparative experience also points to the importance of assessing the Indian Court within the context that created it, both in terms of its relationship with the legislative wing of government and in terms of the particular historical, political, and economic circumstances within which it operates. This means that the institutional changes it has achieved may not necessarily be easily transplanted to other jurisdictions. What it does show, however, is that institutional change is possible and desirable, and indeed the strengths and weaknesses of the Indian Court could well inform comparative developments.

(i) Institutional change

From the early 1980s, the Court began to articulate the obstacles which the adversarial procedure inevitably created for the poor and disadvantaged. Noting that it was only the Anglo-Saxon juridical heritage which made the adversarial system appear sacrosanct, the Court has committed itself 'to innovate new methods and devise new strategies for the purpose of providing access to justice to large masses of people who are denied their basic human rights and to whom freedom and liberty have no meaning'.[3] Thus, in initiating the institutional changes necessitated by a judicial role in progressing positive duties, the Court held:

> Where one of the parties to a litigation belongs to a poor and deprived section of the community and does not possess adequate social and material resources, he is bound to be at a disadvantage as against a strong and powerful opponent under the adversary system of justice, because of his difficulty in getting competent legal representation and more than anything else, his inability to produce relevant evidence before the Court. Therefore, when the poor come before the Court, particularly for enforcement of their fundamental rights, it is necessary to depart from the adversarial procedure and to evolve a new procedure which will make it possible for the poor and the weak to bring the necessary material before the Court.[4]

The first step in the development of the alternative model was the recognition that a narrow concept of standing, which confined the right to bring proceedings to the victim herself, was in itself an insuperable barrier to the poor and disadvantaged. Referring to the 'blinkered rules of standing of British–Indian vintage', the Court began to consider ways in which 'the centre of gravity is to shift, as the preamble of our Constitution mandates, from the traditional individualism of locus standi to the community orientation of public interest litigation'.[5] Hence from the early 1980s, the Supreme Court opened up standing to allow any member of the public to approach the Court for relief on behalf of any person or determinate class of persons who 'by reason of poverty, helplessness or disability or socially or economically disadvantaged position, [are] unable to approach the Court for relief'.[6] The only limits on standing are, therefore, that the individual who moves the Court 'must be acting bona fide with a view of vindicating the cause of justice' and not for 'personal gain, private profit or political motivation'.[7] But given that one function of standing is to present the case to the Court, it may

---

[3] *SP Gupta v Union of India* (1981) Supp SCC 87 (Indian Supreme Court).
[4] ibid.
[5] *Municipal Council, Ratlam v Shri Vardichan* (1980) 4 SCC 162 (Indian Supreme Court) at 163.
[6] *Gupta* (n 3 above) at 210.
[7] *Bandhua Mukti Morcha v Union of India* (1984) 3 SCC 161 (Indian Supreme Court) at 186.

be necessary for the Court to get proper legal assistance, particularly where the PIL is launched by a petitioner in person. In such cases, the Court will appoint a lawyer to act as amicus curiae. Members of the Indian Bar have been praised by a recent Chief Justice for their professionalism in discharging the function of amicus curiae, and their willingness to undertake the work despite the fact that it is not fee-paying.[8]

This comes together with a relaxation of many of the formal requirements of the writ procedure. Thus, states the Court: 'The provision conferring on the Supreme Court power to enforce the fundamental rights in the widest possible terms shows the anxiety of the Constitution makers not to allow any procedural technicalities to stand in the way of enforcement of fundamental rights.' The result is that 'where the affected persons are really helpless the Supreme Court will not insist on a regular writ petition to be filed... the Court will readily respond even to a letter addressed by such individual acting pro bono publico, despite the fact that formal rules exist with regard to filing of petitions'.[9] The result is that many of the path-breaking PIL cases have commenced by letters sent by petitioners to the Supreme Court. It is even sufficient for the Court's attention to be drawn to an issue by a newspaper article. A notification issued by the Supreme Court in 1988 sets out the matters which can be initiated by PIL.[10]

Wide standing, together with the informal initiation of court action, raises a series of challenges, not least among them the need to find an alternative means of fact-finding, which does not depend only on the parties' initiative and is not tested by a system of cross-examination which favours those with skilled legal representation. The Court has addressed this issue by taking on itself the responsibility of gathering and testing facts in a PIL case. Its primary mechanism is the appointment of Commissioners to investigate the facts. Court appointed Commissioners have included district magistrates, district judges, professors of law, advocates, and even journalists.

Together these changes transform the adversarial procedure into one which is regarded as essentially cooperative. The Court has emphasized that PIL litigation is 'not a litigation of an adversary character for the purpose of holding the State... responsible for making reparation, but it is a public interest litigation which involved a collaborative and cooperative effort... for the purpose of making human rights meaningful for the weaker sections of the community'.[11] Indeed, 'it is a challenge and an opportunity to the Government and its officers to make basic human rights meaningful to the deprived and vulnerable sections of the community'.[12] Certainly, law officers appearing for the government in PIL cases view their role in this light, and will make recommendations to the State

[8] Desai and Muralidhar (n 2 above) 167.
[9] *Gupta* (n 3 above).
[10] Desai and Muralidhar (n 2 above) 165.
[11] *Dr Upendra Baxi v State of UP* (1986) 4 SCC 106 (Indian Supreme Court).
[12] *Bandhua* (n 7 above) at 182–183.

to take a constructive role in proceedings rather than polarizing the dispute by defending their position regardless of the circumstances. For example, in the 'Right to Food' case,[13] the Attorney General is on record as accepting that this should not be regarded as adversarial litigation but a matter of concern for all.

Particularly important in the context of the enforcement of positive duties has been the development of the remedial power. Many PIL cases are brought under the writ of mandamus, which gives the court the power to order a public body to carry out a statutory or constitutional duty. Most judicial remedies are geared to the enforcement of duties of restraint, either through injunctive powers or through retrospective awards of compensation. By contrast, mandamus is an express means for compelling public bodies to take action and is therefore a powerful vehicle for the enforcement of positive duties. The Indian Supreme Court has not only used mandamus to issue detailed directions to States or the central government of India to implement its orders, it has also developed the remedy to give it ongoing supervisory powers, using the device of interim orders and 'continuing mandamus', which keep the case open and require ongoing reporting to the Court on the extent of compliance.

Litigants and interested parties return to the Court periodically, generally every two to three months, to report on implementation and request new orders, allowing flexibility as circumstances change. Commissions appointed by the Court are also given the responsibility of supervising implementation, and report regularly to the Court. This makes it possible for the Court to frame far-reaching, forward-looking remedies which can include structural changes, and then to supervise progressive implementation. All of this is backed up by the contempt power, which the Court is not loath to use, even against high-profile government or elected officials. For example, in the long-running forestry cases, the Principal Secretary and the Minister in the Department of Forestry in the State of Maharashtra were committed for contempt for granting permission for saw-mills to operate in forest areas against the orders of the Court. They were each sentenced to one month's imprisonment.[14]

(ii) Social change via the courts

The PIL procedure has infused constitutional litigation in India with a vitality which could not have been achieved without the institutional innovations pioneered by the Court. Hundreds of PIL applications are received each week by the Supreme Court in Delhi, and hundreds more by High Courts all over the country. While a large number are screened out,[15] the Court's interventions in

---

[13] See n 21 below.

[14] *TN Godavarman Thirumulpad Through the Amicus Curiae v Ashok Khot* Contempt Petition (Civil) 83/2005 (2006.05.10) (Indian Supreme Court).

[15] About 50% are declared inadmissible in a brief hearing without reasons given.

response to PIL applications have penetrated many aspects of political and executive action which would be inaccessible to the judicial reach under traditional adversarial proceedings. This has included both civil and political rights and socio-economic rights, and in both arenas, the Court has imposed both negative and positive duties. One of the chief arenas in which the Court has successfully intervened is to enforce the civil and political rights of detainees and remand prisoners; the rights of those detained in mental asylums; and the rights of victims of crime.[16] The PIL jurisdiction has also been a central component in the campaign against corruption both in government and in the judiciary itself. In such cases, the Court has not stopped at the imposition of a duty of restraint on the authorities, preventing them from breaching basic rights. In addition, the Court has frequently enforced a range of positive duties, to create the structures, modify the institutions, facilitate self-help, or provide alternatives.

Particularly noteworthy in this regard is the ongoing litigation on behalf of people with mental illnesses. The case was initiated in 1990 by social activist Sheela Barse, who forwarded to the Court a copy of an article in which she exposed the plight of the thousands of children and adults in Calcutta who were committed to jail under the category of 'non-criminal lunatics' and left there indefinitely in miserable conditions with no recourse to either medical treatment or judicial proceedings. Having received an inadequate response to its direction to the State to provide relevant facts, the Court appointed a Commission to ascertain the facts itself. Consisting of a professor of psychiatry and an academic lawyer, the Commission was required to visit a representative sample of prisons or institutions and gauge relevant facts, including the total number of mentally ill inmates, the procedure for admission, the care and facilities provided, the existence of mental health facilities in the relevant district, the pattern of qualified staff, and procedures for after-care and rehabilitation.[17] The Commission was also required to indicate the most appropriate ongoing monitoring mechanism.

The Court's decision on receipt of the report in 1993 shows the inextricable relationship of positive and negative duties. Not only did it impose an absolute restraint on the State from admitting mentally ill persons to jails, but in addition the State was required to take immediate steps to upgrade mental hospitals, to set up psychiatric services in all teaching and district hospitals, including filling posts for psychiatrists, and integrate mental health care with the primary health care system. The Court retained supervision of implementation, directing that any difficulty encountered in the implementation was to be forthwith brought to the attention of the Court.

Nor was the Supreme Court willing to let the matter rest at West Bengal. It also directed that every other State should take similar measures and that the function

[16] Paradoxically, the Court has been loath to intervene to protect basic civil liberties of those detained under emergency powers: G Subramanium 'Emergency Provisions under the Indian Constitution' in B Kirpal et al (eds) *Supreme but not Infallible* (OUP New Delhi 2000).
[17] *Sheela Barse v Union of India* (1993) 4 Supreme Court Cases 204 (Indian Supreme Court).

of monitoring the implementation of the orders be made over to respective High Courts.[18] Although this has generally been ignored, in one State, Karnataka, the High Court has become a central protagonist in a detailed programme of change, including both duties of restraint and positive duties. With the help of amicus curiae, and a highly engaged set of NGOs and activist lawyers, the designated judge has issued a series of directives to the State government to make proper provision for the mentally ill. These include duties of restraint preventing the imprisonment of the mentally ill, but also wide-ranging positive duties such as the construction of a well-equipped mental hospital with proper facilities for care of mentally ill patients, and the provision of pensions for the mentally ill. Of particular importance is the Court's recognition of structural barriers to change, especially the startling absence of medical expertise in this area. It ordered that all primary medical workers and trainee doctors be trained in psychiatry and psychology as part of their basic education, as well as an increase in the number of places available to train specialist psychiatrists. The Court has not been deterred by claims of lack of governmental resources, but has gone so far as to insist on a budgetary allocation for the purpose of fulfilling the orders. This follows the Supreme Court ruling that a State cannot plead lack of resources as a reason for failing to fulfil its duties.[19] In particular, it cannot avoid its constitutional obligations to provide medical services on account of financial constraints.[20]

Equally successful has been the Court's role in enforcing positive duties to provide food. Although India has a plethora of food distribution schemes, there was little impetus to implement them until the People's Union of Civil Liberties moved the Court to transform the right to food into a fundamental human right.[21] Known as the 'Right to Food' case, the first hearing, in April 2001, took place against a paradoxical background of mounting starvation deaths together with an increase in unused stocks of food. As the Court commented: 'In case of famine, there may be shortage of food, but here the situation is that amongst plenty there is scarcity. Plenty of food is available, but distribution of the same amongst the very poor and the destitute is scarce and non-existent leading to mal-nourishment, starvation and other related problems.'[22] Notably, the right to food derives from the cardinal civil and political right to life. This means that it is not formulated as a progressive duty, to be rolled out subject to the availability of resources, but instead requires immediate fulfilment. It is, however, through

---

[18] *Sheila Barse v Union of India* [1995] 5 Supreme Court Cases 654 (Indian Supreme Court).

[19] *Ratlam Municipality v Vardichand and Others* AIR 1980 SC 67 (Indian Supreme Court).

[20] *Paschim Banga Khet Mazdoor Samity v State of West Bengal* [1996] 4 Supreme Court Cases 37 (Indian Supreme Court).

[21] The information in this and subsequent paragraphs on the 'Right to Food' case are taken from material on the website of the Right to Food Campaign (<http://www.righttofoodindia.org>) and in particular the booklet 'Supreme Court Orders on the Right to Food, October 2005' found at <http://www.righttofoodindia.org/orders/interimorders.html>.

[22] *People's Union for Civil Liberties v Union of India and Others* Writ Petition (Civil) 196 of 2001 (Indian Supreme Court).

the continuing mandamus jurisdiction that the programmatic nature of the right manifests itself. The result has been a series of interim orders from the Supreme Court directing the proper implementation of a range of schemes. These include the Public Distribution System (PDS), which distributes food grain and other basic commodities at subsidized prices through 'fair price shops'; special food-based assistance to destitute households (Antyodaya); and the Integrated Child Development Scheme (ICDS) which seeks to provide young children with an integrated package of services such as supplementary nutrition, health care, and pre-school education, as well as covering adolescent girls, pregnant women, and lactating mothers. Possibly the most far-reaching is the scheme requiring mid-day meals at schools, which the Court strengthened by requiring not just a supply of food, but a proper cooked meal.

As in the mental illness litigation in Karnataka, a key dimension to the success of the 'Right to Food' case is the recognition that a court-centred approach to human rights development and implementation is not sufficient. Instead, the judicial endorsement of a positive duty to provide food has been the focus of a large public campaign around the right to food, where activists on the ground are able to rely on the vocabulary of entitlement to demand compliance. The Court's continuing involvement is both a response to and a catalyst for a well-organized, grass-roots activist campaign of fact-finding, compliance monitoring, and strategic litigation.[23] This has been supplemented by energetic and conscientious Commissioners, who are assisted by a network of advisors at state level.

Also of importance is the nature of the right. As argued earlier, positive duties can be framed either as a simple duty to provide, or transfer goods or benefits, or a duty to facilitate and empower individuals to provide for themselves. While the direct provision of food is essential to prevent immediate starvation, it cannot become a self-sustaining programme and is essentially dependence based unless supplemented by measures which facilitate and empower. The 'Right to Food' case, recognizing this, has incorporated facilitative duties in two respects. The first is a result of the mid-day meals scheme. The NGO spearheading the campaign has detailed the facilitative benefits of cooked mid-day meals:

Mid-day meals help to protect children from hunger (including 'classroom hunger,' a mortal enemy of school education), and if the meals are nutritious, they can facilitate the healthy growth of children. Mid-day meals also serve many other useful purposes. For instance, they are quite effective in promoting regular school attendance, and in that respect mid-day meals contribute not only to the right to food but also to the right to education. Mid-day meals also help to undermine caste prejudices, by teaching children to sit together and share a common meal. They reduce the gender gap in school participation, provide an important source of employment for women, and liberate working women from the burden of having to feed children at home during the day. Aside from

---

[23] I am indebted to Colin Gonsalves for providing me with a rich perspective on this case.

this, mid-day meals can be seen as a source of economic support for the poorer sections of society, and also as an opportunity to impart nutrition education to children.[24]

The mid-day meals scheme has also generated a small amount of employment, and one of the Court's orders has included a direction that in the appointment of cooks and helpers, preference shall be given to Dalits, Scheduled Castes, and Scheduled Tribes.

The second key facilitative right is the right to work. From the very beginning, petitioners argued that assured employment at a living wage is the best protection against hunger. Again, there were already several employment schemes, such as the Sampoorna Grameen Rozgar Yojana (SGRY), which aims to provide additional wage employment in rural areas, using the labour provided to create community, assets, and infrastructural development in rural areas.[25] As with the right to food, the Court's intervention has the effect of transforming a policy document into a fundamental entitlement. This has now been given statutory backing in the form of the National Rural Employment Guarantee Act 2005, which gives the right to be employed on public works doing unskilled manual labour at the statutory minimum wage up to 100 days per household per year, or failing that, to an unemployment allowance.

The Court's intervention does not immediately resolve the problem. Implementation remains patchy and highly dependent on the extent of local activism. The highest levels of compliance are in respect of the school mid-day meal scheme, where the Supreme Court orders have been backed up by lively campaigns for mid-day meals all over the country.[26] The 2005 report by the Commissioners welcomes the fact that several State governments have taken steps to fully implement these court orders, and the Right to Food Campaign booklet estimates that about 10 million children are getting a cooked mid-day meal at school every day. However, the Commissioners add that, in many States, the content of the meal is inadequate, health safeguards are lacking, and social discrimination is common. Nor has anything been done to extend mid-day meals beyond the primary stage.[27] Other programmes have a far poorer implementation record. Most disturbingly, the ICDS only covers 0.3% of adolescent girls, a figure which is even more alarming against a harsh background of discrimination and violence against women and girls. Such halting progress demonstrates the difficulty facing a court without its own executive apparatus for implementing programmatic duties. At the same time, the recalcitrance of State and central government to implement food schemes would have been even greater had the

---

[24] *Right to Food* interim orders booklet, 16.
[25] Government of India *Guidelines for Sampoorna Grameen Rozgar Yojana* (Ministry of Rural Development New Delhi 2002) 1.
[26] *Right to Food* (n 24 above) 18.
[27] Writ Petition (Civil) 196 Of 2001 (PUCL vs. Union Of India & Others) Sixth Report Of The Commissioners December 2005 <http://www.righttofoodindia.org/comrs/comrs_reports.html>.

Court not provided a rallying point for social activism at grass-roots level. Lack of total success should not undermine the very real achievements of the case.

(iii) Courts and transformation: the social conversation

In its early decades of development, the PIL procedure, together with progressive constitutional interpretation, gave the Indian Supreme Court a central role in social transformation on behalf of those who were oppressed and marginalized. As Baxi describes it, a novel conception of judicial power and process developed:

> Adjudication emerges as a form of social conversation among the activist judicial and social/human rights movements...Social conversation on issues of law, rights and justice is no longer a matter of cultivated discourse by, of and for the professional managerial classes (planners, policymakers, judges, lawpersons and related learned professionals). It now becomes a form of conversation among multitudinous narrative voices.[28]

The notion of judicial conversation de-centres the judicial role itself, portraying litigation not as a transfer of hierarchical power to the court, but as a trigger for democratic interaction between judges, government actors, and different social and political groups. Groups without a voice in the political process are able to enter into the conversation and shape its outcome. This in turn highlights the role of social groups themselves in setting the litigation agenda, and therefore shaping the pattern of judicial intervention, not just in terms of the issues that come to court, but also in terms of the perspectives through which the judicial conversation is filtered. Of central importance has been the availability within civil society of activist groups and lawyers willing to commit themselves to participating and who work with their constituents, not as charitable benefactors, but as equal partners. The notion of judicial conversation also highlights the need to achieve governmental cooperation. Coercive remedies such as contempt might have a background impact in spurring on action, but judges can only make good the inactivity of government with the compliance of the same government.

This notion of judicial conversation is well illustrated in the Karnataka case mentioned above. Here the framing of the issues to be addressed was a product of the constructive interaction between the articulation by activists and affected individuals and their families of their needs and perceptions, with the skill of lawyers in presenting such claims in legal terms. In addition, a key to success has been the extent to which the Court has successfully incorporated both government and civil society into the project of change. Viewing his role as one of coordination and facilitation, the designated judge, Justice Bannurmath, of the Karnataka High Court, has encouraged the participants to see themselves as a team working together to find effective solutions. The case can therefore be

---

[28] U Baxi 'The Avatars of Indian Judicial Activism' in S Verma and Kusum (eds) *Fifty Years of the Supreme Court of India: Its Grasp and Reach* (OUP New Delhi 2000).

viewed as a successful means of promoting deliberative democracy by giving a voice to a group which has been rendered wholly impotent in the normal political process and by harnessing the power of the court to insist on equality in the way in which the input of each actor is regarded, notwithstanding their relative power or powerlessness in normal social interaction. From the basis of cooperative deliberation and decision-making, the court's almost unlimited power to issue directions gains democratic legitimacy, and cooperation from government leaves coercive powers in the background. As described by the judge in the Karnataka case, key issues such as budgetary allocation are a product of across-the-table discussions in which government officials and the Court together work out a rational figure for expenditure on particular projects. Because the solution is a result of a fully fledged discussion with the relevant departments of social security and finance, the Court does not feel constrained to defer to government, and government does not challenge the figure arrived at. Particularly interesting is the way in which the judicial conversation can feed into a broader political context by setting in motion the process of legislative change. The next stage in the litigation envisaged by the litigants is for the Court to initiate a national debate, hosted by the local law school, with a wide range of participants who would be charged with drafting a legislative amendment to bring the out-dated Indian mental health legislation into line with international human rights standards.[29]

(iv) Activation or paralysis: the judges and the executive

However, the extent of the transformation in the judicial role necessitated by the PIL jurisdiction and the continuing mandamus remedial structure have raised deeply controversial questions about the proper role of the Court, particularly where positive duties to provide and promote have been at issue. Perhaps most fundamental has been the question of the proper separation of powers between executive and judiciary, which in turn triggers concerns about the nature of democracy. Notably, many of those most active in the field tend to criticize the Court both when it takes too interventionist a line and when it refuses to intervene or fails to intervene effectively. This requires a closer look at when it is appropriate for judges to take a central role in the defining and implementation of positive duties. The formula most often cited is that judges should intervene when government fails. In the context of a highly malfunctioning State, there are a wide range of situations in which judicial prompting does no more than require the government to act in ways it has already committed itself to, but which it has simply failed to honour. Thus, when the Court required the State to build a road to an isolated hill community in order to fulfil the residents' right to life,[30] it was

---

[29] I am indebted to Leilla Ollipally, Justice Bannurmath, and Jayna Kothari for their helpful insights on this litigation.
[30] *State of Himachal Pradesh v Umed Ram Sharma* AIR 1986 SC 847 (Indian Supreme Court).

in fact only requiring the proper implementation of a scheme already instituted by the relevant authority, but one which had never been brought to fruition. Similarly, and more far-reaching, the Court's intervention in ordering the State to provide food as an essential positive duty arising from the right to life was based on the failure of governments, both at the centre and State level, to properly distribute food which was stored in various parts of the country.

The role of the Court in stepping in where government fails is, however, more complex than it seems at first sight. Appointment of Commissions can, in some cases, create a parallel structure of decision-making deep within the area of executive competence. Court appointed Commissions have a wide-ranging remit not just to find facts, but also to consider possible solutions as a basis for positive duties to be imposed by the Court. Judicial Commissions then parallel and mirror executive structures which should have been in place. For example, in a case challenging the failure of the Delhi authorities to deal with waste and pollution in the city, the terms of reference of a judicially appointed committee took commissioners to the centre of executive policy-making. Its remit covered formulating proposals for economically feasible, safe, and eco-friendly hygienic processing and waste disposal practices; suggesting necessary modifications to municipal bye-laws; and formulating standards and regulations for management of urban solid waste.[31] There are many who consider that the Court has had the effect of perpetuating government inactivity. The prospect of a Court appointed Commission either gives the executive a pretext for further inaction, or makes action seem futile because judges will decide in any event.

Empirical work would be needed to establish the proof of this claim, but certainly the impression given by the Court to many of those affected by its actions is as often one of unhelpfully suffocating government initiative as of constructively spurring recalcitrant executives into action. An example is the long-running question of the upper limits which private universities can charge in terms of fees. Although the Court has not yet insisted that the right to primary education be fulfilled, it has held that private university education can only be permitted if fees are capped at an upper limit.[32] In the exercise of its continuing jurisdiction, the Court has appointed a committee to determine the payable sum. Annual disputes between students, universities, and State governments inevitably land up in High Courts in various parts of the country, with students refusing to pay fees and facing suspension while universities insist on higher limits. Questions are also raised as to the fact that the appointment of Commissioners is entirely in the gift of the Court. The Court selects Commissioners on the basis of its own views of who would have the appropriate standing or expertise, without being required to follow any procedure or open application process. Although the Commissioners

---

[31] *Almitra Patel v Union of India (16 January 1998)* [1998] INSC 35 (Indian Supreme Court).

[32] *Mohini Jain v State of Karnataka* AIR 1992 SC 1858 (Indian Supreme Court); *Unni Krishnan v State of AP & Ors* AIR 1993 SC 2178 (Indian Supreme Court).

generally serve the Court very well, some safeguards in terms of transparency and accountability should be in place. In addition, it may be necessary to ensure that the Commissioners are drawn from a wider section of society than the limited pool the courts tend to draw from.

(v) Straying too far? Relaxing the criteria

A further source of criticism of the Court concerns the rigour of its fact-finding procedures in PIL cases.[33] Commissioners are able to pursue their investigative function in any way they please and will often visit the contested area and hear representations from a wide range of interested parties on the ground. Their report and any other evidence is presented by affidavit, without the facility for cross-examination. There are many who argue that such a procedure is likely to elicit a greater appreciation of the complex polycentric matters at issue than a bipolar adversarial system and cross-examination which encourages defensiveness rather than cooperation. Others, while not wishing to retreat to the adversarial system of fact-finding, nevertheless doubt whether the use of affidavits gives a sufficiently rigorous foundation for the highly complex orders promulgated by the Court. Commissioners are part-time and temporary appointments, required to take time out of their busy, and usually highly paid, jobs to serve the Court for a small consideration, and this might make it difficult for them to achieve the highest standard of fact-finding necessary to ground a PIL.[34] It is arguable that PIL is best suited to cases where the facts are reasonably straightforward or uncontested. Alternative means of accessible justice, such as tribunals, might fill the gap thus created. Such specialist tribunals could well deal with complex situations without relying only on affidavit evidence. Environmental tribunals have in fact frequently been proposed in India, but they have not yet been established.

Also problematic is the fact that the PIL procedure brings polycentric cases before the court, without necessarily giving it the tools to deal with the range of issues implicated in a complex policy field. In making the transition from immediate relief, as is frequently the case in imposing merely a duty of restraint, to structural change which requires the design, institution, and implementation of complex policies, positive duties can overtax the resources of the Court. A particularly problematic example concerns the forest cases. As will be seen below, the protection of the forests has had a severe impact on the life of poor and tribal people living near the forests, leading both to wholesale eviction of indigenous people on the ground that they were 'encroachers' and deprivation of their

---

[33] I am indebted to Justice Madan Lokur for many of the insights in this and subsequent paragraphs. The commentary and any errors are of course my own.

[34] Alternatively, the Supreme Court of India (SCI) has deputed District Justices to perform similar functions as permanent commissions with routine reporting obligations.

livelihood in the forests. Even this picture is, however, deceptively simple. It was perhaps predictable that the ban on commercial sale of timber would affect the main source of income of numerous farming families as well as the local economy of shops and services which depended on the farmers' spending power. Less predictable but equally problematic were the negative implications for forests themselves. One study shows that pine trees, instead of being sold as high-value timber, are being sold for one-tenth of the price as firewood, on which there is no ban, and that, since timber has no value, farmers prefer to convert forested lands into agricultural plots.[35] On the other hand, there are those who argue that it is romantic to regard the life of forest dwellers as symbiotic with that of the forest and that many of the practices of the tribal communities are unsustainable and destructive to biodiversity. One study claims that in the north-east where the larger tracts of forests are owned by tribal councils, the rate of deforestation is far higher than in the forests managed by forests departments.[36]

(vi) Who is the 'public'? The role of the public interest litigant

The role of the Court has become particularly contentious now that access to the courts via the PIL process has spread well beyond its original rationale. Far from only serving the poor and disadvantaged who would not otherwise have access to the court, PIL is now widely available to anyone claiming the public interest. The result is that procedural safeguards are circumvented even when the normal writ procedure would not render the court inaccessible. Cases contesting the treatment of wild monkeys in Delhi jostle with cases contesting the right of private schools to conduct admissions interviews for very young children. It has been argued that this has increased the workload of High Courts and the Supreme Court, which in itself obstructs access to justice for the most disadvantaged and decreases the Court's ability to provide justice. But whether PIL cases make a significant contribution to the vast increase in the Court's docket remains controversial. Certainly, the statistical case is not made out.

More fundamentally, widening access beyond the original constituency of poor and disadvantaged has resulted in a crucial change in the perspective from which the case is presented to the Court. Those who initiate the case have the power to frame the issues for the Court. Widening access therefore runs the risk that those who already have political and economic power will drown or even silence the voices of the poor and disadvantaged. In this context, as Baxi puts it, the social conversation easily moves along an 'axis of discursive inequality'.[37]

---

[35] R Dutta and K Kohli 'North East: Apex Court Rules the Forests' *India Together* 5 March 2005.
[36] Submission to the Ministry of Tribal Affairs, Government of India on Behalf of the Wildlife Trust of India on the Draft Scheduled Tribes (Recognition of Forest Rights) Bill 2005, 10 July 2005.
[37] Baxi (n 28 above) 173.

Indeed, the partial reversal in the Court's attitude to the poor and disadvantaged reflects, at least in part, the change in the character of the public interest litigant. The power of the initial litigant to shape the case is not, of course, absolute. The decision as to whether to litigate and how to present it may itself be the product of deliberative participation. Nor does the litigant have the last word on the perspective from which to view the case. Framing the issue is only the beginning of the conversation. Regardless of who initiates the case, the interests of the poor or disadvantaged can be addressed by interveners. However, this is an empty promise for those who are insufficiently organized or who do not have the resources to keep in touch with Court developments. More frequently, they will be drawn into the litigation after the original orders have been passed, to redress the implications of judicial intervention to which they suddenly find themselves exposed.[38] Alternatively, the Court itself could raise relevant issues, but this is no substitute for participation. Ultimately, a conversation between equal participants is premised on the ability of the poor and disadvantaged to make themselves heard. This is not always the case.

This role of the litigant in framing the issue can be seen in the controversial forestry cases initiated by a petition to prevent illicit felling of timber in India's forests.[39] In this case, the petitioner was an ex-estate owner, whose vast tracts of forest in Kerala had been taken over by the forest department in the early 1990s, threatening trees his family had protected for generations. In response to the petition, the Court issued a series of interim directions requiring an immediate cessation of all ongoing activity within any forest in any State throughout the country (unless it had the prior approval of the central government), including a ban on the felling of trees in the tropical forests. Total and immediate cessation of all sawmills and mining in forests was ordered, and a complete ban imposed on the movement of cut trees and timber from any of the seven North-Eastern States to any other State of the country. This ban, however, did not only capture large commercial enterprises, it also seriously affected tribals and other poor people living within and around forests, who depended on the forests for fuel, fodder, minor forest produce, and construction timber.[40] Their position was made even more difficult by a further order in 2002 directing State governments to summarily evict all illegal encroachment of forestlands since 1980. Because the indigenous rights of many tribal forest dwellers were not established, this led to widespread eviction of indigenous peoples throughout the country, a result aggravated by the

---

[38] For example, an interlocutory order was passed on 5 April 2006 ordering removal of slum dwellers from the Nangla Machi slum in Delhi without hearing the people affected (SP (C) No 3419/1999). The affected people then brought a special petition requesting that they be heard. See *Ram Rattan et al v Commissioner of Police*, Special Petition, 9/05/06.

[39] *TN Godavarman Thirumulpad v Union of India* (1997) 2 SCC 267 (Indian Supreme Court).

[40] The Court did hold that in respect of some States, 'those tribals who are part of the social forestry programme in respect of patta lands, other than forests, may continue to grow and cut according to the Government Scheme provided that they grow and cut trees in accordance with the law applicable', but this was only a limited concession.

widening of the definition of 'forest' to include all areas conforming to the dictionary definition and not just those officially registered as such. One of the key problems was the paucity of proper participation by the indigenous people themselves, either in the initial litigation or in government decision-making. Although many interveners on behalf of tribals and forest dwellers appeared at subsequent hearings, this was only in response to the impact on these people of the Court's original directions.

The power of the litigants to frame the perspective can further be illustrated by contrasting cases initiated by slum-dwellers asserting rights to livelihood, with those initiated by environmentalists or middle-class property owners asserting rights to a cleaner city. Thus, it was in response to petitions by pavement-dwellers themselves that the Court in the seminal case of *Olga Tellis* articulated the rights of slum-dwellers to livelihood and therefore to remain in the city.[41] The role of the litigants is apparent from the opening paragraphs of the case, which clearly present the petitioners' perspective. The Court not only describes their plight with great sympathy, narrating the conditions of appalling squalor in which they, together with nearly half the population of Bombay, lived. It also stresses their 'respectability': they were in employment and had paid rent (to local slumlords) for their shelters. 'It is these men and women who have come to the Court to ask for a judgement that they cannot be evicted from their squalid shelters without being offered alternative accommodation.' By 1996, when cases were increasingly initiated by environmentalists and middle-class property owners, slum-dwellers were no longer characterized as rights-bearing citizens. In the waste-disposal case of *Almitra*,[42] initiated by a public interest litigant committed to the improvement of the urban environment, the Court characterized the provision of alternative accommodation as rewarding wrongdoers. According to the Court: 'The promise of free land, at the taxpayers' cost, in place of a jhuggi, is a proposal which attracts more land grabbers. Rewarding an encroacher on public land with a free alternate site is like giving a reward to a pickpocket.'[43]

From this, it can be seen that the agenda of PIL is shaped as a dialectic between social activists and courts. Although the PIL was originally intended to give access to those who would otherwise not have a voice, it is easily captured by articulate and well-organized interest groups. How then can this dilemma be addressed? Underlying this question is a debate both as to what constitutes the public interest and as to who can legitimately represent it. As far as the public interest is concerned, there is clearly an area in which it is obvious that litigants are representing private trade or industrial interests. Early cases held that standing would not be granted to those pursuing private interests. It is open to State governments to contest the bona fides of PIL petitioners, and they regularly do so, sometimes

[41] *Olga Tellis v Bombay Municipal Corporation* AIR 1986 SC 180 (Indian Supreme Court), initiated by two pavement-dwellers and a journalist.
[42] *Almitra Patel* (n 31 above).
[43] ibid.

successfully. Beyond that, however, as the range of litigated cases demonstrates, the definition of public interest is wide and inclusive. Perhaps this is inevitable, given the impossibility of a single public interest in a highly diverse and complex society such as India. This places the emphasis on who can be said to 'represent' the public interest. Baxi argues that the meaning of representation is itself contested. While representation usually entails 'speaking for others', deliberative democracy aims to 'speak with others'. Viewed in this light, for the court to impose criteria of representation might only detract from the ability of PIL to redefine representativity as a conversation between and among co-equal citizens.[44] At the same time, it must be recognized that the conversation between co-equal citizens can only take place if the participants can in reality participate on equal terms. The aim of PIL was always to prevent the court from simply replicating the disparities in power and economic position in the wider society. To keep this ideal alive requires ongoing vigilance. The primary source of such vigilance must be social activism itself, rather than the top-down control of the court. A key issue is therefore the willingness and ability of social rights activists to bring social action petitions in the appropriate contexts, and to formulate the claim in such a way as to open up areas of conversation which the ordinary paths of 'legality' bypass and negate. However, the court also has a role to play in ensuring that the voice of all is actually heard, not just in response to a question already framed but in the framing of the question itself.

These dilemmas are well illustrated in the Narmada dam litigation, where the problems raised by allowing the Court to determine the representativity of the plaintiff are highlighted. In this case, an environmental group brought a PIL to ask the Court to restrain the government from proceeding with the construction of the dam on the Narmada River, which would displace tens of thousands of people. Here the Court refused to accept the petitioner's credentials in representing the weaker sections of society. The petitioner was an organization which had campaigned against the dam largely for environmental reasons, and although this included a concern for the interests of those ousted by the project, the Court did not regard the petitioner as an authentic representative of those interests. Instead, it accepted the government's view that affected tribals and people of weaker sections would in fact gain from resettlement, since many of them were living as labourers or marginal farmers and would be given a house and land of their own. Indeed, it was contended that opponents of the dam were simply 'playing the card of tribals and weaker sections' on behalf of the land-owning class, who were opposing the project because it would deprive them of cheap labour. In coming to the conclusion that the oustees would in fact be better off as a result of the project, the Court gave no indication that it had made any attempt to find a means whereby these groups could articulate their own position. It was again only in subsequent hearings that these groups were able to articulate their

---

[44] U Baxi, interview, 23 February 2007 Delhi.

concerns as interveners, and this was only after the Court had allowed construction to proceed *pari passu* with rehabilitation measures.

One possibility is to attempt to confine PIL to those who would not otherwise have a voice, thus returning PIL to its original constituency of the poor and disadvantaged. It is arguable that where litigants do not speak for those whose poverty or other social disadvantage is a bar to access to justice, they should be bound by the rigours of normal civil procedure, including narrow rules of standing, rigorous fact-finding, and limited remedial powers. For example, middle-class environmental groups agitating for slum clearance would need to bring a claim in nuisance and follow the regular court procedure to do so. However, this may present practical problems in screening out the appropriate cases; and may in any event simply transpose the problem of identifying appropriate litigants to an earlier phase of the process. The power of the court to define who speaks would thereby be unnecessarily enhanced. An alternative might be an approach which gives greater emphasis to opening up the procedure to all concerned, from the very beginning of the litigation. The claim to represent the public interest in cases such as environmental litigation should be scrutinized, and avenues opened up from the very beginning of the litigation to ensure representation for diverse parts of the public. Thus, as we have seen above, Michelman has argued that a Constitutional Court should 'reach for the inclusion of hitherto excluded voices of emergently self-conscious social groups'.[45]

(vii) Consensus and controversy: the appropriate role of the court

PIL appears to be most successful when the court intervenes to require implementation of policies which have already achieved broad consensus but through apathy, disorganization, or failure to prioritize have not been put into action. The 'Right to Food' case, as we have seen, turned existing policies into fundamental rights and elaborated on them. The Court can also be effective in its intervention in cases where there is a conspicuous gap in policy-making in areas affecting the most fundamental rights, such as the right to dignity and equality of mentally disabled people. A particularly important area in which the Court has been instrumental in filling a gap in legislation is that of sexual harassment. In response to a PIL, the Court held that sexual harassment constitutes a violation of women's constitutional right to dignity, and drafted quasi-legislative guidelines, drawing on internationally recognized norms.[46] Here, however, the institutional limitations of a court taking on a legislative role quickly became apparent. The process of drafting a statute in line with the Court's prescriptions

---

[45] FI Michelman 'Law's Republic' (1988) 97 Yale Law Journal 1493 at 1529.
[46] *Vishaka v State of Rajasthan* (1997) 6 SCC 241 (Indian Supreme Court) and see I Jaising 'Gender Justice and the Supreme Court' in B Kirpaland et al (eds) *Supreme but not Infallible* (OUP New Delhi 2000) 312–315.

has proved very difficult, because of the diversity of situations the law needs to address. This is exacerbated by the Court's delineation of the issue as one for the public sector only.[47]

Where, however, the PIL challenges an existing policy backed by powerful political forces, and established in the name of economic development, the Court's grasp of its fundamental rights mission becomes more unsteady. This has been painfully clear in an era in which the forces of globalization and the rhetoric of economic development have permeated Indian policy-making. In such cases, the public interest is easily transmuted to exclude the fundamental rights of the most disadvantaged, either through a utilitarian calculus or through equating the benefit to some parts of the population with the public interest as a whole. Using familiar legal formulae, such as separation of powers, legality and deference, courts have in several dramatic cases endorsed the position of the powerful and the privileged at the expense of the poor and marginal. Indeed, some would argue that the deference to globalization and multi-national capital makes sense of the Court's simultaneous assault on pollution, corruption, and labour rights.[48] This can be seen in three broad areas: urban development, protection of the environment, and dam development.

(viii) Urban development

Although India has had severe housing shortages and chaotic urban planning for many years, urban development comes into focus in a different way when the aim is to create cities which are attractive to inward investment and global capital. In this light, urban development requires orderly planning, effective services, anti-pollution measures, and public spaces; all of which immediately undermine the claim to urban citizenship of the slum- and pavement-dwellers, the hawkers and the homeless, who now constitute nearly a quarter of the population in 26 big Indian cities.[49] Instead of aiming for integration, through housing, services, and schools, the focus is on removal. The Indian Supreme Court, faced with powerful demands for eviction and displacement, has taken refuge in a narrow concept of legality which relies on absence of proprietary rights to shut down any claims at the threshold. The result is to characterize all those without property rights as encroachers, trespassers, and even petty criminals. Yet the guiding principle behind human rights is to challenge legality when it deprives people of their rights. By failing to regard slum-dwellers as urban citizens with equal rights, the courts have strayed from their human rights role.

---

[47] I am grateful to Indira Jaising for this insight.
[48] U Baxi, interview, 23 February 2007 Delhi.
[49] <http://www.censusindia.gov.in/Tables_Published/Admin_Units/Admin_links/slum1.html>.

This can be seen in the string of cases concerned with eviction of slum-dwellers. Constituting well over 40 million people,[50] slum-dwellers have found themselves pitted against pedestrians, town-planners, middle-class homeowners, environmentalists, and local authorities in their struggle for minimum human rights. While lip service is often paid to the duty to rehabilitate, relocation is frequently to unserviced sites inaccessible to schools or work, where displaced people are required to pay for a piece of land with little real utility to themselves. In such cases, the Court has neither imposed a duty of restraint (against eviction) nor used its extensive remedial powers to insist on implementation of positive duties to provide housing and infrastructure. The result is that evicted slum-dwellers are forced back into the illegal settlements as their only means of making a living. This can be dated back to *Olga Tellis* itself, which, although using the vocabulary of a right to livelihood, in fact imposed only a duty to consult those facing eviction. Particularly serious was the refusal to insist that alternative pitches with proper infrastructure be provided as a condition precedent to removals.[51] In one sense, the Court's reluctance to enforce such positive duties is difficult to explain since the Court could have followed its own example in the 'Right to Food' case and insisted on the implementation of existing policy documents, thus turning a policy commitment into a fundamental right to livelihood and shelter. In particular, the Delhi Master Plan aims to deal systematically with Delhi's housing problems through integration of slum-dwellers into housing with the necessary infrastructure and accessibility to sources of work. The plan, which includes a significant land allocation, has been consistently ignored.

(ix) Environmental cases

Overlapping with housing issues, and similarly caught between a fundamental rights approach and the utilitarianism of global capitalism, are environmental concerns, an arena in which the Court has been a major player.[52] Many of the environmental cases upheld by the Court have of course benefited the poor as well as the middle classes. The Court's intervention after public-spirited individuals drew its attention to the dangerous leak of oleum gas from factory premises in Delhi[53] and the discharge of toxic effluents into the soil in Udaipur[54]

---

[50] <http://www.censusindia.gov.in/Tables_Published/Admin_Units/Admin_links/slum1.html>.

[51] *Olga Tellis* (n 41 above) 586.

[52] M Lokur 'Environmental Law: Its Development and Jurisprudence' Greenlaw Lecture IX, Greenlaw Lecture Series, World Wide Fund for Nature, India 1–27.

[53] *M C Mehta v Union of India* (1986) 2 SCC 176, (1986) 2 SCC 325, (1987) 1 SCC 395 (Indian Supreme Court).

[54] *Indian Council for Enviro-legal Action v Union of India* (1996) 3 SCC 212 (Indian Supreme Court).

are good examples. In the famous *Vehicular Pollution* cases,[55] the Court was faced with government statistics showing that vehicles contributed to 70% of the air pollution in Delhi and other major cities. In response, it ordered strict measures to decrease such pollution, including the conversion of all public transport in Delhi to use Compressed Natural Gas rather than petrol. The resulting drop in pollution clearly benefits all. Such cases are, however, consistent with a judicial approach which views cleaner cities as an essential way of attracting global capital. Other aspects of the environment raise more complex conflicts of interest. In one of its earliest decisions, concerned with illegal quarrying which was destroying the Musoorie hills near Delhi and interfering with the water system, the Supreme Court was able to take into account the effect of closing the mines on workers' jobs. Thus, as well as prohibiting the mining, the Court directed that a task force be set up to engage workers in the task of aforestation and soil conservation of reclaimed land.[56] However, in the clash between the drive for cleaner cities and the needs of the urban poor, the former has invariably triumphed. Although rehabilitation and resettlement are sometimes ordered, as has been seen above, their efficacy is seriously weakened by allowing resettlement to be postponed while environmental measures proceed.

A particularly ferocious instance of the Court privileging environmental issues over people was the action in May 1997 of the Bombay High Court in ordering the eviction of informal settlement dwellers adjacent to the Sanjay National Park. The Court was responding to a petition filed in 1995 by the Bombay Environmental Action Group (BEAG), asking the Court to 'remove forthwith' the 'encroachers' in order to ensure protection of 'the environment and all its aspects'. Not only did the Bombay High Court direct the relevant authorities to evict persons from their homes, it also specifically ordered the demolition of shelters and the destruction of all belongings and construction materials.[57] As many as half a million slum-dwellers were potentially affected. A similar pattern can be seen in the decision to clear one of the biggest and oldest slums in Delhi, home to 150,000 people and 40,000 homes, which had existed for many years on the banks of the Yamuna River. The slum was demolished in 2004 by order of the High Court of Delhi, in response to a petition brought by citizens concerned at the pollution and encroachment on the river. About a fifth of the residents were resettled on the outskirts of Delhi, without local services or transport into the city. The rest were left to their own devices. Although the High Court

[55] *M C Mehta v Union of India* (1998) 6 SCC 60; (1998) 8 SCC 648; (1999) 6 SCC 14; (2000) 9 SCC 519; (2001) 3 SCC 756; (2001) 3 SCC 763; (2001) 3 SCC 767; (2002) 4 SCC 352; (2002) 4 SCC 356; (2003) 10 SCC 560 (Indian Supreme Court).
[56] *Rural Litigation and Entitlement Kendra v State of Uttar Pradesh* (1985) 2 SCC 431; (1985) 3 SCC 614; (1986) Supp SCC 517; (1980) Supp 1 SCC 514; (1989) Supp 1 SCC 537; (1989) Supp 2 SCC 384; (1991) 3 SCC 347 (Indian Supreme Court); and see Lokur (n 52 above) 4–6.
[57] Writ Petition No 305 of 1995 in the Bombay High Court; see U Ramanathan 'Illegality and Exclusion: Law in the Lives of Slum Dwellers' International Environmental Law Research Centre Working Paper 2004–2, 9.

directed that proper basic amenities, including power, water, sewerage, schools, and transportation be provided in the rehabilitation colonies, it refused to stay the eviction until these has been complied with. By 2006, little had been done to implement these directions. While no one is in any doubt that the Yamuna is seriously polluted, the extent to which the slums contribute is controversial. One study puts the contribution of slums to such pollution at less than 1%.[58]

(x) Development and dams

A third area in which the PIL has required the Court to face up to powerful political and economic interests in the name of development concerns the much-contested Narmada dam project. This concerned the construction of a dam on the Narmada River, which would displace many people and submerge natural forestland. The claimed benefits included providing irrigation to drought prone areas, drinking water facilities to thousands of villages and urban centres, as well as power generation. Proposals for the project, initiated in 1947, had been the subject of numerous reports and consultations, as well as a detailed award by a statutory tribunal. Financed by a loan from the World Bank, construction eventually began in 1987 and the first ten sluices were closed in February 1994. Almost immediately, a PIL was filed, asking the Court to restrain the government from proceeding with the construction of the dam. The facts were heavily contested. The petitioners claimed that the environmental clearance given in 1987 was based on incomplete evidence and the proper studies had not been undertaken. They also claimed that the right to life of those who were ousted by the dam had been breached, since it was impossible to fully substitute for their way of life through rehabilitation measures. In any event, they argued, there was insufficient public interest to justify the displacement, given that serious doubts had been raised about the benefits of the project, in particular, that it would only bring water to the margins of drought-prone areas and even then would have little real effect. For this, they relied on the 1992 report of an Independent Review set up by the World Bank, which concluded that decisions had been made on the basis of questionable or unfounded assumptions without a full understanding of the consequences, that the benefits were overstated and the environmental impact not adequately addressed. Most serious, it found rehabilitation of all those displaced was not possible.[59] The government cited its own alternative assessment, which referred to the many benefits the scheme would bring, particularly since it was making use of water which otherwise would flow unused into the sea. Even the extent of the displacement was contested, with the government

---

[58] R N Barucha *Yamuna Gently Weeps* <http://www.yamunagentlyweeps.com>.
[59] *Narmada Bachao Andolan v Union of India* (2000) 10 SCC 664 (Indian Supreme Court) para 64.

claiming that the project would affect 'only' 245 villages, of which 241 were only partially affected.[60]

Faced with such strongly opposing currents, the Court decided to defer to the political process. In its view, the decision as to whether to have an infrastructure project, and how it was to be executed, were part of the policy-making process, a field into which courts should not transgress. Its assessment of the development of PIL is illuminating:

PIL was an innovation essentially to safeguard and protect the human rights of those people who were unable to protect themselves. With the passage of time, PIL jurisdiction has been ballooning so as to encompass within its ambit subjects such as probity in public life, granting of largesse in the form of licences, protecting environment and the like. But the balloon should not be inflated so much that it bursts. Public interest litigation should not be allowed to degenerate to becoming publicity interest litigation or private inquisitiveness litigation.[61]

The Court reiterated its role in protecting the fundamental rights of the people. But, it continued:

In exercise of its enormous power, the court should not be called upon to or undertake governmental duties or functions. The court cannot run the Government... In a democracy, welfare of the people at large and not merely of a small section of the society has to be the concern of a responsible government... For any project which is approved after due deliberation the court should refrain from being asked to review the decision just because a petitioner in filing a PIL alleges that such a decision should not have been taken because an opposite view against the undertaking of the project, a view which may have been considered by the government, is possible. When two or more options or views are possible and after considering, the government makes a policy decision, it is then not the function of the court to go into the matter afresh and in a way sit in appeal over such a policy decision.[62]

In particular, where there were conflicts of interest, such as the interest of the people of Gujurat in having access to drinking water, and the people whose houses and land would be submerged, it was for the government to resolve, and the Court should not sit in appeal.

The majority of the Court achieved this outcome in two ways. First, it held that the petitioners were too late to challenge the construction of the dam itself. Although it accepted that complete data with regard to the environment were not available when the government gave clearance in 1987,[63] it was held that the petitioners should have acted immediately to challenge the project, rather than waiting until hundreds of billions of public money had been spent. 'It is against the national interest and contrary to established principles of law that decisions to

---

[60] ibid para 54.
[61] *Narmada Bachao Andolan* (n 59 above) para 230.
[62] ibid para 233–234.
[63] *Narmada Bachao Andolan* (n 59 above) para 47.

undertake developmental projects are permitted to be challenged after a number of years during which period public money has been spent in the execution of the project.'[64] It was therefore only its concern for the protection of the fundamental rights to life of the oustees in respect of the relief and rehabilitation measures that the Court was prepared to entertain the petition.

Secondly, the Court used a very light touch standard of review, asking only whether decisions had been taken bona fide and with 'application of mind'. On the basis of the very many discussions and documents received by the government, the Court held that it was not possible to conclude that the environmental clearance had been given without proper application of mind. However, there is a middle ground between substituting for the decision of the relevant authorities, and deference to authority decision-making. This can be seen in the dissenting judgment of Bharucha J. While he did not claim that the Court should make the decision, he did hold that where the impact on the environment could have disastrous consequence for many generations, the Court's constitutional responsibility under Article 21 (the right to life) required the Court to ensure that the project did not go ahead until those best fitted to do so have had the opportunity of gathering all necessary data and assessing it. Such data had not, in his view, been fully gathered. Environmental clearance was based on next to no data in regard to the environmental impact of the project, and therefore, in his view, could not be considered clearance at all.

As far as the right to life of the oustees was concerned, the majority was content to accept the contention of the government that the planned resettlement and rehabilitation would leave oustees better off than before. Thus, it was held not only that displacement of the tribals and other persons would not per se result in violation of their fundamental or other rights, but also that on their rehabilitation at new locations they would have more and better amenities than those they enjoyed in their hamlets; and their gradual assimilation in the mainstream of the society would lead to betterment and progress. The majority was in any event prepared to go along with a utilitarian calculus, which saw the cost borne by those ousted by the dam as well compensated for by the benefits to others including fulfilling the right to water of people who suffer due to water shortage.[65] Thus, the Court refused to require the scheme to be put on hold, either to carry out further impact assessments, or to institute rehabilitation measures. Instead, the Court directed only that the resettlement and rehabilitation measures should be implemented *pari passu* with the raising of the height of the dam. This again contrasts with the dissenting judgment, which insisted that the rehabilitation projects be both designed and implemented before the reservoir was filled, rather than, as the majority held, simultaneously with the development of the dam. In practice, it is clear that promises to rehabilitate have been reneged on and States

---

[64] ibid para 48.
[65] *Narmada Bachao Andolan* (n 59 above) para 248.

have disputed the legitimacy of many claims on such grounds as they are not permanently affected or are the sons of the original oustees. Nevertheless, in subsequent hearings, while insisting that rehabilitation be implemented, the Court has refused to halt construction until such rehabilitation has been accomplished.

(xi) Conclusion: a peril and a promise

How then should the innovative PIL procedure be assessed in respect of the promotion of positive duties arising out of human rights? Baxi argues that 'the growth in constitutional faith overloads adjudicatory power with great expectations, which it does not quite efficiently manage and which it may not always fulfil'.[66] The result has been that 'judicial activism is at once a peril and a promise, an assurance of solidarity for the depressed classes . . . as well as a site of betrayal'.[67] Indeed, he concludes: 'Courts are, at the end of the day, never an instrument of total societal revolution: they are at best . . . instruments of piecemeal social engineering . . . never a substitute for direct political action.'[68]

This suggests that the PIL jurisdiction should not be judged by expectations it cannot fulfil, but instead be tailored to achieve what it was intended for. A central aspect of this mission is to step in when government fails to act to achieve positive freedom and fulfil human rights. At the same time, there is no reason to believe that courts will always succeed where government has failed. Even under the PIL procedure, courts have limited fact-finding facilities, and appointed committees do not in themselves have the resources to ensure that court decrees are fulfilled. In that sense, courts cannot substitute for recalcitrant governments. Nor can they replace political activity. What courts can do, however, is to act as a catalyst for the democratic pressures which ultimately make recalcitrant governments act. At its most basic, the PIL procedure enables ordinary people to require governments to be accountable, that is, to come to court and explain and justify their actions or inactivity. Beyond that, the PIL procedure, with its open doors to all interested parties, facilitates genuine conversation, requiring governments to listen and interact with civil society, and groups within civil society to listen and interact with each other. Most importantly, it permits the conversation to take place on equal terms. The judicial forum makes it possible to restore what Baxi calls the republican virtue of civility, that is, that everyone is treated as an equal citizen.[69] To maintain this, courts should take care to avoid capture by those who already have political power in society, remaining true to their original mission of ensuring that the poor and disadvantaged are given an equal voice within judicial proceedings. Courts should also remain clearly focussed on their human rights role, both in respect of positive duties and duties of restraint. This entails avoiding both the temptation to range too far from fundamental human rights (as in

[66] Baxi (n 28 above) 159.   [67] ibid 161.
[68] Baxi (n 28 above) 164.   [69] U Baxi, interview, 23 February 2007 Delhi.

whether small children should be interviewed for private schools) and the temptation to retreat into a narrow concept of legality or deference to authority.

But should the court involvement end with the conversation? Or should it go much further, as the Indian Court has done, to set the direction for change and then police its implementation? Judicial decisions must be taken; thus, it is inevitable that there should be moments of closure in the conversation. However, as Habermas shows, such moments are only pauses in the discourse. Moreover, as Baxi puts it, there are 'civil' and 'uncivil' means of applying closure. The way in which closure is effected can open up new beginnings, but can also constitute a point of no return. The ideal would be for the court to energize the political process, rather than paralyzing it by taking over its functions. Positive duties should be primarily fulfilled by the initiative of the democratic process itself, with the courts acting as facilitators rather than substitutes. Moreover, in order to achieve a just closure, the court should see its role as not a freewheeling political one, but one which is structured by the human rights values from which it gains its legitimacy. The danger of the PIL procedure is that its openness to many voices might lure courts into reaching closure in terms of interest bargaining rather than through a deliberative mechanism whereby equal parties to a conversation flesh out and apply human rights values. Notions of the public interest as a pluralist's bazaar, in which interest groups bargain according to their economic and political strength, are not appropriate in the judicial forum. At the same time, its openness to many perspectives is also its strength, provided that in transcending the limitations of the bipolar adversarial process, PIL is used to facilitate deliberation in place of interest bargaining.

The court's continuing role in supervising the implementation of positive duties carries similar risks and strengths. By allowing litigants and interveners to return repeatedly to the court, PIL ensures that closure is dynamic and flexible, a continuation of the social conversation in order to find the most effective way of achieving its human rights mission. On the other hand, if it takes over too many executive functions, the ongoing supervisory jurisdiction of the court, whether through commissions or otherwise, can itself become rigid and inaccessible, particularly if it means a Supreme Court hearing every few months. Energizing the political process requires the creation of structures which can themselves manage implementation, which are responsive to the range of interests, and which can deal with polycentric implications, with judicial supervision acting as a facilitator rather than a substitute. This is of course a delicate tightrope to walk, but is nevertheless a goal to be aspired to.

6

Achieving Compliance: Positive
Duties Beyond the Courts

A. Introduction

The previous chapters have reached beyond the divide between justiciability and non-justiciability in relation to positive human rights duties. It has been shown that positive duties have both justiciable and non-justiciable dimensions. Courts have a role to play, particularly by enhancing democratic deliberation. However, because positive duties require goal-oriented action from individuals or bodies, they raise a series of challenges to compliance systems which extend well beyond court-based remedies. Unlike duties of restraint, which are bi-modal in that a body is either in breach or not in breach, positive duties can be carried out in a variety of different ways. They require initiative, planning, execution, and implementation, all of which necessitate internal motivation and organizational change. They also call for cooperation between different organizations which provide aspects of the same right.

This chapter examines ways in which such non-justiciable compliance mechanisms can be understood and constructed. It argues that such mechanisms should be more than an attempt to replicate court-based remedies in a different forum. They should self-consciously model themselves on the different nature of positive duties as compared to duties of restraint. Particularly important is the movement away from a fault-based notion, which focusses on finding an individual perpetrator who has breached a right. Instead, the focus is on the body in the best position to bring about change. This means action is proactive and collective rather than retrospective and individualized. Rather than leaving enforcement to the ad hoc initiative of an individual, it aims to stimulate an internalization of the demands of human rights. The primary motivation should be acceptance by the actors of the validity of the duty, assisted by incentives, with sanctions or penalties viewed only as the fall-back. Also of key importance is the role of participation and involvement of a wide range of stakeholders and other individuals or groups.

Such mechanisms hold out great promise in achieving institutional change and a culture of human rights. However, they lie at the interface between law and policy. This means that there is always the risk that positive human rights duties will become severed from their roots as fundamental human rights and merge with policy-making, which is dependent on political will and the balance of interests. Non-judicial methods also open up some fundamental questions as to the distinction between norm-formation, interpretation, and enforcement. A central strength of proactive approaches is the possibility of continuing review and revision in the interests of greater effectiveness. Enforcement, interpretation, and creation of norms interact in order to continually move the process forward. Here too there is a risk of encroaching on the fundamental core of the right. The challenge is therefore to ensure that such mechanisms are firmly centred on fundamental rights rather than political discretion. This may well require a combination of judicial and non-judicial compliance mechanisms.

In many ways, the challenges raised by positive human rights duties resemble those raised more generally by regulation in the Welfare State and post-Welfare State. Section B therefore draws on modern developments in regulatory theory in order to illuminate both the challenges of positive human rights duties and potential solutions. Section C turns to possible applications of these theoretical insights. The Open Method of Coordination in the EU is used as a central example, because it is primarily aimed at positive duties to provide and facilitate, particularly those linked to the right to work and general welfare. It is acknowledged that in many ways the EU is *sui generis*, because of its unique powers to bind its members, but given that it is a sophisticated example of the mechanisms under discussion, it nevertheless casts valuable perspectives on both international and national possibilities. The model is also useful in assessing non-judicial reporting mechanisms. The chapter briefly considers some key aspects of international reporting mechanisms, and then assesses the South African Human Rights Commission as an example of a domestic reporting mechanism as well as some US examples of experimentalism at local level. It concludes by drawing together the various elements considered in Chapters 4, 5, and 6 into a 'synergistic' approach, in which political, judicial, and non-judicial mechanisms potentially work together to produce positive outcomes.

B. Challenges

Goal-oriented duties are challenging for legal regulation because effective compliance defies a monolithic solution. Instead, compliance with positive human rights duties necessitates problem-solving and continuing review by actors themselves. For this reason, traditional models of legal enforcement based on formal legal rules are inappropriate. Formal legal rules, as defined by Teubner,[1]

---

[1] G Teubner 'Substantive and Reflexive Elements in Modern Law' (1983) 17 Law and Society Review 239.

are designed to give an unambiguous legal response to factual situations. Their underlying rationale is to protect a sphere of autonomy within which individuals are free to pursue private interests and chosen values. Duties of restraint fit well into this model, both because they aim to protect a sphere of autonomy, and because their binary character makes it possible to design specific legal rules. But duties to take action cannot be formulated in such terms. In principle, they fit better into what Teubner calls a substantive model of legal rationality. Rather than protecting individual freedom, this model directly regulates behaviour by imposing substantive requirements. Well-established in the Welfare State, it aims to compensate for the inadequacies of the market. However, the Welfare State mode of regulation has come under fire from all directions. Market-oriented theorists argue that it stifles initiative, which can only be generated by a competitive market. Social welfare oriented theorists regard it as bureaucratic and often ineffective. In practice, attempts to impose substantive outcomes on organizations can lead to unexpected consequences. An organization might simply not react; or it might react by creating bureaucratic procedures, which substitute for goal-oriented action; or it might create defensive structures which justify inaction.

The weaknesses of substantive regulation have led to a wealth of literature both diagnosing the causes and prescribing solutions. One of the most interesting diagnoses has come from systems analysis. According to systems analysis, law is not capable of controlling behaviour through direct 'command-and-control'. This is because society is not hierarchically organized, with law at the apex. Instead, society is structured non-hierarchically into multiple sub-systems, such as the market, the administration, religion, or culture. Sub-systems are not only functionally differentiated. In addition, each has its own 'language' or mode of function which is not capable of being understood or translated by other sub-systems.[2] In its extreme form, systems theory posits that there is no higher-level shared language. Instead, each system translates external stimuli into its own language and reacts reflexively according to its own internal logic. This means that there is no way of directly regulating society nor of integrating diverse systems through deliberate action. Drawing on the biological metaphor of 'autopoiesis', systems theory posits that sub-systems only influence each other by reflexively adjusting their own internal systems to the mutual environment in which they operate. In other words, at best, a particular system can alter itself, presenting a modified environment or irritant to which other sub-systems react according to their internal logic.[3] For example, within the political sub-system, legislation is viewed as an instrument of communication with the legal sub-system, operated

[2] ibid; C Scott 'Regulation in the Age of Governance: The Rise of the Post-regulatory State' in J Jordana and D Levi-Faur (eds) *The Politics of Regulation* (Edward Elgar Cheltenham 2004); J Black 'Constitutionalising Self Regulation' (1996) 59 Modern Law Review 24; J Black 'Proceduralising Regulation, Part II' (2001) 21 OJLS 33.
[3] J Habermas *Between Facts and Norms* (Polity Press 1997) section 2.1.

through the courts. The legal sub-system, does not, however, receive the legislation as intended by the political system. On the contrary, the instrumental objectives of the political system are of no interest to the legal sub-system. Instead, it filters the legislation through the lens of its internal norms, such as a strict standard of proof in the criminal law. This might cut across the regulatory objectives of legislation by making it too difficult to penalize breaches of a particular standard.[4]

This analysis leads to the conclusion that law cannot directly regulate another system, since law is only one system among many. Attempts by the law to change the behaviour of another sub-system using command and control regulation merely result in what Teubner calls the 'regulatory trilemma'. One possibility is that intervention is ignored by the targeted sub-system. A second is that regulation might damage the ability of the targeted sub-system to reproduce itself. For example, juridification of collective bargaining could undermine the dynamic of voluntary interest bargaining and therefore its ability to reach stable solutions. Thirdly, regulation might damage the legal sub-system itself, in that the perceived ineffectiveness of law results in a crisis of legitimacy.[5]

The only way to avoid the regulatory trilemma is to adopt a new model by which law adjusts itself, creating an altered environment in the hope of inducing adjustment in other systems indirectly through its own adjustments. This is known as reflexive law. According to Teubner, reflexive law gains its legitimacy neither from the protection of autonomy, nor the collective regulation of behaviour, but by the need to coordinate semi-autonomous systems.[6] Accepting the fact and the desirability of decentralized decision-making, reflexive law rejects authoritative prescription, seeking instead to 'support integrative mechanisms within autonomous social subsystems'.[7] This 'structural coupling' recognizes the inner logic of social systems and attempts to find ways to steer them. Thus, there is increasing interest in constructing models of reflexive law which relate to other sub-systems, not by imposing specific rules or goal-oriented substantive law, but by understanding and working with the dynamic of other sub-systems.[8] An example is collective bargaining law. Such laws do not directly intervene in the bargain struck between employers and unions; instead they seek to structure bargaining relations so as to equalize bargaining power. This affects the quality of outcomes but not their precise content.[9]

Systems theory on its own leads to a relatively pessimistic vision of the possibilities of ensuring genuine compliance with positive human rights duties.

---

[4] Scott (n 2 above).
[5] Teubner 'After Privatization: The Many Autonomies of Private Law' (1998) 51 Current Legal Problems 393–424.
[6] Teubner (n 1 above) 254.
[7] ibid 255.
[8] Scott (n 2 above) 9.
[9] Teubner (n 1 above) 256.

Because formal knowledge is tied to a single system, there is little space for individual agency, and almost none for express coordination.[10] However, systems theory on its own is not a sufficiently coherent theory to allow us to apply it in an unadulterated form. It has several weaknesses. First, in arguing for a horizontal vision of society, it ignores power structures, both within and between sub-systems. This means that it pays no attention to how decisions are made and in particular to the quality of democracy and equality in such decision-making. Secondly, it goes too far in its assumption of the opacity of sub-systems and the impossibility of communication. Other thinkers are more optimistic about the possibilities of communication and coordination through law. Habermas, for example, while recognizing the special codes of language in the systems of market and administration respectively, argues that it is possible to have differentiated functional specifications within the boundaries of a multifunctional language.[11] Thirdly, it is not self-evident that the sub-systems work within sealed borders, or even that lines of demarcation are clear. In a world of privatization and contracting out, there is growing mobility between the marketplace and the administration, both in function and personnel. This is true too for law. The notion that legislation is a part of the political and not the legal sub-system presumes a narrow court-centred view of law. In addition, there are many ways in which laws can be seen to emerge from a variety of sources apart from the State.

The increasingly popular notion of reflexive law has taken on board some of these criticisms. Recent advocates of reflexive law take from systems theory an appreciation of the need to shape regulatory mechanisms in ways which connect with the internal logic of other systems. At the same time, the idea of reflexive law has come some way from its origins. The recognition of horizontal decision-making units has tended to extend beyond hermetically sealed 'systems' such as law or the administration, to refer instead to organizations, public bodies, or corporate entities. Reflexivity in turn has come to refer to the possibilities for autonomous decision-making in a decentred polity.[12] This in turn has made it possible to consider local decisions as decentralized law-making. This 'second generation regulatory approach' is described by Susan Sturm as an approach that 'encourages the development of institutions and process to enact general norms in particular contexts. "Legality" emerges from an interactive process of information gathering, problem identification, remediation, and evaluation.' The participants in the

---

[10] O Gerstenberg and C Sabel 'Directly-deliberative Polyarchy: An Institutional Ideal for Europe?' in C Joerges and R Dehousse (eds) *Good Governance in Europe's Integrated Market* (OUP Oxford 2002) 338–340.

[11] Habermas (n 3 above) para 2.1.

[12] See, for example, O de Schutter and S Deakin 'Reflexive Governance and the Dilemmas of Social Regulation' in O de Schutter and S Deakin (eds) *Social Rights and Market Forces: Is the Open Coordination of Employment and Social Policies the Future of Social Europe?* (Bruylant Bruxelles 2005).

process, whether State bodies or non-governmental institutions, are treated as 'lawmaking bodies, rather than simply as objects of state or market regulation'.[13]

These inroads into the purism of systems analysis allow us to take a more optimistic view of the ability of law to influence behaviour. The regulatory problem is not so much one of impermeable systems, but of the impossibility of devising appropriate and dynamic solutions for the wide diversity of units required to take steps to achieve human rights goals. This points to the importance of devolved decision-making. Attempts to specify solutions from above stifle local initiative and forfeit the cooperation of local actors. Instead, the heterogeneity of organizations subject to the duties should both be recognized and cultivated in order to find creative and dynamic methods of problem solving. Viewing the issue in this light opens up the potential to incorporate principles of deliberative democracy into local decision-making. This points us towards the solutions proposed under the label of Directly Deliberative Polyarchy (DDP).[14] DDP recognizes the limits of legal regulation but also rejects the view that free enterprise within the market is the only alternative. The aim is to find a democratic solution to the need for creative problem-solving both within and between units. This approach is particularly aimed at situations in which there are too many sites to monitor through centralized compliance mechanisms; or where the diversity of sites means that different means are appropriate in each case. It also aims to address situations in which the complexity of the problem to be solved requires continuous review and reflection, and where cooperation between units is necessary to achieve the desired outcome. It is superior to market allocation in that the service or good provided emanates from a fundamental right and therefore its provision is obligatory rather than a result of exchange or bargaining power.[15]

DDP harnesses the energy and knowledge of local actors by granting them autonomy to experiment with solutions of their own devising within broadly defined areas of public policy.[16] The focus is on finding ways to stimulate problem solving, encouraging organizations to identify ways in which to carry out their duties which are most appropriate to their own context. Instead of insisting on specific actions, the thrust of the compliance mechanism would be to facilitate deliberative procedures, whereby the decision-makers in an organization are able to work out the appropriate response. Deliberation is more than discussion or consultation; it aims to achieve a problem-solving dynamic where participants are ready constantly to review and revise their conclusions in the light of their exposure to their own and others' experience and perspectives. This in turn generates a greater likelihood that local norms will be developed which will be real and effective. This operates within a regulatory framework in which

---

[13] S Sturm 'Second Generation Employment Discrimination: A Structural Approach' (2001) 101 Columbia Law Review 458 at 463.

[14] J Cohen and C Sabel 'Directly-deliberative Polyarchy' (1997) European Law Journal 313.

[15] ibid 321, 334.

[16] Gerstenberg and Sabel (n 10 above) 291.

the role of legislation is to set general goals and to facilitate deliberation; the role of the administrative bodies is to provide the infrastructure for the exchange of information; and the role of the courts is to require decision-making to proceed in a deliberative way.[17]

This approach resonates with the deliberative democratic model used in previous chapters. However, the same tensions emerge as in the earlier discussions of deliberative democracy. There are three particularly salient sources of strain. The first is the relationship of deliberation to pre-existing values and goals. In the context of positive human rights duties, deliberation cannot be an end in itself. Because it is based on a human right, it is targeted at securing the exercise of the right. Secondly, deliberation must lead to action. Otherwise, positive duties have no normative value. This puts particular weight on the ability of deliberative structures to reach decisions. As Black points out, it is by no means inevitable that deliberation will lead to conclusions. Thirdly, close attention needs to be paid to the participants in the process. It is easy to regard a sub-system or organization as a horizontally organized entity, in the same way as systems are regarded as non-hierarchically related to each other. However, there are very real power structures within organizations, and the ways in which participants to deliberation are identified is crucial. This manifests itself too in the nature of the communication process itself. While Habermas assumes that language is an unambiguous medium of communication, Young shows that this conceals a particular view of rationality, which privileges speech that is formal and general, and values assertive and definitive approaches rather than that which is tentative or exploratory. This in turn can operate as a form of power, silencing or devaluing the speech of those who do not engage on these terms.[18] As Black concludes:

We have to recognise the possibility of forms of communication that do not correspond to the ideal of communication that Habermas posits, in which there may not be orientation to mutual understanding, to public reason, and a commitment to take on obligations arising from the interaction…We have to allow for manipulation by communicants, for insincerity, for lack of trust and belief in the others' motives, or quite simply for the fact that people may not be interested in communicating at all.[19]

It is therefore necessary to find the right balance between external imposition of the goal to be achieved and local autonomy as to how to achieve the goal. This is particularly complex where the goal is one of progressive realization. Effective monitoring of the priorities set by local decision-makers is necessary to prevent the process becoming one of pure discretion. But at the same time, deliberation

---

[17] Cohen and Sabel (n 14 above) 334–335.

[18] I Young 'Communication and the Other: Beyond Deliberative Democracy' in S Benhabib (ed) *Democracy and Difference: Contesting the Boundaries of the Political* (Princeton Paperbacks Princeton 1996) 127–128; I Young 'Justice and Communicative Democracy' in R Gottlieb (ed) *Radical Philosophy: Tradition, Counter-tradition, Politics* (Temple University Press Philadelphia 1993) 130.

[19] J Black 'Proceduralising Regulation, Part II' (2001) 21 OJLS 33 at 47.

should not be stifled by tying deliberators to particular outcomes. This is further complicated by the permeability of means and ends. The interpretation of the means to achieving the right bears closely on the meaning of the right itself, so that while the right anchors deliberation, deliberation also shapes the right and the consequent duty. Similarly, the duty requires action, but action must continually be deliberatively reviewed to better achieve the right. Finally, deliberation requires equality among participants, both in their presence and their ability to present their perspective and this is a key aspect of deliberative democracy.

This discussion suggests that, in designing compliance mechanisms, it is necessary not only to understand the conditions under which a deliberative process takes place but also to affirmatively create them.[20] The autopoietic analysis highlights a particular problem in the translation of legal norms into action by wholly or partially closed sub-systems. It therefore points towards the need to involve in a fundamental way the actors within the system if a desired change is to be achieved. At the same time, it is crucial to alter the usual ways of reacting within the system. Decision-making within organizations is not necessarily deliberative or democratic; in fact, it is more often autocratic or bureaucratic. Therefore, regulation should be fashioned in a way which reflexively leads to an alteration in internal structures, creating the conditions for deliberation among relevant actors, so that they can reach a mutual understanding of the goal to be reached, and the most effective means of reaching it. In particular, participants must be willing to revise their initial perceptions in the light of the discussion. There also needs to be a regular process of review, where further deliberation takes place in the light of experience of the workings of any given solution, with a crucial role being played by the differing perceptions of various participants. Experience has shown that this does not happen without some external triggers, in the form of incentives or sanctions. Attempts at voluntary codes have proved that, while some organizations may readily respond, others will simply ignore attempts at change which have no ultimate sanction or incentive.[21] The challenge is to find a way to establish a relationship between internal deliberation and external incentive or deterrent structures, while at the same time being responsive to different organizational dynamics.

Empirical studies have shown that one way of doing so is through a 'pyramid of enforcement'. This envisages that most regulatory interaction will be in the form of persuasion, or education and advice, the aim being to trigger a deliberative mechanism within the organization which will take appropriate action. A critical element in the process is to ensure that deliberation draws in all affected groups and individuals, not just those who already have power of decision-making and may be resistant to change. If compliance is not forthcoming, enforcement

---

[20] de Schutter and Deakin (n 12 above) 3.
[21] B Hepple, M Coussey, and T Choudhury *Equality: A New Framework Report of the Independent Review of the Enforcement of UK Anti-discrimination Legislation* (Hart Oxford 2000).

activity is escalated, becoming most severe at the apex of the pyramid, where revocation of a licence or contract, or criminal sanctions might be imposed.[22] The difficulty of the model is its reliance on a regulator capable of escalating sanctions in response to failure to react, particularly where the coverage of regulation extends to a large number of public or private organizations. Some studies find that in fact regulators tend to choose the strategy which is appropriate rather than progressing consistently up the pyramid.

Black explores further ways in which deliberative structures might be harnessed to achieve compliance. To enlist deliberation, which can lead to action in respect of positive duties, might require active mediation by a regulator which has the ability to overcome some of the obstacles identified above. The difficulties of communication even between participants in the same system require a regulator who is capable of translating the different languages used by participants in a way which all can understand. This is more difficult than it seems, because the blockage is not simply one of using different words as signifiers of the same concept, but of the different logical and motivational underpinnings of the discourse. For example, it is necessary to recognize non-rational forms of communication, such as storytelling and rhetoric together with 'rational' approaches. Even more important, as Black argues, if translation is to facilitate the inclusion of all those who want to deliberate, it cannot be a translation into one dominant language. Instead, it must be multiple, from the language of each to that of the others.[23] The influence of the regulator's own frame of reference and 'language' should not be ignored.

This section has set out the main contours of a non-court-centred regulatory system appropriate for positive human rights duties. The aim is to design reflexive law so that it stimulates deliberation and dynamic problem-solving within organizations while at the same time retaining the mandatory nature of human rights duties. This requires a dynamic dialectic between external and internal stimuli. External standards set broad framework goals, which emanate from the nature of the right itself. They also mandate procedures which facilitate deliberative democracy. Within this framework, it is left to bodies subject to the duty to devise intermediate goals and priorities and to fashion appropriate means to achieve those goals. This internal process remains normative because of the requirement of accountability: that is, that decision-makers should provide a transparent account of their reasons for decisions, which in turn invites further deliberation from service users or the wider public. Accountability is not, however, simply explanatory. Progress towards change needs to be monitored and compared to benchmarks which are in turn generated through a participative process involving both internal and external actors. Further stimulation towards ongoing change is provided by peer review; or discussion between units with the

---

[22] Scott (n 2 above) 12; Hepple, Coussey, and Choudhury (n 21 above) 56–58.
[23] J Black 'Proceduralising Regulation, Part II' (2001) 21 OJLS 33 at 51.

aim of continually improving and revising the approach in the light of the experience of other organizations.

There remain problematic issues. Whether deliberative problem-solving can be stimulated at all, and if so, whether it will lead to a dynamic process of review and creative change, is far from clear-cut. The search for the appropriate mix is an ongoing one. But the fact that there are no ready answers is not a reason to reject this approach. Instead, experimentalism applies to the process of developing the appropriate model itself. In the next section, some of these ideas are tested by considering ways in which compliance mechanisms for positive duties could be developed.

C. Applying the Model: Compliance Mechanisms for Positive Duties

(i) The right to work: the European Employment Strategy and the Open Method of Coordination

The European Union (EU) is an interesting arena within which to test changing paradigms of enforcement, because of the increasing use of 'new methods of governance' instead of formal law in Teubner's sense. Such strategies are part of a general move in EU law and governance 'away from binding rules and towards securing the active co-operation of all those involved in the regulatory chain'.[24] Because they are not based on formal law, new methods of governance are generally not considered to be based on fundamental rights or positive duties. Nevertheless, they resonate with the elements of positive duties discussed in this book so far. In particular, they require positive action to achieve rights-based goals; they go beyond mere policy in their expectations of progressive action rather than discretion; and they emphasize prospective, institutional change, rather than individualized enforcement.

New methods of governance are controversial within the EU because they allow those involved in carrying out EU social programmes a central role in developing and furthering the norms according to which such programmes function. Legal frameworks are correspondingly broad and malleable. Because these methods breach traditional divisions between law-making, implementation, and enforcement, they are viewed by some as a retreat from 'hard law' into pure discretion. For others, however, they are transformative, drawing on the local knowledge, initiative, and creativity of those involved in implementation.[25]

---

[24] N Bernard 'New Governance Approach to Economic, Social and Cultural Rights' in T Hervey and J Kenner (eds) *Economic and Social Rights under the EU Charter of Fundamental Rights* (Hart Oxford 2003) 255.

[25] C Sabel and W Simon 'Epilogue: Accountability without Sovereignty' in G de Burca and J Scott (eds) *New Governance and Constitutionalism in Europe and the US* (Hart Oxford 2006).

Particularly important is their dynamic nature, in that actors are continually involved in reviewing, refining, and developing norms in order better to achieve the prescribed aims. At the same time, the 'softness' of the legal framework means that new methods of governance risk becoming purely political, with no normative dimension. For this reason, it is necessary to pay particular attention to establishing mechanisms of accountability, and appropriate incentives and sanctions to ensure that the norms are in fact carried out. Sabel and Simon argue that such accountability can be achieved by peer review.

Peer review is the answer of new governance to the inadequacies of principal—agent accountability. Peer review imposes on implementing 'agents' the obligation to justify the exercise of discretion they have been granted by framework-making 'principals' in the light of pooled comparable experience. In peer review, the actors at all levels learn from and correct each other.[26]

It is in the light of this assessment that the European Employment Strategy (EES) can be evaluated. The EES is of particular interest, because of its potential use as a mechanism for enforcing the positive duties which arise from the right to work. It was initiated in 1997, in order to implement the newly acquired duty on the EU to 'contribute to a high level of employment by encouraging co-operation between member states'.[27] In particular, the Treaty requires the EU and Member States to cooperate to provide a strategy 'for promoting a skilled, trained and adaptable workforce and labour markets responsive to economic change'.[28] This is an expressly proactive and mainstreaming approach. The Treaty specifies that the 'objective of a high level of employment shall be taken into consideration in the formulation and implementation of Community policies and activities'.[29] More specifically, it requires annual guidelines to be formulated which Member States must take into account in their employment policies.[30]

Particularly innovative, and of most interest for our purposes, is the compliance mechanism known as the Open Method of Coordination (OMC). Instead of a stark dichotomy between untrammelled policy and justiciable rules, the OMC harnesses the active participation of Member States, coordinated by EU institutions. It is based on a creative tension between centrally established guidelines and domestically formulated objectives. Thus, the Commission is charged with establishing Union-wide employment guidelines, drawing on a common analysis of the causes of unemployment and of the type of policies which would 'turn back the tide of unemployment on a lasting basis'.[31] The guidelines set

---

[26] ibid 7.
[27] Treaty of the EU, Article 127.
[28] Article 125.
[29] Article 127.
[30] Article 128.
[31] *Presidency conclusions* Extraordinary European Council meeting on Employment Luxembourg, 20 and 21 November 1997 para 13 <http://ec.europa.eu/employment_social/elm/summit/en/backgr/home.htm>.

targets which can be regularly monitored under a common procedure for assessing results. Member States adapt the targets into national objectives which can be transposed into national regulatory mechanisms to form the basis of annual National Employment Action Plans. Crucial to this process is the recognition that the differing situations of Members States will result in differing solutions and emphases, with Member States deciding for themselves the deadlines for achieving the desired result in the light of available administrative and financial results. The central role played by Member States in norm-making and compliance makes it more likely that norms will be appropriate and bring with them a sense of ownership and commitment. At the same time, the involvement of EU institutions means that the guidelines are more than flexible regulatory tools. There is also a stress on participation below government level in Member States—the strategy calls for the central involvement of social partners in drawing up national plans.

Annual reports are submitted to the Commission which, having examined the report, makes recommendations to the Member State involved. The result is that employment creation is not left to the discretionary policy-making process of Member States, but combines active participation of Member States with the normative pull of the EU. Nor is the normative dimension purely vertical. Particularly important is the dynamic of horizontal peer review, with national plans being the subject of deliberation between Member States, the idea being to foster learning in order to advance the best practice solution. The process culminates in the Joint Employment Report, which sums up present achievements and sets priorities for the following year.

The EES carries many of the hallmarks of the mechanisms described above to achieve compliance with positive human rights duties. It moves beyond the traditional conception of rights as individual claims, based on proof of fault against a named perpetrator. Instead of an individualizable 'right to work' which is enforceable in court, it places a positive duty on the State both to diagnose the causes of unemployment and to remedy them. This means that, rather than responding retrospectively to individual claims of breach, it is proactive and collective, aiming to achieve institutional change. Responsibility for change does not rest in an alleged perpetrator, but with those most able to act. Nor is it an immediate, determinate duty, but must be realized progressively. Equally importantly, the EES is premised on participation of stakeholders through the policy chain.[32] Rather than fixed norms requiring compliance, norms are seen as best established through the participation of multiple stakeholders, with peer review functioning as a crucial means of accountability. This closely corresponds to the model of accountability through peer review described by Sabel and Simon.

In practice, the OMC falls short of these ideals in several respects. The 2003 Taskforce report on the EES concluded that implementation of the strategy

---

[32] Bernard (n 24 above) 263–267.

remained a major political challenge.[33] This is true on both sides of the regulatory dialectic. Three major issues are highlighted. The first is peer review itself. The Taskforce takes the view that the existing peer review, while a valuable tool, has not been sufficiently effective in generating a mutual exchange of good practice and debate. More needs to be done to reinforce an environment in which governments see themselves as learning organizations open to good ideas from others. The second concerns the extent and nature of participation. National Action Plans, argues the Taskforce, need to have political legitimacy through involving national parliaments, and consulting both social partners and civil society. 'To succeed, it is essential that governments build up reform partnerships, by mobilising the support and participation of the various stakeholders, and securing public conviction in the need for reforms.'[34] Even this does not go far enough towards requiring participation to be genuinely deliberative rather than simply consultative or premised on interest bargaining. Although paying lip service to the notion of partnership, the Taskforce still talks in terms of government mobilizing support, persuading stakeholders and educating the public, rather than genuinely working towards a synthesis of ideas.

The third major problem concerns the difficulty of ensuring that employment creation is seen as a mandatory duty rather than a discretionary policy. The Taskforce points to the fact that reforms have been too slow and patchy in many Member States, and recommends that the EU play a stronger monitoring role. This requires the use of the EU budget as a lever to promote investment in research and human capital, to support cooperation and to follow up on Member States' proposed reforms.

This raises the question of whether the EES is simply a regulatory tool, or whether it has harnessed reflexive self-government and deliberative democracy in a way which can enforce positive human rights duties. It could be argued that 'experimentalism' is inimical to human rights, because it inevitably exposes the fundamental right itself to reinvention, and therefore erosion. This can be seen by considering job security. According to the EU Commission: 'Security in today's labour markets is not a matter of preserving a job for life. In a more dynamic perspective, security is about building and preserving people's ability to remain and progress in the labour market.'[35] This means that job security does not preserve a particular job, but facilitates transitions between jobs, adapting social protection systems to support labour market mobility and easing transitions between different statuses such as work, training, career breaks, or self-employment.[36] Employment rights are no longer attached to the employment relationship, but to the worker. State provision would therefore consist of providing for the portability of benefits across different employments rather

---

[33] European Commission *Jobs, Jobs, Jobs: Creating More Employment in Europe* (2003).
[34] ibid.
[35] European Commission (n 33 above) 29.
[36] ibid 27.

than protecting the worker in a particular job.[37] There are even suggestions that this entails removing termination rights such as notice periods and compensation for dismissal.

Alternatively, it could be argued that this does not undermine the right, but changes the focus from a duty of restraint to a positive duty. Rather than emphasizing a duty of restraint, in the form of protection against dismissal, the right triggers a positive duty on the State to facilitate employment. This in itself is transformative, particularly in its expectation of the State as provider of resources. Improving the quality of work is expressed as a requirement on the State to invest in education and training in order to develop human capital. This entails giving everyone access to secondary education, and to lifetime learning.[38] This is particularly true for the maintenance of security in a flexible labour market, which requires investment in continuing training, for low-skilled and older workers.[39] The State has a duty to facilitate the integration of migrants and ethnic minorities through participation in education and training, and addressing the specific needs of immigrant women.[40] Its duty to integrate women into the workforce requires an increase in the availability, affordability, and quality of childcare and eldercare.[41] Finally, making work pay requires, where necessary, the supplementation of low wages with in-work benefits as an incentive for workers to accept low-paid jobs while maintaining wages at a level reflecting productivity.[42]

There remain several challenges. The first is how to resolve conflicts between duties of restraint, such as the right not to be unfairly dismissed, with duties to provide. Dismissal rights themselves are far from a panacea, in that they rarely give the worker the opportunity to remain in the job itself, but instead at best give lump sum monetary compensation. The positive duty has the potential to constitute a genuine improvement. However, there is no reason why the positive duty should be seen as a substitute for the duty of restraint. Unfair dismissal rights should remain part and parcel of the right to work. Secondly, it is necessary to take care that the duty on the State is not transmuted into a duty on the worker. As Ball has argued, the correlative of shifting from traditional employment rights to the State's duty to provide is that a corresponding burden is placed on the individual worker.[43] If job security no longer lies in the right to remain within a job, but in the ability to update skills, to be geographically mobile, and to respond flexibly to new developments, then much of the responsibility lies on the worker herself, to invest in her own human capital, and to accept and respond to the

---

[37] A Supiot *Beyond Employment* (OUP Oxford 2001).
[38] *Draft Joint Employment Report 2003/2004* (2004) 17, 30.
[39] ibid 26.
[40] *Draft Joint Employment Report* (n 38 above) 36.
[41] ibid 18, 35.
[42] *Draft Joint Employment Report* (n 38 above) 38.
[43] S Ball 'The European Employment Strategy: the Will but not the Way?' [2001] 30 Industrial Law Journal 353.

pressures of change. It is also by no means guaranteed that the labour market will continually demand more and different skills, so that retraining may not guarantee employment.

A third challenge lies in the provision of resources. Paradoxically, EU-imposed budgetary constraints could impede the provision of sufficient resources. The Taskforce report confronts this possibility squarely, suggesting that Member States facing budgetary conflicts should divert sufficient resources. 'If the need to find adequate resources in order to implement reforms gives rise to budgetary problems, redirection of spending and greater efficiency in the use of public funds should be guiding principles.'[44] However, this is by no means reliable.

Possibly the most important challenge is to ensure that the strategy is genuinely participative. Participation in decision-making both at EU and national level has been disappointing.[45] One of the reasons for the limited role of the social partners has been their difficulty in agreeing among themselves. Deliberative democracy also assumes a high level of commitment within civil society to participate in the process: yet it seems that such commitment has generally been lacking. In addition, national NGOs express concern that consultation does not necessarily mean participation in decision-making. This concern is reinforced by the evaluation carried out by the European Anti-Poverty Network, which highlights the lack of real influence of social NGOs in shaping the National Action Plans within the social inclusion strategy.[46] This casts some doubt on the real potential for deliberative democracy within the OMC. As Borras and Greve conclude: 'Rather than constituting a democratic watershed in EU politics, the OMC runs the risk of ending up in a sort of "democratic legitimacy limbo", at the crossroads between the insufficient accomplishment of the deliberative and participatory democratic ideals, the virtual nonexistence of democratic representation channels (by the European/ national parliament(s)), and the absence of output legitimacy owing to its indistinguishable results.'[47]

The overall evaluation of the EES and the OMC is therefore complex. On the one hand, it represents an exciting new set of parameters by which to improve the position of workers. It places clear responsibilities on the State as provider, and provides participative and proactive forms of norm-setting and norm enforcement. On the other hand, it carries clear dangers. Basic entitlements could be undermined without proper substitutes. Participation without proper rights

---

[44] European Commission (n 33 above) 57.

[45] CDL Porte and P Nanz 'The OMC—a Deliberative-democratic Mode of Governance? The Cases of Employment and Pensions' (2004) 11 Journal of European Public Policy 267–288 at 281.

[46] KA Armstrong 'Tackling Social Exclusion Through OMC: Reshaping the Boundaries of EU Governance' in T Börzel and R Cichowski (eds) *State of the Union: Law, Politics and Society* (Vol. 6) (OUP Oxford 2003) 27.

[47] S Borras and B Greve 'Concluding Remarks: New Method or Just Cheap Talk?' (2004) 11 Journal of European Public Policy 329–336 at 345.

to association and without checks on representativity could mean capture by powerful interests.[48]

(ii) Reporting mechanisms and socio-economic rights

In the international system, non-judicial compliance mechanisms have always been regarded as the appropriate method for enforcing socio-economic rights, but these have taken the limited form of a requirement to report periodically to the appropriate committee. The insights of systems analysis suggest that it is not surprising that duties to report tend to have little effect in securing actual compliance. The duty, where it is not wholly ignored, is translated into a duty to describe existing policies rather than to frame policies to comply with positive duties. This can be seen by examining the dissonance between the aims of the reporting procedure and its practical realities. The ICESC identifies three aims to the reporting procedure: to facilitate the ongoing monitoring by a State of its rules, procedure, and practice in implementing the Covenant; to facilitate public scrutiny of relevant government policies; and to provide a basis on which the State, together with the Committee, can evaluate progress towards realization of the obligations in the Covenant. However, reporting is generally regarded as a mere descriptive exercise by State parties, who do not see themselves as obligated to design policies to forward their obligations. There is little public awareness of the Covenant, and often little awareness even among government actors and agents of their duties. Alston describes a similar pattern for the European Social charter (ESC). Not only does it take up to a decade to complete a single reporting round, by which time 'the likelihood of attracting any significant public attention has long since passed'. In addition, the governmental report is likely to be a dense and technical account of government activities, rather than a roadmap towards achieving social goals.[49]

For many, the answer to this weakness in enforcement of socio-economic rights lies in creating individual justiciable rights. At international level, much energy has been expended in an effort to agree an optional protocol to the ICESCR allowing individual and collective communications.[50] This would allow the Committee to receive communications from individuals alleging violation of a Convention right, and to reach a decision on the merits. Certainly, the right of individual and collective communications under the ESC has breathed new life into this often forgotten sister of the European Convention of Human Rights. In

[48] See further S Fredman 'Transformation or Dilution: Fundamental Rights in the EU Social Space' [2006] 12 European Law Journal 41–60

[49] P Alston 'Strengths and Weaknesses of the ESC's Supervisory System' in G De Burca and B de Witte (eds) *Social Rights in Europe* (OUP Oxford 2005) 51.

[50] Draft Optional Protocol to the International Covenant on Economic, Social and Cultural Rights Prepared by the Chairperson-Rapporteur, Catarina De Albuquerque A/HRC/6/WG.4/2 23 April 2007.

particular, the relevant ESC committee has been able to sharpen the meaning of the relevant rights through adjudicating particular complaints.

However, this does not obviate the need for mechanisms which trigger pro-active fulfilment of positive human rights duties even if there has been no individual complaint. In the last decade, the ICESCR Committee has been refining its approach to compliance apart from individual remedies. On the surface, the process has many of the hallmarks of the reflexive, deliberative systems described above, with an emphasis on accountability, participation, and ongoing problem-solving through peer review and central coordination. The resulting process in fact looks remarkably similar to that of the OMC. The Committee has responsibility for setting framework goals, while State parties are required to identify policy measures derived from such goals, and specify available resources and ways of achieving the specified measures. National plans should be drawn up identifying targets or benchmarks and appropriate indicators to measure progress both nationally and comparatively. The dialectical relationship between the Committee and the State party takes the form of 'scoping' or joint consideration of progress, and the reasons for any difficulties that may have been encountered.[51] In the following five years, the State party should use this experience to continually review and upwardly revise its implementation policies. Also similar to the OMC are the requirements of accountability and participation, which are both stressed in the General Comments. However, like the OMC, the new model does not give enough emphasis to deliberation. Although State parties are urged to stimulate participation of the people, it is not clear whether participation is to be informative, consultative, or genuinely deliberative.

The slow-moving pace of the ICESCR reporting process makes it difficult to say whether any change has been produced. Certainly, the ICESCR lacks the power of the European Commission to create external sanctions or incentives for change. Thus, the creative tension between external and internal stimuli is missing. Instead, its coordinating powers, and particularly its scoping role, depend very much on the energy and inventiveness of the Committee's members and officials in engaging responses from State parties. In addition, much depends on the ability of local activists, communities, and NGOs to make political use of the reporting procedure. Overall, the ability of the ICESCR to achieve change in this direction is inevitably limited.

(iii) Domestic compliance mechanisms: human rights commissions and triggers for change

To what extent does the deliberative model set out in this chapter have the potential for strengthening domestic non-judicial compliance methods and what are

---

[51] CESCR General Comment 14, The right to the highest attainable standard of health (Twenty-second session 2000), E/C.12/2000/4.

the challenges that such a model brings? At domestic level, non-judicial compliance mechanisms are frequently the responsibility of human rights commissions. This section examines this question by briefly considering the role of the South African Human Rights Commission and some US alternatives.

The South African Human Rights Commission is specifically charged with monitoring human rights, including the positive duties to which it gives rise.[52] It has express powers to investigate and report on the observance of human rights and to take steps to secure appropriate redress where human rights have been violated. This includes wide powers to require information from relevant organs of the State on the measures they have undertaken to fulfil their duties. In principle, this gives the Commission the potential to initiate a dynamic and deliberative approach. However, its original approach was simply to require organs of State to report on their progress, rather than to engage in an interactive manner. This ran into the problems which systems theory would expect when a regulatory approach attempts to superimpose goals and methods which appear alien to the body subject to the regulation. Reporting has typically been haphazard and inconsistent. Information is of poor quality and often unknown reliability. Clearly, the duty to report is viewed as a bureaucratic exercise on the periphery of the body's primary functions.

More recently, protocols have been developed which aim to achieve consistency in the quality and type of information gleaned. However, these appear to have increased the bureaucratic load without necessarily improving real responsiveness. In the reporting period 2003–04, protocols sent to national organs of State were not returned by key departments, including housing, health, and correctional services. At provincial and municipal level, only a minority of authorities responded. In some cases, responsible officials were issued with subpoenas to appear before the Commission if a report was not forthcoming. The Commission noted that this tended to produce a quicker response and a greater sense of personal accountability. But this has not created any ongoing momentum. Little assistance has been forthcoming from the legislature, which could in principle put pressure on departments to comply. However, although Parliament has received six reports over the past ten years from the Commission, there has been no debate on the Commission's reports, and the annual parliamentary committee session devoted to the reports has been brief and unsatisfactory. Even if a debate were to be held to raise awareness, it is not clear that it would have any ongoing effect.[53]

The Commission has made some constructive changes to improve on this record. First, it suggests that part of the problem is lack of capacity in public bodies to gather, store, and analyse information and therefore proposes to give

[52] South African Constitution, s 184.

[53] CF T Thipanyane 'The Monitoring of Socio-economic Rights by the South African Commission in the Second Decade of the Bill of Rights' (2007) 8 Economic and Social Rights Review 11.

more assistance in this respect. It also recognizes that, rather than viewing reporting as a one-way and one-off exercise, bodies should be required to respond to its
recommendations, and reflect such responses in their annual reports. It has also
decided to shift its focus from protocol-based desktop monitoring to a combination of desktop monitoring and fieldwork verification.[54]

Nevertheless, so long as the reporting duty is seen as peripheral to the primary
duties and functions of the body, little progress will be made. The key challenge
therefore is to enlist cooperation and ongoing interaction with relevant organs of
State and with stakeholders. The above analysis has suggested that a fruitful way
forward would be to institute a process, similar to the OMC, whereby participants at all levels of governance are encouraged to enter into discussion with the
Commission and each other in order to appraise their own functioning, discover
alternative possibilities, and, most important, air common problems of coordination in order to search for an ever improving set of solutions. One possible mechanism to do so is the public hearing. The aim of the public hearing is expressly
not to duplicate a court of law, but instead to constitute a platform for dialogue.
Although the Commission has powers to subpoena persons or institutions to
participate, it has generally chosen not to do so. Instead, it aims to create an environment for an open, frank discussion in the spirit that all interested parties are
commonly and genuinely committed to finding ways of fulfilling the positive
duty in question.[55] Unfortunately, however, while public hearings have facilitated the active participation of groupings within civil society, senior and responsible officials in relevant organs of State have not regarded them as a forum within
which deliberative decision-making and problem-solving should take place in an
interactive way. Nor has the Commission been able to enlist the cooperation of
such officials in acting on the recommendations which emerge.

Susan Sturm's description of equal opportunities programmes for women in US
universities shows how some of these obstacles can be overcome by a combination
of internal and external drivers for change.[56] In this scheme, an external funding body made the availability of research money conditional on the institution
of procedures for change aimed at specified goals. These external triggers were
matched by an internal driver in the form of a very senior member of the faculty
who had both the authority and the internal motivation to achieve change. The
process was deliberative and participative, but targets set in the deliberative process were also subject to external review.

While there are undoubtedly problematic issues in the implementation and
design of such schemes, the underlying principle remains the most attractive way of creating a compliance system which directly addresses the resistance highlighted by systems theory and demonstrated in practice in the South

[54] South African Human Rights Commission 'Sixth Economic and Social Rights Report'
August 2006, xiv.
[55] ibid 6.
[56] Sturm (n 13 above).

African context. These principles include the ability to enlist the cooperation of the regulated body through a combination of external incentives and deterrents, and internal responsibility through a named and responsible senior official. Regulation should be through the identification of broad goals deduced from the right in question and fleshed out by deliberative problem-solving and peer review at local level. Accountability and progressive realization are provided through a dynamic interchange with a commission or political body, and through peer review.

D. A Synergistic Approach

Chapters 4, 5, and 6 have considered judicial and non-judicial approaches to achieving fulfilment of positive human rights duties. This section draws together the strands to argue for a synergistic approach, in which the separate components potentially work together to produce a whole that is greater than the sum of the parts. The major components of a synergistic approach are the State, the courts, a commission or similar body, civil society, and the stakeholders or rights-bearers. Considering each of the drivers separately gives a disappointing result. However, when all the processes are brought together, the result is a closer approximate of the model set out above. The result is not necessarily apparent to all the actors involved. This makes it difficult to achieve a synergistic approach unless one or more of the actors are able to take a holistic and strategic view.

There are several intertwined aspects of this approach. One is the proactive role of a human rights commission or similar body, responsible for finding a means of building positive duties into the mainstream activities of the public body. We have seen that reporting is not sufficient; instead there needs to be a dynamic process of engagement through a mechanism which involves a combination of peer review, and participation by stakeholders, with incentives and ultimately deterrents. A second is the use of litigation or the threat of litigation to set in motion a process of deliberation and discussion. Such a process is able to go beyond the limits of the ordinary court processes in its ability to provide creative and appropriate solutions. At the same time, the supervisory role of the court ensures that the result is a genuine fulfilment of the duty to fulfil the relevant right.

A particularly good demonstration of a synergistic approach is that of the 'Right to Food' campaign. As we saw in Chapter 5, much of the success of that campaign has been due to the imaginative and energetic approach of an NGO, which has worked hard to combine grass-roots organization, political activism, and strategic litigation to achieve compliance with the duty to fulfil the right to food. A further demonstration of a synergistic approach comes in the arena of HIV/AIDS in South Africa, where a combination of local activism, litigation, and NGO involvement has sustained the process of ongoing deliberation, problem-solving, and implementation. The strategic direction in this area has been set by one major actor, the Treatment Action Campaign (TAC), an NGO which was established in 1998 as a response to the increasing numbers of South Africans who were dying of AIDS because they were not able to afford life-saving medication. With a registered membership in 2005 of well over 10,100 individuals, TAC's primary purpose is to facilitate access to affordable treatment for people living with HIV/AIDS in South Africa. It uses a combination of grass-roots organization, education, political lobbying, and litigation in order to further its aim of achieving compliance, by a highly recalcitrant State, with the positive duties arising under the rights to life, the rights to health, and the right to dignity in the Constitution. This is a particularly good illustration because it comes in the context of the failure of the political process to achieve compliance with the constitutional right of access to health care, driven by what has been called 'AIDS denialism' on the part of a government ideologically opposed to acknowledging the role of HIV in causing AIDS. This section focusses on the ways in which the interaction between litigation and political strategies have been used to further this aim.

As will be recalled from Chapter 4, one of the major victories of TAC has been the *TAC* case, in which the Court ruled that the Constitution required the government to 'devise and implement within its available resources a comprehensive and co-ordinated programme to realise progressively the rights of pregnant women and their newborn children to have access to health services to combat mother-to-child transmission of HIV'. The Court's decision on its own was not, however, enough to ensure implementation. There remained deep resistance among State authorities at both provincial and national level. For this, close monitoring at ground level was required. Unlike the *Grootboom* decision, where neither the Court nor activist groups were able to take on this role, such monitoring has been mobilized and coordinated by TAC and other NGOs. In at least one province, it took a further application to the High Court for a contempt order before the province complied even materially with the order which had been made by the Constitutional Court.[57]

In addition, litigation continued to be used as a means of triggering a process of deliberation. Following the success of the *TAC* case, a decision was made to launch further litigation, with the aim of establishing treatment for all those living with AIDS. The threat of such litigation, together with extensive campaigning, finally led to the adoption of a comprehensive strategy for HIV/AIDS care, management, and treatment in the form of an Operational Plan for the five years beginning in November 2003. According to the AIDS Law Project, which works closely with TAC, the plan demonstrated that the South African government had absorbed the lessons of the litigation, namely that public policy had

---

[57] *Treatment Action Campaign v MEC for Health, Mpumalanga & Minister of Health* Transvaal Provincial Division case no 35272/02 and see G Budlender and K Roach 'Mandatory Relief and Supervisory Jurisdiction: When is it Appropriate, Just and Equitable?' [2005] 122 South African Law Journal 325–351.

to be fashioned in a way that directly takes account of its legal obligations as set out by the Constitutional Court.[58] Even here, however, there was resistance to implementation, requiring further combinations of political campaigning and litigation to get the process started and to ensure that interim medication was obtained.

As with the Court decision, the policy framework also required close monitoring. An important development was the establishment of the Joint Civil Society Monitoring Forum (JCSMF), composed of 11 civil society organizations. This aims to provide an ongoing and accurate assessment of the plan's implementation, acting as an early warning system for problems and helping communicate successes. Equally important has been the realization of the need to mobilize communities themselves to monitor and support the rollout of treatment in local areas. In many respects then, the activist groups have been able to create a model of localized deliberative democracy with the aim of holding the authorities to account, as well as of problem-solving at local level, and sharing best practice solutions through the framework of the monitoring forum. In this respect, TAC views itself as a 'critical vehicle through which the poor and the marginalised access their rights'.[59] What has been conspicuously lacking however is the whole-hearted participation of national and provincial health departments and health care workers. Although the Forum has attempted to engage senior civil servants in this process, both in order to provide information and to respond to discussion, most have failed even to acknowledge these invitations.[60]

When monitoring and consultation yield no results, further litigation has been successfully used both to secure that specific duties were fulfilled and to prompt further and wider consultation. This was the case in respect of prisoners living with HIV/AIDS who were being denied access to anti-retroviral treatment in Westville Correctional Centre in Durban. This was a clear breach of the Constitutional right of detained persons to medical treatment,[61] as well as being contrary to the Operational Plan. The High Court in this case moved quickly and decisively, ordering the State immediately to remove all restrictions on treatment and to file an affidavit within two weeks setting out the steps it intended to take to make such treatment available to all prisoners who needed it. The State predictably took a highly defensive legal stance and used all the opportunities presented by the adversarial procedure to obstruct the claim, despite the very real risk that some of the prisoners might die in the meanwhile. Tragically, one of the applicants did die, having waited 32 months from diagnosis to treatment. Eventually, however, a deliberative process began, given a sense of urgency by the prospect of continued proceedings in the Court. This successfully yielded a plan, not just for the prison in question but for all correctional centres in the country,

---

[58] Aids Law Project Annual Report 2003, 24.
[59] Treatment Action Campaign Annual Report 2006.
[60] ibid 8.
[61] South African Constitution, s 35(2)(e).

and one in which consensus was reached on all major matters. It was here that the fragility of a deliberative process in the face of strong political intransigence was revealed. At the last moment, the State resiled from the agreement, and resort to the Court was again needed.[62]

Ultimately, the combined efforts of litigation, local activism, NGO involvement, and coordinated efforts by civil society achieved what could be called a genuinely deliberative approach. In March 2007, the draft of the new National Strategic Plan for 2007–11 was produced and placed before a consultative meeting of 500 people, where it was interrogated and debated, with proposals for amendments being put forward and incorporated into the final version, which was later approved by the Cabinet. According to the AIDS Law Project, this was a 'genuinely national consultative meeting' and 'a genuine exercise of democracy'.[63]

The importance of a synergistic approach is highlighted by an evaluation of the TAC advocacy strategy in 2005, which concludes that the most successful examples of litigation were those which were part of a robust and well-orchestrated public campaign, which in effect created the demand for the litigation to occur. But equally important was TAC's strategy of creating numerous opportunities for government to avoid litigation by entering into informed, transparent, and participative discussion. The least successful examples of litigation occurred when legal strategies were conducted without a public groundswell of opinion or where there was insufficient familiarity with the facts. At the same time, achieving a court victory was not enough: a well coordinated strategy was necessary to monitor implementation and ensure service delivery.[64]

It will have been noted that one actor is conspicuously missing from the synergy: the Human Rights Commission. In fact, one of the chief sources of disillusionment with the Human Rights Commission has been its failure to intervene in the TAC case, and its ineffectiveness in monitoring. This has meant that it is only because of the vigour of TAC that litigation and non-judicial strategies have been able to be combined to achieve a deliberative outcome. To achieve a full synergy, a far more active role of a human rights commission can be envisaged, in particular one which could aim to draw State officials more wholeheartedly into the process than has been achieved so far.

---

[62] J Berger 'Implementing the Operational Plan in Prisons' AIDS Law Project 18 month Review 2006–7, 21–26.
[63] ALP Annual Report 2006–7, 18.
[64] Treatment Action Campaign Evaluation June 2005, 25.

PART III

SUBSTANTIVE RIGHTS AND POSITIVE DUTIES

7

Equality

Equality is a pivotal concept linking negative and positive human rights duties. It is both an unquestioned member of the category of civil and political rights; and central to the class of socio-economic rights. In its distributive form, it is a vital principle of the Welfare State. However, instead of recognizing this integral connection equality is fragmented into distinct and often rival concepts. The fragmentation is reinforced by the allocation of different types of duties to various understandings of equality. In its most formal civil and political sense, the right to equality is generally associated with duties of restraint, while positive duties are associated with socio-economic equality. Nor are they necessary complementary: duties of restraint have been used to trammel or even defeat positive duties arising from equality.

More recently, however, the artificiality of the distinction between negative and positive duties within the equality guarantee has become increasingly evident. This is in part due to the ineffectiveness of duties of restraint in addressing discrimination and inequality. It has become clear that, without a positive duty to promote equality, patterns of discrimination and social exclusion will remain unchanged.

This chapter argues that real progress can only be made through a unified approach to equality, one which includes both positive and negative duties. This entails particular challenges so far as justiciability is concerned. Consistently with earlier chapters, it is argued here that courts should not shy away from positive duties, but instead use their position to enhance accountability and deliberative democracy. However, framing an appropriate role for the judiciary does not exhaust the question. Even more important is the development of positive duties outside of the courts. There is a growing momentum in this direction, as the ineffectiveness of court-centred, restraint-based approaches becomes more and more evident. Significant progress has been made in this direction. But there is always a risk that the resulting positive measures become dislocated from their human rights source and are formulated in terms of pure policy. Section A considers the interaction between positive and negative duties within developing concepts of equality. Section B examines the role of the judges. Section C examines proactive measures outside of the courts, using the framework developed in Chapter 6.

It should be noted at this point that positive duties to promote equality do not necessarily entail reverse discrimination. While reverse discrimination is not precluded, there is a range of techniques to promote equality which do not require such a strategy. These include providing welfare, training, flexible working, or childcare; or altering institutional structures which disadvantage some groups. The debate about the legitimacy of reverse discrimination has been fully aired in other contexts[1] and is not dealt with here. The focus in this chapter is on wider questions of whether the right to equality gives rise to a positive duty in the first place, and if it does, how that duty should be constructed and enforced.

A. Recognition and Redistribution: Negative and Positive Dimensions

Equality as a civil and political right has been primarily concerned with duties of restraint. This manifests as an injunction that the State be restrained from treating similarly situated individuals differently. A paradigm example is the equality guarantee in the Fourteenth Amendment of the US Constitution, which provides: 'No state shall...deny to any person within its jurisdiction the equal protection of the laws.' The stress on duties of restraint arises from the assumption that agents are only responsible for inequalities which they have deliberately caused through their own prejudiced behaviour. This means that the right to equality restrains prejudiced action, rather than requiring positive steps to be taken to prevent inequalities from arising or to address inequalities not due to the perpetrator's own actions. Yet it is now well established that inequality and discrimination are not necessarily caused by any one individual. This assumption also confines remedial action to a complaints-based model of enforcement through litigation. Because the duty is no more than one of restraining deliberate action, an individual rights-holder must find a perpetrator and prove breach before her inequality can be addressed. Not only does this fault-based orientation impose a heavy burden on the individual rights-holder. In addition, the many forms of structural discrimination which cannot be traced to individual action go unremedied. Finally, the focus is on groups defined by race, gender, or other status rather than their poverty or socio-economic position. Prohibiting differentiation according to socio-economic status would inevitably lead to a concept of equality with distributive connotations, bringing a positive duty in its wake. In order to avoid this result, the focus has been on characteristics which an individual cannot change and are unrelated to her own merit or desert. Race, gender, and more recently, disability, sexual orientation, and age fall into this category.

---

[1] S Fredman *Women and the Law* (Oxford Monographs in Labour Law OUP Oxford 1997) 385–403; S Fredman *Discrimination Law* (Clarendon Law Series OUP Oxford 2002) ch 5; S Fredman 'Reversing Discrimination' [1997] 113 Law Quarterly Review 575–600.

This emphasis on duties of restraint within the human rights field sharply contrasts with the approach to distributive inequalities. Positive measures are clearly central to any policy dealing with socio-economic inequality. However, unlike equality in the civil and political rights field, such positive measures are not considered to be human rights duties. Instead, socio-economic inequality has generally been regarded as a matter of social policy, to be dealt with through the political system on the basis of majoritarian politics. Thus, equality has developed along two quite separate trajectories: one in the form of human rights giving rise to negative duties based on status wrongs, and the other in the form of redistributive social policy, giving rise to positive measures without the backing of human rights.

These two separate approaches are helpfully illuminated by the conceptual apparatus of recognition and redistribution developed by Fraser, Honneth, and others.[2] 'Recognition' is based on Hegel's understanding of individual identity, according to which an individual only becomes an individual by virtue of recognizing others and being recognized by them.[3] Individual identity derives from social relations, including the social hierarchies which arise from cultural value patterns.[4] It is here that invidious inequalities arise. As Fraser shows, status hierarchies are defined not by relations of production, but of esteem, respect, and prestige enjoyed relative to other groups in society.[5] Subordination or misrecognition occurs when cultural value patterns constitute some as inferior, excluded, or invisible;[6] whereas equality consists of the equal ability to participate in social life.[7] Distribution, by contrast, is concerned with power differentials corresponding to the distribution of wealth in society, and the consequent relationships of power and subordination attached to economic hierarchies.

The attempt to avoid positive duties in respect of the right to equality is increasingly difficult to sustain as the interaction between recognition and redistribution becomes ever more evident. It is by now more than familiar to acknowledge that economic disadvantage is disproportionately concentrated among groups experiencing status-based discrimination. Women, ethnic groups, the disabled, the young, and the old, are unduly represented amongst the poorest in society. These structures of inequality are left intact by understandings of equality which assume that responsibility for change rests only with those who have committed acts of deliberate or manifest prejudice. This demonstrates clearly that equality requires more than restraint. In addition, it calls for a duty on the State to take positive measures to promote equality, including, where appropriate, allocation of resources.

[2] N Fraser and A Honneth *Redistribution or Recognition* (Verso London, New York 2003) 13.
[3] GWF Hegel *Phenomenology of Spirit* (OUP Oxford 1977) 104–109. See Chapter 1 above.
[4] Fraser and Honneth (n 2 above) 13.
[5] N Fraser 'Redistribution or Recognition' in Fraser and Honneth (n 2 above) 14.
[6] ibid 29.
[7] Fraser in Fraser and Honneth (n 5 above) 29.

The development from formal to substantive equality goes a long way towards recognizing the centrality of positive duties. Substantive equality transcends equal treatment, recognizing that treating people alike despite pre-existing disadvantage or discrimination can simply perpetuate inequality. Instead, as Sen argues: 'Equal consideration for all may demand very unequal treatment in favour of the disadvantaged. The demands of substantive equality can be particularly exacting and complex when there is a good deal of antecedent inequality to counter.'[8] Substantive equality expressly addresses the interaction between recognition and redistribution, focussing not on status per se, but on those groups for whom status differentiation is correlated with disadvantage. This is combined with the key insight that societal discrimination extends well beyond individual acts of prejudice. This makes it clear that substantive equality must include some positive duties.

Logically too, it is difficult to confine the right to equality to a duty of restraint. Even in its most formal sense, it requires the State to act in a particular way, namely, to treat similarly situated individuals equally. This might be a preventative duty, where the State actively oppresses a particular group. However, where the less favourable treatment arises because the State has provided a benefit to one group and not another, the right to equality would translate into a positive duty to extend the benefit to the excluded group. It is for this reason, as will be seen below, that the non-discrimination clause in the ECHR has been able to transform negative duties associated with civil and political rights into positive duties to make provision.

The acknowledgement of positive duties is the first step in the analysis. The next step requires a closer examination of the nature of positive duties and what they entail. As was shown in previous chapters, positive duties are more challenging than duties of restraint. Whereas the latter simply prohibit specified action, the former require complex decisions as to the objects to be achieved and the means to do so. In the case of substantive equality, neither the aims nor the means have been conclusively articulated. It is usual to frame the objectives in terms of equality of opportunity or equality of results. Both, however, are too vague to provide a secure enough guide. Providing equal opportunities aims to equalize the starting point, so that all participants can compete on the same terms. However, what this means in terms of positive measures is open to a variety of interpretations. Provision of equal opportunities could consist of simply changing procedures, such as removing exclusionary criteria from job specifications. At the other end of the spectrum, it could entail a radically substantive approach, requiring structural change and socio-economic equality.

Equality of results is, in turn, a far from straightforward concept. It is most easily understood in the context of the workforce, where equal pay or equal

---

[8] A Sen *Inequality Re-examined* (OUP Oxford 1992).

representation of men and women can be specified and quantified. It is more difficult for services, reflected in measurements of vague notions such as customer satisfaction or confidence levels. Even where results are easily specified, however, they need to be kept in context and analysed with a sensitivity to qualitative as well as quantitative factors. A narrowing of the pay gap might mean that pay in a particular sector has diminished as a whole, perhaps because economic circumstances have forced down male wages or because men have been leaving the occupation, with a consequent decline in status through a negative process of feminization. Alternatively, a rise in the proportion of women in a grade might reflect greater conformism of women to male norms, for example, by leaving childcare to other, usually very low-paid, women. Similarly, fair participation focusses on those within the workforce; leaving out of account those who cannot access the labour market in the first place.

A more nuanced approach to the aims of proactive models goes beyond the opportunity-results conceptual framework. Instead, I have argued for four potential aims of equality.[9] First, it should promote respect for the equal dignity and worth of all, thereby redressing stigma, stereotyping, humiliation, and violence because of membership of an out-group. Sexual harassment, racist abuse, humiliation of old people, and homophobic bullying at schools are all examples of situations in which the primary claim is based on dignity. Secondly, it should entail an accommodation and positive affirmation and celebration of identity within community. Thirdly, it should break the cycle of disadvantage associated with out-groups. Finally, it should facilitate full participation in society. The content of positive duties can more easily be specified in relation to these four aims or dimensions. So far as respect for dignity and worth of the individual, it is not sufficient that the State be restrained from perpetrating stigma, violence, or stereotyping. This would not reach the many situations when breach is by a private individual. Instead, the State has a positive duty to protect individuals against others. The accommodation dimension similarly necessitates positive duties. To demand that an individual conform to the dominant norm as a price for inclusion would undermine the principle of recognition. Thus, equality in the recognition arena gives rise to a positive duty to accommodate different identities. Even clearer is the need for positive duties where there is a redistributive dimension. Recognizing the correlation between status and disadvantage, substantive equality should aim to break the cycle of disadvantage associated with membership of status-groups. At the same time, the nature of the redistributive intervention is crucial. The central aim is to empower and facilitate genuine choice. This means more than providing benefits to passive and subordinated beneficiaries, but instead requires

---

[9] S Fredman *The Future of Equality in Great Britain* (Working Paper No 5 Equal Opportunities Commission Manchester 2002); S Fredman 'Recognition and Redistribution' [2007] South African Journal of Human Rights (forthcoming).

the use of resources to create a sense of universal citizenship and solidarity. The positive duty therefore needs to integrate the recognition and redistribution aims; ensuring that redistributive measures do not reinforce status hierarchies. An example would be the assumption that women are dependants or that households are a single unit.[10]

The final aim of substantive equality is to facilitate full participation in society. Participation is fundamental to deliberative democracy. The positive duty to promote participation therefore goes to the heart of positive human rights duties as a whole. Participation is a multi-layered concept. At its most basic, it entails political participation.[11] As has been recognized in several jurisdictions, equality law should specifically compensate for the absence of political power of minority groups;[12] groups 'to whose needs and wishes elected officials have no apparent interest in attending'.[13] However, participation goes beyond the political arena. It also entails taking part in decisions in a wide range of situations affecting individuals or groups, including at the workplace, in education, in health care, and in community organization. As Sen has argued: 'Political rights, including freedom of expression and discussion, are not only pivotal in inducing political responses to economic needs, they are also central to the conceptualisation of economic needs themselves.'[14] This is particularly true in the area of status equality, where decisions made on behalf of groups excluded by gender, race, minority status, disability, or sexual orientation may well be patronizing and misguided unless those affected are actively drawn into the process.

Many critics of republicanism and deliberative democracy point to the unrealistic expectation that ordinary people have the time or desire to participate on such a wide scale. This has in fact manifested in the form of 'consultation fatigue', whereby a few over-extended organizations find themselves playing the role of participant in too many contexts. In addition, deliberative democracy may well favour the well organized and the more articulate. There is therefore a role for a positive duty to facilitate participation, through building capacity or other means. In addition, there is clearly a positive duty to provide the basic subsistence and education without which individuals cannot be full participants. Participation also entails redressing under-representation of status groups in the workforce and overcoming social marginalization and exclusion.

---

[10] See further Chapter 8.

[11] J Habermas *Between Facts and Norms* (Polity Press 1997) para 1.3.1.

[12] *United States v Carolene Products Co* 304 US 144, 152 n4 (US Supreme Court); *Andrews v Law Society of British Columbia* [1989] 1 SCR 143 (Supreme Court of Canada).

[13] JH Ely *Democracy and Distrust: A Theory of Judicial Review* (Harvard University Press 1980) 151.

[14] A Sen 'Freedoms and Needs' *The New Republic* (10 and 17 January 1994, 31, 32) cited in HJ Steiner and P Alston *International Human Rights in Context* (2nd edn OUP Oxford 2000) 269.

B. Equality and the Courts

(i) Principles of justiciability

The above discussion has demonstrated that the right to equality gives rise to a range of positive duties, many of which require complex policy decisions with clear distributive consequences. This gives rise to the familiar objections to justiciable positive duties. However, the equality context makes this question particularly challenging against the background of the modern Welfare State. This is because the principles behind the Welfare State are broadly in line with those behind the positive duty to advance substantive equality: both aim to redress disadvantage. Thus, positive measures within the Welfare State could be said to advance substantive equality without any further intervention by the courts. Indeed, intervention by courts has historically been associated with imposing a duty of restraint which interferes with substantive measures of this sort, explaining some of the hostility to judicial intrusion.

Does recognition of positive equality duties therefore suggest judicial deference? This context is particularly sensitive in that welfare by its nature requires differential treatment, targeting benefits at particular categories of individuals defined according to capacity or need. To what extent should such categories be subject to challenge in court on the ground that they breach the duty to fulfil equality? A successful challenge by an excluded person or group would inevitably have the effect of requiring that the benefits be extended to that group. Thus, even if there were no right to the benefit in the first place, the court's decision would impose a duty on the State to provide the benefit more widely, with a corresponding right in members of the excluded class. On the other hand, the State's policy decisions in the distributive regime do not necessarily fulfil the positive duties arising from the right to equality. In particular, distributive decisions might cause or entrench inequalities in the recognition sphere. The Welfare State has advanced gender equality in many important respects; but it has also reinforced gender inequalities, particularly by assuming that women are dependent on men.

This suggests that there is an important role for courts within the democratic parameters argued for in Chapter 4. As Sunstein puts it, 'judges have limited wisdom and limited tools. Their role is therefore catalytic rather than preclusive.'[15] Courts' role therefore is to advance accountability, deliberative democracy, and participative equality. By requiring decision-makers to justify their decisions, courts enhance the democratic process by exposing such explanations to public scrutiny and debate. Courts are also in a position to improve the deliberative dimension of decision-making, preventing like-minded people from pushing

---

[15] CR Sunstein *Designing Democracy What Constitutions Do* (OUP 2001) 11.

each other towards extreme and polarized decision-making by increasing the range of opinions that are aired in the process. This is particularly so when those affected have little or no real prospect of participating equally in the political process.

What then can courts legitimately add to the political definition of equality within the socio-economic sphere? It is here that the multi-dimensional understanding of equality set out above comes into play. Decision-makers must show that their choice of eligibility criteria not only redresses disadvantage, but also promotes respect and dignity, accommodates diverse identities, and facilitates participation or counters social exclusion. Redistributive decisions should not be made on the basis of criteria which undermine status equality, such as stereotypical assumptions and unwarranted generalizations. Indeed, it is exactly in this area of interaction that intervention might be most needed. For example, assumptions about women's dependency on male breadwinners have permeated the structure of benefits; and similar assumptions in respect of homosexuality or disability have led to distortions in the delineation of eligibility criteria. These are precisely the type of situation in which courts should be able to intervene.

(ii) Justiciability in practice

This section considers the extent to which the above principles been realized in courts in various jurisdictions. It will be seen that while there remains considerable reluctance on the part of courts to acknowledge the positive duties to which the right to equality gives rise, some important strides have been made.

The most traditional approach can be seen in the US Supreme Court, which has relied on two familiar arguments to resist claims that the right to equality gives rise to positive duties. The first is that the State is responsible only for inequalities it has actually caused; poverty is not seen as the responsibility of the State and therefore the State cannot be under duties to take steps to redress inequalities which arise as a result. The second is to point to the court's limited legitimacy and competence in the distributive arena. Both these arguments were used by the US Supreme Court in *San Antonio v Rodriguez*,[16] where the judges emphatically rejected the argument that unequal treatment of a group because of their poverty constituted a breach of the Fourteenth Amendment. The case challenged the funding system of schools, which was based on local taxes. The claimants argued that this discriminated against those who lived in poor areas. The Court made it clear that there was a bright line between recognition and redistributive claims. As Powell J put it:

The system of alleged discrimination and the class it defines have none of the traditional indicia of suspectness: the class is not saddled with such disabilities, or subjected to such

[16] *San Antonio Independent School District v Rodriguez* 411 US 959, 93 S Ct 1919 (US Supreme Court).

a history of purposeful unequal treatment, or relegated to such a position of political powerlessness as to command extraordinary protection from the majoritarian political process.[17]

The Court also rejected the claim on grounds of judicial legitimacy and competence. Questions of this sort were inappropriate for strict scrutiny since they involved 'the most delicate and difficult questions of local taxation, fiscal planning, educational policy, and federalism, considerations counselling a more restrained form of review.'[18] Both these arguments are problematic. In limiting the State's responsibility to its deliberate action, the court ignores the role of the State in setting up the funding framework which resulted in the inequalities. This shows clearly that it is artificial and illogical to attempt to distinguish between positive and negative duties on the grounds of whether the State's deliberate action has resulted in the inequalities. In addition, as has been argued throughout this book, instead of declining jurisdiction on grounds of limited competence, courts should use their position to require authorities to give a democratically acceptable account of the reasons for lack of action, and ensure that all groups have a proper participatory role in decision-making. Poverty is as much a reason for political marginalization as any other.

At the other end of the spectrum are cases which clearly demonstrate the principles of justiciability set out above. The South African case of *Khosa*[19] concerned the restriction of child benefit and old age pensions to South African citizens, excluding permanent residents, who lived legally in South Africa without having achieved citizenship. Permanent residents claimed this breached both their constitutional right to social security and the equality right to be treated in the same way as citizens. The Court recognized that some classifications are necessary for a State to provide benefits appropriately and efficiently. It therefore saw its role as that of determining the reasonableness of the classification, without substituting its own decision for that of the decision-maker. Its understanding of reasonableness reflects at least three of the dimensions of substantive equality identified above. First, the classification did not meet the distributive criterion of redressing disadvantage: permanent residents were a vulnerable group and would in any event be subject to stringent means testing. Secondly, the exclusion of permanent residents had a strong stigmatizing effect, creating the impression that they were inferior to citizens and less worthy of social assistance. Finally, it breached the participation criterion: permanent residents were in effect 'relegated to the margins of society and deprived of what may be essential to enable them to enjoy other rights vested in them under the Constitution'.[20]

---

[17] ibid 1294.

[18] *San Antonio* (n 16 above) 1302.

[19] *Khosa and Mahlaule v Minister for Social Development* 2004 (6) BCLR 569 (South African Constitutional Court).

[20] ibid para 77.

A second case demonstrating use of the principles of justiciability above is the decision of the Supreme Court in the Canadian case of *Eldridge*.[21] This case similarly concerned a positive duty arising from the equality guarantee, in this case whether there was a duty to provide sign language interpreters for deaf persons when they receive medical services. In upholding the positive duty, notwithstanding its distributive consequences, La Forest J's judgment draws out all four of the dimensions of equality set out above. The equality clause in section 15(1) of the Canadian Charter, he declared, 'expresses a commitment—deeply ingrained in our social, political and legal culture—to the equal worth and human dignity of all persons'.[22] Secondly, it entailed the 'accommodation of differences... [which] is the essence of true equality'.[23] Thirdly, its aim was to rectify and prevent discrimination against particular groups 'suffering social, political and legal disadvantage in our society'; and particularly those who had suffered disadvantage by exclusion from mainstream society. Finally, it endorsed the centrality of participation in society, by recognizing that for deaf people, communication was crucial to prevent marginalization.

The respondents resisted the implication of a positive duty on the ground that the equality guarantee in section 15(1) only applied to deliberate action. It did not oblige governments to implement programmes to alleviate disadvantages that they had not caused. Here the Court clearly distanced itself from the US Court's requirement for deliberate action as a precondition for State responsibility. Such a position, according to La Forest J, 'bespeaks a thin and impoverished vision of s. 15(1)'.[24] Adverse impact could constitute a breach of the equality right even in the absence of deliberate State action. The logical consequence was that in many circumstances, governments would be required to take positive action, for example by extending the scope of a benefit to a previously excluded class of persons.[25]

Particularly important was the Court's insistence that any limits on the State's positive duty should be dealt with at the stage of justification,[26] thereby requiring at least accountability and potentially also furthering deliberative democracy. To pass muster, the objective of the impugned legislation must be pressing and substantial, and the means to attain this end must be reasonable and demonstrably justifiable in a free and democratic society. In addition, the impugned provision must do no more than minimally impair the Charter guarantee; and the attainment of the legislative goal should not be outweighed by the abridgement of the right. Applying these criteria, the Court concluded

[21] *Eldridge v British Columbia* [1997] 3 SCR 624 (Canadian Supreme Court).
[22] ibid para 54.
[23] *Andrews v Law Society of British Columbia* [1989] 1 SCR 143 (Supreme Court of Canada) per McIntyre J at 169.
[24] *Eldridge* (n 21 above) para 73.
[25] ibid.
[26] Canadian Charter, s 1.

that the government had 'manifestly failed to demonstrate that it had a reasonable basis for concluding that a total denial of medical interpretation services
for the deaf constituted a minimum impairment of their rights'. Particularly
striking is the fact that, in applying this standard, the Court scrutinized and
rejected the State's budgetary argument, on the basis that the estimated cost of
providing sign language interpretation for the whole of British Columbia was
only $150,000, or approximately 0.0025% of the provincial health care budget
at the time.

This case contrasts strikingly with the later cases of *Law v Canada*,[27] and
Gosselin, in which the same Court was reluctant to insist that the State be
accountable for a failure to fulfil a positive duty arising from equality. This led
it to deny that there was a positive duty in the first place. Both these cases, as in
Eldridge, involved a claim that the State's exclusion of a group from a specific
benefit amounted to an unlawful breach of the equality principle. In both cases,
the result of a decision in favour of the claimants would have been to require
the State to extend the benefit further, and in both cases, the Court declined
to do so. In the *Law* case, survivors' pensions were only immediately available
to surviving spouses over 45 or with children. The applicant argued that this
discriminated against her on grounds of her age, claiming that she too should
have been entitled to the benefit. The Court did not deny the fact of disadvantage, but rejected the view that the imposition of disadvantage undermined the
claimant's dignity. According to Iaccobuci J, the law was not discriminatory
because it did not 'perpetuate the view that people in this class are less capable or
less worthy of recognition or value as human beings or as members of Canadian
society'. Even more problematic was the decision in *Gosselin*, in which an applicant challenged a scheme according to which full benefit was only available to
welfare recipients over 30. Those under 30 received significantly less unless they
participated in a designated work activity or education programme. In practice,
there was a significant shortfall in places available, and those which were available were relatively short-term. Thus, many young people, including the claimant, experienced real poverty. Nevertheless, the majority of the Court concluded
that 'the provision of different initial amounts of monetary support to each of
the two groups does not indicate that one group's dignity was prized above the
other's.[28] In effect, then, the Court was only prepared to restrain the State from
impinging on individuals' sense of dignity or self-respect, rather than positively
requiring it to distribute benefits.

On closer inspection, it can be seen that in both these cases, the Court's rejection of a breach of substantive equality had the effect of freeing the State from any
obligation to justify its choice of criteria. Instead, the Court went so far as hold
that, when legislation had an egalitarian purpose, there was no need for the State

---

[27] *Law v Canada* [1999] 1 SCR 497 (Canadian Supreme Court).
[28] *Gosselin v Quebec* 2002 SCC 84 (Canadian Supreme Court) para 61 (McLachlin J).

to do any more than act on the basis of an informed generalization.[29] In both the *Law* and *Gosselin* case, the categorization was based on the assumption that younger people have better labour force prospects than older people. Although in both cases this correlation was disputed, the Court was prepared to take judicial notice of the broad generalizations offered by the State. Thus, stated Iaccobuci J, '[i]t seems to me that the increasing difficulty with which one can find and maintain employment as one grows older is a matter of which a court may appropriately take judicial notice'.[30] Similarly, McLachlan J in *Gosselin* held that this was not a stereotype but an informed generalization which a government was entitled to make. Nor did it matter that this might not be true of the whole group, so that some were unfairly excluded from the benefit. According to McLachlan J: 'Perfect correspondence between a benefit program and the actual needs and circumstances of the claimant group is not required.'[31] Indeed, she insisted, 'we cannot infer disparity between the purpose and effect of the scheme and the situation of those affected, from the mere failure of the government to prove that the assumptions upon which it proceeded were correct'.[32]

Yet it is precisely in this kind of situation that democracy requires more, rather than less, attention to the State's duty to be accountable. This is true whether or not the State's reasons are ultimately acceptable. In *Law*, it may well have been the case that the State's justification fulfilled the principles in the multi-dimensional understanding of equality set out above. However, in *Gosselin*, there was plenty of evidence that the exclusion perpetuated disadvantage in a highly marginalized group of young benefit claimants; and it is not as easy to see that the justification would have held up.

One Court which has been surprisingly open to acknowledging positive equality duties is the European Court of Human Rights (ECtHR), followed to some extent by the British courts. Article 14 of the ECHR provides as follows: 'The enjoyment of the rights and freedoms set forth in this Convention shall be secured without discrimination on any ground such as sex, race, colour, language, religion, political or other opinion, national or social origin, association with a national minority, property, birth or other status.' Article 14 is often criticized for its parasitic nature. Rather than being a freestanding equality guarantee, it only prohibits discrimination in the enjoyment of rights in the Convention itself. This aspect is expected to be remedied by the introduction of the new Protocol 12, which decouples the equality guarantee from the substantive rights. Nevertheless, Article 14 has considerable power in respect of positive duties. This is for two main reasons. The first is that the wording of the provision is essentially in positive terms: Convention rights *must be secured* without discrimination on the specified grounds. Secondly, the ECtHR has interpreted the role of the 'gateway' rights expansively. There is no need to prove that a

---

[29] *Law* (n 27 above) para 105.   [30] ibid para 101.
[31] *Gosselin* (n 28 above) para 55.   [32] ibid para 56.

Convention right has been breached to trigger Article 14. The Court has said on many occasions that Article 14 comes into play whenever 'the subject-matter of the disadvantage constitutes one of modalities of the exercise of a right guaranteed', or the measures complained of are 'linked to the exercise of a right guaranteed'. These principles have led the Court to acknowledge expressly that positive duties can arise from the equality guarantee. In a similar line of reasoning to that seen in *Eldridge* above, the Court has held that if a State chooses to provide a benefit, it must do so without discrimination. This inevitably entails a positive duty to provide the benefit to the wrongfully excluded group unless the State can justify the exclusion.

The thrust of adjudication is therefore to determine whether the State has properly accounted for its decision to exclude the group in question. The Court, acknowledges that in a modern State, categorization is essential. 'The competent national authorities are frequently confronted with situations and problems which, on account of differences inherent therein, call for different legal solutions; moreover, certain legal inequalities tend only to correct factual inequalities.'[33] It is through the duty to provide acceptable reasons for categorization that the court exercises its chief supervisory role. To be acceptable, a distinction must have an objective and reasonable justification. This refers to both the aim and the means: there must be a legitimate aim, and a reasonable relationship of proportionality between the means employed and the aim sought to be realized.[34]

A recent example is found in *Petrovic v Austria*,[35] where a complaint was made about the exclusion of fathers from the right to a parental leave allowance that was available to mothers. It was argued that the exclusion breached Article 14 in conjunction with Article 8, which protects the right to respect for family life. Here the Court held that Article 8 on its own did not impose a positive obligation on the State to provide the financial assistance in question. Nonetheless, it held that the allowance was intended to promote family life, thereby demonstrating the State's respect for family life. It therefore came within the scope of Article 8, triggering the equality guarantee in Article 14.[36] This meant that unless the State could justify the restriction, it would be under a positive duty to provide the allowance to fathers and not solely to mothers.

However, its position as a supra-national court has made the Court quick to accept the justifications offered by States. The result is that in practice the positive duty is rarely imposed. In *Petrovic* itself, it was held that since there was no accepted standard among Convention countries of giving fathers the right to paternity benefits, the State's justification was acceptable. No attempt was made to consider the strength of the justification nor the reasons presented. This can be

---

[33] *Belgian Linguistic Case (No 2)* (1968) 1 EHRR 252 (European Court of Human Rights), para 10.
[34] ibid.
[35] *Petrovic v Austria* (2001) 33 EHRR 14 (European Court of Human Rights).
[36] ibid paras 27–29.

contrasted with the opinion presented to the Court by the Commission, which pointed out that the State's attempt to justify the distinction on the grounds of protection of the health of the mother was not logical. Parental leave payments related to periods subsequent to the first eight weeks of maternity leave, which were aimed to give the mother time to recover from the pregnancy and birth. The parental leave payments aimed instead to enable the beneficiary to personally take care of the newborn child. 'The Commission cannot see why fathers, who are willing to do so, could not take over this task... The lack of a common standard cannot absolve Contracting States which have opted for a specific scheme of parental leave payments from granting these benefits in a non-discriminatory manner.'[37]

The UK courts have been more assertive in this respect, but this has depended very much on the court's perception of the legitimacy of the exclusionary category. For issues of race, gender, and, most recently, sexual orientation, the courts will subject the justification offered to intense scrutiny, being prepared to evaluate and even reject the State's evidence, even if this has distributive implications.[38] On the other hand, where the ground of distinction is not thought to be so serious, distributive claims by the State are likely to attract substantial deference.[39] Thus, in *Ghaidan*, the UK House of Lords struck down a statutory provision which excluded same-sex partners from inheriting statutory tenancies from their partners, in a situation in which both married and unmarried heterosexual partners could so inherit. The result was that the State was under a positive duty to extend the provision of council housing to same-sex partners. This was despite the fact that there was no duty to provide a home in the first place. Following *Petrovic*, the House of Lords accepted that once the State has chosen to intervene in a factual area characteristic of those protected by Article 8, Article 14 is engaged if there is relevant discrimination in the mode of that intervention. Since this clearly affected the applicant's home, Article 14 was engaged. Unlike the courts in *Law* and *Gosselin*, the House of Lords did not attempt to protect the State from having to provide a justification. It concluded that, in fact, no acceptable reasons had been given. According to Lord Nicholls: 'One looks in vain to find justification for the difference in treatment of homosexual and heterosexual couples... Here, the difference in treatment falls at the first hurdle: the absence of a legitimate aim.'[40]

This approach can be contrasted with that in *Michalak*,[41] which like *Ghaidan*, concerned the rights of family members to succeed to social housing. In this case,

[37] *Petrovic* para C38.
[38] *R on the Application of Hooper v Secretary of State for Work and Pensions* [2005] UKHL 29 (House of Lords); *Ghaidan v Godin-Mendoza* [2004] UKHL 30, [2004] 2 AC 557 (HL).
[39] *Wandsworth Borough Council v Michalak* [2003] 1 WLR 617 (CA); *Douglas v North Tyneside Metropolitan Borough Council* [2003] EWCA Civ 1847 (CA).
[40] *Ghaidan* (n 38 above) para 18.
[41] *Michalak* (n 39 above).

however, the relative was not a same-sex partner but a distant relative who had been sharing the house. The UK Court of Appeal accepted that a distant relative was analogous to a close relative, and therefore that the burden shifted to the State to defend its categorization. However, in this case, there was no question of a right of 'high constitutional importance' being involved. Instead, the Court emphasized that local authority housing was a valuable resource, and therefore that this is pre-eminently a field in which the courts should defer to the decisions taken by a democratically elected Parliament.[42]

C. Beyond the Courts: Positive Duties to Promote Equality

The limited nature of judicial intervention has triggered a surge of new energy aimed at formulating positive duties to promote equality outside of the courts. Rather than a duty of restraint, requiring proof of individual fault through a litigation process, proactive models insist that responsibility for addressing inequality lies with those best placed to bring about change. This section examines some of the recent formulations of a positive duty to promote equality. It will be seen that the proactive model has important advantages over the more established restraint-based model. However, the proactive model is frequently assumed to be based in policy rather than rights. This leaves such models highly dependent on political commitment. The key challenge is therefore to structure the duty round the concept of a fundamental right, without reverting to individualized complaints mechanisms with all their inbuilt weaknesses. This can only be done by a wholehearted recognition that the right to equality gives rise to both positive duties and duties of restraint. I begin by contrasting the proactive model with the traditional fault based model. I then draw on the experience of several jurisdictions in assessing the newly developing proactive model and the particular challenges it poses.

(i) Proactive models: principles and practice

The ineffectiveness of a litigation-centred approach to addressing status inequality is a direct result of limiting the right to equality to a duty of restraint. Given that the right can only be breached by deliberate action aimed at the individual right-holder, the focus of litigation is inevitably on the need to prove fault. Structural and institutional inequalities which cannot be traced to an individual perpetrator are outside of the scope of enforcement. It also means that if there is no individual with the energy and resources to bring a claim, there is no mechanism for redress. The court's intervention is therefore inevitably random and ad hoc,

---

[42] ibid para 41.

depending on litigants' ability to bring a claim.[43] Litigation is lengthy and costly and many complainants have retired or even died before their claims are resolved. Even if a case is pursued successfully, the result is limited to compensation for the individual or group of complainants, with no ongoing obligations to correct the institutional structure which gave rise to the discrimination. The model cannot therefore produce significant or systematic progress towards the goals of equality.[44] Individual claims are also adversarial. Because they are based on proof of fault, such claims are resisted by employers or the State. Instead of viewing equality as a common goal, to be achieved cooperatively, it becomes a site of conflict and resistance.[45] Finally, the focus on restraint assumes that the State is a potential threat to liberty, rather than a potential force for enhancing equality. In fact, the immense power of the State means that it is particularly well situated to take on responsibility for correcting inequalities, regardless of whether it caused them in the first place.

Proactive models aim to remedy each of the deficiencies of the complaints-led model. First, and most important, is the recognition that responsibility for achieving equality is not limited to those who can be proved to have caused it. Instead of merely a duty of restraint, equality entails a positive duty on those with the power and capacity to bring about change. The aim is no longer to determine fault and punish conduct, but to address the institutional basis of inequality through the duty to take positive measures.[46] This relieves individual victims of the burden and expense of litigation, placing the initiative instead on policy-makers and implementers, service providers or employers. Secondly, change is systematic rather than a response to those few who have the resources to complain. The structural causes of inequality can be diagnosed and addressed collectively and institutionally so that the right to equality is available to all, not just those who complain.

Finally, in moving away from the 'command and control' model, proactive approaches aim to harness the energy and initiative of local actors, who are best acquainted with the problems and potential solutions. Likewise, there is an insistence on participation and involvement by those directly affected. This means that instead of fixed and predetermined legal rights or obligations, the proactive model produces norms which are dynamic and renegotiable, capable of being implemented programmatically and subject to constant review. Proactive models have also been able to link up different sorts of equality concerns, both from the direction of redistributive justice and from that of recognition. Thus, policies on social inclusion and employment creation are interwoven and expressly linked to gender and other equality groups. Proactive models also range well beyond the

---

[43] Pay Equity Taskforce and Departments of Justice and Human Resources Development Canada *Pay Equity: A New Approach to a Fundamental Right* (2004) 106.
[44] ibid 108.
[45] Pay Equity Taskforce (n 43 above) 98.
[46] ibid 147.

employment focus of traditional anti-discrimination law, to include pensions, tax, education, transport, health, corporate policies, benefits, conflict, violence, and criminal justice.[47]

Proactive strategies lie on the interface between law and politics and it is therefore useful to distinguish between them according to the extent to which they mobilize or interact with legal norms. The approach which is most policy-led is that of mainstreaming. Mainstreaming is a 'social justice-led approach to policy making in which equal opportunities principles, strategies and practices are integrated into the every day work of government and other public bodies'.[48] Although these policies originate from equality norms, they are autonomous from them. Mainstreaming strategies have been attempted in various places, including local government in the UK, Canada, and several other EU Member States.[49]

More specific are those models which place a statutory duty on public bodies to promote equality.[50] In Britain, the Race Relations Act 1976, as amended in 2000, places a positive duty on public bodies to have due regard to the need to promote equality of opportunity and good relations between people of different racial groups ('the British race duty').[51] More recently, this has been supplemented by a proactive duty in respect of gender,[52] and a separate duty in respect of disability.[53] A similar, but more wide-ranging, duty applies in Northern Ireland. Under section 75 of the Northern Ireland Act 1998, all public bodies have a duty in carrying out their functions to have due regard to the need to promote equality of opportunity between specified groups, including between men and women, between persons with dependants and those without, between persons with and without disabilities, and between persons of different religious belief, political opinion, racial group, age, marital status, or sexual orientation ('the section 75 duty').[54] Such statutory duties do not, however, give rise to individual rights enforceable in courts.

Most specific are those which apply to employment or pay equity, both in the public and private sectors. Thus, in Northern Ireland, fair employment legislation[55] (separate from the section 75 duty) requires employers periodically to review the composition of the workforce and its employment practices to determine

---

[47] Platform for Action *Fourth World Conference on Women* (Beijing 1995).
[48] F MacKay and K Bilton *Learning From Experience: Lessons in Mainstreaming Equal Opportunities* (Scottish Executive Social Research 2003) 1.
[49] ibid.
[50] C McCrudden 'Review of Issues Concerning the Operation of the Equality Duty' in E McLaughlin and N Faris (eds) *Section 75 Equality Review—An Operational Review Volume 2* (Northern Ireland Office Belfast 2004); C McCrudden 'Mainstreaming Equality in the Governance of Northern Ireland' in C Harvey (ed) *Human Rights, Equality and Democratic Renewal in Northern Ireland* (Hart Oxford 2001).
[51] Race Relations Act 1976, s 71(1).
[52] Sex Discrimination Act 1975, s 76A.
[53] Disability Discrimination Act 1995 (DDA 1995), s 49.
[54] Northern Ireland Act 1998, s 75.
[55] Fair Employment and Treatment (Northern Ireland) Order 1998 No 3162 (NI 21).

whether members of each of the two main communities (Protestants and Roman Catholic) are 'enjoying fair participation in employment in the concern'.[56] If this is not the case, then the employer is required to institute positive action in order to make progress towards fair participation. Similarly, in Canada, provincial legislation places a proactive duty on employers to achieve pay equity between men and women. A recent and powerfully argued Taskforce Report has summed up the strengths and weaknesses of the models currently in use, making recommendations for future federal pay equity legislation.[57]

(ii) Achieving compliance

These models have exciting new potential to bring about real change. They also raise major challenges. The insights from regulatory theory presented in Chapter 6 demonstrate that simply imposing external norms on a body is unlikely to achieve real change. Unless the impetus is found internally, these models will not achieve their aim of ultimately transforming the organizational culture. Real change in organizational culture therefore depends on the interplay between the enlightened self-interest of public or private managers on the one hand, and the drive and energy of affected participants on the other.[58] At the same time, self-regulation becomes pure voluntarism unless it is made to be responsive to some external impetus. Equally difficult has been the challenge of achieving real participation from those involved.

Possibly the greatest challenge is to achieve the appropriate balance between internal autonomy and external stimuli. Some models have so little normative force that they could constitute a retreat from rights to mere policy. In this respect, their basis in fundamental rights needs to be reasserted. This is particularly evident in respect of mainstreaming. A recent study demonstrated that political will is the key to progress in most mainstreaming strategies.[59] It is difficult to sustain positive action strategies without strong political and managerial support[60] and lack or loss of political will can turn mainstreaming into a mere gesture or even a pretext for inaction.[61] Thus, the success of gender mainstreaming at EU level is highly dependent on whether individual Directors General sympathize with its overall aims. Where gender mainstreaming has 'resonance' in a department, it flourishes; where it does not, very little happens.[62] Paradoxically, it works best when there is high level representation of women

---

[56] ibid s 55.

[57] Pay Equity Taskforce (n 43 above).

[58] B Hepple, M Coussey, and T Choudhury *Equality: A New Framework Report of the Independent Review of the Enforcement of UK Anti-discrimination Legislation* (Hart Oxford 2000) 57.

[59] MacKay and Bilton (n 48 above) 97.

[60] ibid 74.

[61] MacKay and Bilton (n 48 above) 143.

[62] M Pollack and E Hafner-Burton 'Mainstreaming Gender in the European Union' [2000] 7 Journal of European Public Policy 432–456.

in the policy-making or implementation machinery. Yet this is precisely what it aims to achieve in the first place.

A similar pattern is evident in the British and the Northern Irish duties, where the statutory formulation deliberately gives a wide margin of autonomy to the decision-making body. Rather than a duty to take action, public bodies are under a duty to pay 'due regard' to the need to eliminate unlawful discrimination and promote equality of opportunity. This leaves the authority to decide whether to take any action, having taken account of the equality issues along with its other priorities. In the recent case of *Elias*,[63] it was held that the duty is only breached by a failure to 'properly consider whether there was any potential discrimination'.[64] The judge held that to discharge the duty, it is necessary to make a careful attempt to assess whether a scheme raises issues of discrimination and the extent of any adverse impact, as well as to examine whether there are other possible ways of eliminating or minimizing such impact. However, if after considering these matters, the authority adopts precisely the same scheme, it would have done so after having due regard to the obligations under the statute.[65]

In Northern Ireland, the due regard standard has not proved problematic because it is part of a carefully crafted framework creating the appropriate impetus for action. This is based on a 'three legged stool', incorporating the public body, the Northern Ireland Commission and civil society, which has performed an active and constructive role. This has meant that the 'due regard' standard has in effect been interpreted as requiring action to be taken.[66] However, this has not been the case in Britain. It is too early to judge the impact of the gender and disability duties. But the impact of the race duty, which came fully into force in 2001, has been below expectations. It has successfully changed the discourse in many public bodies from a focus on tackling discrimination to one of delivering equality. It has also been the catalyst for some significant changes at the national level: embedding race equality performance measures into the targets which are set for government departments for instance; and equally into the monitoring of public bodies such as local authorities and hospitals by audit and inspection bodies. The new approach has not, however, led most public bodies to

---

[63] *R (on the application of Diana Elias) v Secretary of State for Defence, Commission for Racial Equality* [2005] EWHC 1435 (Admin) (QBD (Admin)) (Elias J's decision was not subject to appeal, and still stands).

[64] *R (on the application of Diana Elias) v Secretary of State for Defence, Commission for Racial Equality* [2005] EWHC 1435 (Admin) (QBD (Admin)); *Elias v Secretary of State for Defence* [2006] EWCA Civ 1293 (Court of Appeal).

[65] In the particular case, it was held that this duty was breached by the Secretary of State, as no regard at all was given to the potentially racially discriminatory nature of the particular policy challenged.

[66] Equality Commission for Northern Ireland Reviewing the Effectiveness of Section 75 of the Northern Ireland Act 1998 (May 2007) <http://www.equalityni.org/archive/pdf/Reviewing EffS75ECNIRpt0507.pdf>.

review their practices and implement reforms in the way Parliament intended.[67] The duty has frequently become an exercise in procedure and paperwork, rather than in institutional change. According to a government consultation paper, the general view is that it is an 'overly bureaucratic, process—driven and resource intensive'.[68]

This is a good illustration of the ways in which regulatory attempts can misfire if not properly tuned to the system in hand. If standards are too vague to give clear guidance, those involved will attempt to discharge the duty in a way that disrupts the system as little as possible. One way forward, then, is to define the objectives to be achieved more carefully. While decision-makers within the body in question should play a central role in determining the strategy, the objectives of that strategy need greater specification. In practice, too little thought has been given to this issue. The standards in gender mainstreaming strategies are particularly open-ended, referring generally to the transformation of the culture of governments and the need to improve the quality of public policy and governance.[69] The British and Northern Irish legislation on the face of it formulates the goal in a more specific manner: the duty is to pay due regard to the need to promote equality of opportunity.[70] However, as we have seen, equal opportunity is a particularly difficult standard to apply. In addition, opportunities are very difficult to quantify and they are frequently reduced to results for the purposes of monitoring or impact assessment.

This has led to calls for more outcome-oriented objectives. Equality of results could indeed be a more specific target, but only in narrowly defined circumstances. These would include pay equity provisions, where the focus is on equalizing the pay of women and men doing work of equal value. Similarly, equality of results is appropriate where the aim is to improve the participation of an under-represented group in a workforce. Thus, Northern Ireland fair employment legislation aspires to the result-oriented aim of fair participation in employment. Results are much more difficult to specify outside of the workforce, for example in service delivery. In addition, as argued earlier, focussing on results might be too superficial a goal, since apparent changes in outcomes could mask persistence of underlying structures.

It is for these reasons that reform proposals in respect of the British duty are now actively seeking to define the goals to which the duty should aim. Indeed, the four dimensional understanding of equality set out above was expressly adopted in an influential consultation paper produced by a government body charged with

---

[67] See, for instance, *Common Ground: Equality, Good Race Relations and Sites for Gypsies and Irish Travellers. Report of a CRE Inquiry in England and Wales 2006*. The inquiry took evidence on implementation of the duty from 236 local authorities.

[68] Women and Equality Unit *Advancing Equality for Men and Women: Government Proposals to Introduce a Public Sector Duty to Promote Gender Equality* (2005) para 30.

[69] MacKay and Bilton (n 48 above) 142.

[70] Race Relations Act 1976, s 71(1); Northern Ireland Act 1998, s 75.

recommending reform.[71] It is therefore useful to assess existing duties according to the extent to which they aspire to equality goals in this four dimensional sense. It will be recalled that these are (i) the promotion of respect for the equal dignity and worth of all, thereby redressing stigma, stereotyping, humiliation, and violence because of membership of an out-group; (ii) accommodating difference; (iii) redressing disadvantage; and (iv) promoting participation.

To some extent, these goals are already in evidence. The promotion of respect and dignity is now expressly endorsed in the new gender duty in Britain, which includes harassment as well as equality of opportunity in the definition of its goals. The disability duty goes even further and provides not only that public bodies must have due regard to the need to eliminate harassment of disabled persons, but also to promote positive attitudes towards them.[72] Less expressly, but also important has been the way in which pay equity strategies in Canada have advanced the recognition of the value of women's work, improving both women's own self-respect and the respect accorded to them in the workplace.[73] The goal of accommodating difference is found in the disability duty, according to which due regard must be paid to the need to take account of disabled persons' disabilities, even where this involves treating them more favourably than others.[74] Similarly, there are several proactive duties which could be said to expressly or implicitly advance the third goal, namely, that of redressing disadvantage. This is reflected in an asymmetric approach, targeting the disadvantaged or under-represented group. Thus, gender mainstreaming is specifically aimed at women, as are proactive pay equity schemes.

Nevertheless, the objectives to which the positive action should be aiming remain too vague and unarticulated. Also, more attention needs to be paid to the interaction between the four equality objectives. This is particularly true of the appropriate relationship between recognition and redistribution. In Northern Ireland, policy measures were put in place to reduce the disadvantage experienced disproportionately by Catholics. This caused intense debate as to whether the aim was to address disadvantage per se, including disadvantaged Protestants; or to redress Catholic disadvantage. This ambiguity in the aims threatened to paralyze implementation.[75] The OMC on social inclusion resolves the ambiguity by expressly targeting disadvantage rather than identity groups.[76] However, this is

---

[71] Discrimination Law Review: A Framework for Fairness: Proposals for a Single Equality Bill for Great Britain (Department for Communities and Local Government, June 2007) <http://www.communities.gov.uk/publications/communities/frameworkforfairnessconsultation> para 5.29.

[72] DDA 1995, s 49A(1).

[73] Pay Equity Taskforce (n 43 above) 62.

[74] DDA 1995, s 49A(1)(e).

[75] B Osborne and I Shuttleworth (eds) *Fair Employment in Northern Ireland: A Generation On* (Blackstaff Press Ltd Belfast 2004) 8.

[76] KA Armstrong 'Tackling Social Exclusion through OMC: Reshaping the Boundaries of EU Governance' in T Börzel and R Cichowski (eds) *State of the Union: Law, Politics and Society (Vol. 6)* (OUP Oxford 2003) 12.

to ignore the ways in which redistributive policies can entrench status inequality if sufficient care is not taken to integrate the two. This is clearly evident in respect of gender. Focussing on women alone risks representing the problem as one of 'women's' disadvantage, rather than one requiring change in both men's role as well as women's. Thus, within the EES, there is a tendency to focus on supply side factors, such as training and flexible hours for women, rather than insisting also on change in demand side factors and particularly from employers.[77]

Having specified the goals, the next step is to establish a programme of action, known as an equality plan. This has several benefits. Given that the duty is pro-grammatic, rather than immediate, it ensures that an organization plans properly and allocates responsibilities in a way which survives personnel changes. It also enhances transparency, and functions as a blueprint for accountability in respect of whether action has actually been taken. In the British race duty, public bod-ies are required to produce an equality plan or scheme which sets out each of the steps to be taken. All policies need to be screened to determine whether they pose a risk for particular groups. Those which do pose such a risk need to be fully assessed for their impact on racial groups and adjustments or changes need to be made accordingly. The public duty in Northern Ireland requires public bodies to produce a scheme setting out its arrangement for assessing compliance; for assessing and consulting on the likely impact of policies on equality of opportun-ity; for monitoring any adverse impact of policies, for publishing results of the assessments, for training, and for ensuring and assessing public access to infor-mation and to service provided by the authority.[78] The Northern Ireland duty of fair representation in employment requires employers to review the composition of their workforce every three years to establish whether there is fair participation of each of the two relevant communities. If they find there is not, then they must compile an affirmative action programme. Similarly, Canadian pay equity plans require a review to determine female dominated occupations and compare their pay to a male dominated comparable group. The absence of such a structured approach in the EU may be one reason why mainstreaming in the EU is so reliant for its success on finding resonance within the bureaucracy.

Thirdly, mechanisms for monitoring the effectiveness of the strategy and for periodic review in the light of experience are essential. But this too is not without its challenges. The above discussion has assumed that 'success' is clearly measur-able and uncontested. Measures of success take the form of targets or objectives to be achieved over time, accompanied by indicators to measure progress. However, such indicators are themselves contestable, and subject to negotiation and agree-ment. Successful mainstreaming in particular requires the development of indi-cators that are sensitive to gender. As Mackay and Bilton note, indicators are not

---

[77] J Rubery 'Gender Mainstreaming and Gender Equality in the EU: The Impact of the EU Employment Strategy' (2002) 33 Industrial Relations Journal 500–522 at 503.
[78] Northern Ireland Act 1998, Sch 9.

'facts' which exist 'out there' for the policy-maker to use. Rather, they are created and 'validate particular world views and prioritise selected areas of knowledge'. Many traditional indicators characterize families as single units, represented by the head of the household, who is defined as the male breadwinner. Internal relations within the family are therefore obscured and women are seen primarily as mothers or caregivers. The main indicators used at an international and national level, such as GDP (Gross Domestic Product), ISH (Index of Social Health), and the HDI (Human Development Index) are all 'gender invisible'. The influence of the choice of indicator can be seen by considering Canada. The United Nations has ranked Canada first in the world in terms of human development, but this drops to second place when the status of women is factored in. Particularly striking is the ranking which emerges in respect of an indicator which concentrates on the gender pay gap. Canada ranks 47th out of 55 countries the UN compares in terms of women's wages as a percentage of men's, behind all industrialized countries studied and behind many developing nations.[79]

The fourth ingredient is the regulatory body itself. It has been shown that voluntary compliance is not on its own sufficient.[80] It is here that the compliance pyramid described in Chapter 6 comes into play.[81] The first tier is one of encouragement and support, to promote a cooperative rather than an adversarial approach and to promote and preserve long-term relationships and avoid an adversarial climate. Also key are expert assistance and training. The diagnosis of discrimination may require complex decisions as to the appropriate pool of comparison. For example, where there is a duty of fair representation in the workforce, it is necessary to determine which part of the population is the relevant benchmark: is it the population as a whole, the working population, the relevantly qualified population, or the population in a particular region?[82] Pay equity comparisons can be particularly complex; the Canadian Pay Equity Taskforce envisages a specialist pay equity oversight body as providing relevant statistical information and methodological guidance.[83]

The next layer of compliance consists in scrutinizing reports and equality plans. Whether the relevant commission is required to approve every plan is to some extent determined by numbers. In Northern Ireland, the numbers are far more manageable than elsewhere: hence the requirement to obtain advance approval of the equality scheme.[84] Thus, the public equality duty covers about 160 bodies, each of whom needs to submit an equality scheme and then report annually on

---

[79] MacKay and Bilton (n 48 above) 46ff.
[80] Hepple et al (n 58 above) 57; Pay Equity Taskforce (n 43 above) 395.
[81] Hepple et al (n 58 above) 59.
[82] C McCrudden, R Ford, and A Heath 'The Impact of Affirmative Action Agreements' in B Osborne and I Shuttleworth (eds) *Fair Employment in Northern Ireland: A Generation On* (Blackstaff Press Belfast 2004) 125.
[83] Pay Equity Taskforce (n 43 above) 163, 406.
[84] Northern Ireland Act 1998, Sch 9.

its progress. Compliance has been high: in their review in 2003, the Commission stated that of 160 designated bodies, 156 submitted reports and four failed to do so. In other contexts, it is necessary for the relevant commission to take a strategic view. In respect of fair representation at work, the relevant Northern Ireland commission began by investigating larger enterprises in both the public and private sectors, and then moved on to considering smaller enterprises.[85] The Hepple report concluded that it would not be feasible in Britain to require advance approval of equality schemes by the commission, because of the large number of public authorities and the limited resources available. In any event, it took the view, based on the Northern Ireland experience, that this could have the effect of externalizing the responsibility for implementing the plan, rather than building up the energy and resources from within.[86]

These compliance-oriented approaches are not, however, sufficient without the possibility of sanctions. Voluntary action is much more likely when the possibility of sanctions exists as a default. Thus, in Northern Ireland, the relevant commission has had to make remarkably little use of its considerable investigatory powers, because employers have been willing to enter into voluntary affirmative action agreements. This is only the case, however, because those sanctions exist: the purely voluntary approach previously pursued yielded no such results.[87] Many of the proactive models stress that innovative remedies are required, remaining within the spirit of a proactive model, and not regressing to an original fault-based approach. Considerable investigative and review powers can be vested in the commission, leading to the issue of a compliance notice by the commission itself, backed up by recourse to a court of law with injunctive powers to insist on compliance. A different model would give the individual some power to initiate compliance proceedings, by means of an individual complaint either to the commission or directly to a court. The Canadian Taskforce suggests that there be recourse to a pay equity tribunal which, rather than being adversarial, uses conciliation and arbitration methods and with a range of innovative remedies. It too, however, recommends the court as the final enforcement body, so that cooperative solutions can always be backed up by judicial remedies if they fail.[88] The Northern Ireland fair representation legislation leads to a possible legally enforceable affirmative action agreement.[89] The Hepple report, however, recommended that instead of entrusting this function to a specialist regulatory agency, it should be built into existing performance management frameworks. Inspection and audit should be carried out by bodies with established inspection

---

[85] McCrudden et al (n 82 above) 122.

[86] Hepple et al (n 58 above) 62.

[87] B Osborne and I Shuttleworth (eds) *Fair Employment in Northern Ireland: A Generation On* (Blackstaff Press Ltd Belfast 2004) 7.

[88] Pay Equity Taskforce (n 43 above) 401, 406.

[89] Fair Employment and Treatment (Northern Ireland) Order 1998 No 3162 (NI 21) Article 13; see McCrudden et al (n 82 above) 122–150.

and audit functions, such as the Audit Commission, and the inspectorates of prisons, schools, and police.[90]

(iii) The deliberative dimension: participation and the participants

Perhaps the most important element in proactive schemes is that of participation. We saw in Chapter 6 that institutional change is more likely to succeed if it incorporates decision-makers and stakeholders in both decision-making and implementation. At their most ambitious, proactive models aim to move beyond conflict and interest-based bargaining to a form of deliberative democracy, whereby interests are not taken as fixed or predetermined, but are themselves moulded by the process of decision-making to achieve a new public-regarding synthesis.[91] Rather than leaving norms to be determined in legislatures or courts, the proactive model incorporates relevant stakeholders into both the process of norm setting and its implementation. Norms are set in a dynamic and responsive way, and implementation and norm setting interact. Nevertheless, however bright the ideal of participation shines, there remain important areas of contestation and conflict. These centre on two main issues: the function of participation and the choice of participants. Each is dealt with in turn.

Functions of participation

It is not always made clear what function participation performs. This is complicated by the fact that participation can both be an end and a means. As an end, it aims to enhance participation in society by marginalized groups. For example, gender mainstreaming aims to increase the participation of women in decision-making structures. At the same time, participation is a means to achieve greater legitimacy and effectiveness in policy-making. In this instrumental sense, it plays several overlapping roles: to impart information, to glean information, to influence decision-making, and to achieve compliance.

The first function, to impart information to those affected, aims at transparency and accountability. Transparency is essential to deliberative democracy, since without proper information, public debate cannot take place.[92] Publication requirements are one way to achieve transparency. The British race duty requires results of all monitoring processes to be published, while the Canadian Pay Equity Taskforce recommends posting of information at each stage of the process.[93] By contrast, there is little by way of specific requirements of transparency in the EU mainstreaming process. The EES has similarly been criticized for lack

---

[90] Hepple et al (n 58 above) 64.
[91] CR Sunstein 'Beyond the Republican Revival' [1988] 97 Yale Law Journal 1539.
[92] CDL Porte and P Nanz 'The OMC—A Deliberative-democratic Mode of Governance? The Cases of Employment and Pensions' (2004) 11 Journal of European Public Policy 267–288.
[93] Pay Equity Taskforce (n 43 above) 231.

of transparency: decision-making by the relevant European level committee takes places behind closed doors.[94] There is even less transparency at national levels.[95]

The second function of participation is to glean information from those affected in order to improve the quality of decision-making. Those who are at the receiving end of discrimination are in the best position to detect it and to suggest change.[96] A third function of participation is to influence decision-making. From the perspective of deliberative democracy, the process of decision-making moves forward from interest-based bargaining to a deliberative ethic, during which decision-makers are able to redefine their goals as a result of discussion and debate.[97] In this respect, participation should facilitate the voice of groups who are excluded from traditional representative decision-making[98] with the aim of introducing new perspectives and refashioning outcomes. Non-State actors are empowered and new channels of political participation are stimulated.[99]

Few positive duties, however, go far enough to achieve a deliberative model. The British race relations duty and the Northern Ireland public duty both suggest that participation is only in the nature of consultation, without giving consultants the right to participate in making the decision itself. The Canadian Taskforce, by contrast, stresses the importance of participants having actual decision-making powers. It proposes a workplace pay equity committee, with affected women comprising at least half the membership, which has power to make the final decision.[100] Disputes can be referred to an outside tribunal in the form of the Pay Equity Commission. Such a structure is more difficult to envisage outside of the workplace. The EU High Level Report on industrial relations includes the useful idea of 'social concertation', which involves community groups as well as trade unions in the participation process.

Finally, participation is part of effective implementation or delivery of the policy. Although the process of compliance is not driven by individuals, those affected are in a good position to insist that duties are fulfilled. Participatory functions are more easily fulfilled by NGOs or in the workplace, where there are established consultation structures, than in respect of the provision of services and other public functions, where the community is more amorphous. The British legislation measures user satisfaction levels as one of the indicators of compliance, but this is at best a passive form of participation.

---

[94] J Zeitlin 'Conclusion: The Open Method of Coordination in Action: Theoretical Promise, Empirical Realities, Reform Strategy' in J Zeitlin, P Pochet, and L Magnusson (eds) *The Open Method of Coordination in Action: The European Employment and Social Inclusion Strategies* (PIE-Peter Lang 2005).

[95] ibid 39.

[96] Pay Equity Taskforce (n 43 above) 160, 223.

[97] CDL Porte and P Nanz 'The OMC—A Deliberative-democratic Mode of Governance? The Cases of Employment and Pensions' (2004) 11 Journal of European Public Policy 267–288, 273.

[98] Armstrong (n 76 above) 25.

[99] Zeitlin (n 94 above) 37–38.

[100] Pay Equity Taskforce (n 43 above) 230.

The participants in the process

Given the pivotal functions of participants, it is of key importance to determine who should perform these roles. An obvious first step is to turn to the traditional structures of representative democracy, in the form of legislatures at national, local, and regional levels. Yet, such structures have played a minor role or even been deliberately marginalized. This is particularly true within the OMC process. The European Parliament was given no more than a consultative role, and even this has been sidestepped. In fact, Zeitlin doubts whether conventional legislatures could play a useful role in the deliberative process of the OMC without 'transformation of the conventional conception of parliaments' role in democratic polities as authoritative principals delegating detailed implementation of legislation to administrative agents, whose behaviour they seek to control through a combination of ex ante incentives and ex post sanctions'.[101] Certainly, where Parliaments do play a greater role, it is not in the conventional sense of legislating, but instead as advocates for the strategy. Thus, in implementing mainstreaming in Canada, a parliamentary gender caucus is advocated as a champion of mainstreaming by raising awareness, lobbying, promoting equal participation of women and men; and by scrutinizing parliamentary structures, procedures, and matters under debate.[102] Local authorities are seen as playing a more central role, but often this is in implementation, as under the British race duty, rather than as participants in decision-making.

Outside of State structures, the aim is to bring civil society and other stakeholders into the decision-making process. But little attention is paid to why particular groups are chosen and civil society is not itself defined. The process of selection of participants favours better organized groups in civil society, running the risk of marginalizing even further those who are not well organized.[103] It also assumes that the participants are representative of all the interests in their constituency. However, the trade unions, employers groups, and NGOs do not necessarily fully represent marginalized groups. Rubery notes that there is little evidence, within either the EU strategy or the National Action Plans of any awareness of possible gender bias arising from the lower representation of women in trade unions and collective bargaining.[104] Similarly, the Canadian Taskforce points out that trade unions themselves might replicate both structures of segregation within the workforce, with women dominated sectors having less industrial muscle than those dominated by men.[105] In any event, many of the worst affected areas are non-unionized. Thus, the Taskforce suggests including representatives of the women affected rather than relying solely on trade unions.

[101] Zeitlin (n 94 above) 42–43.
[102] MacKay and Bilton (n 48 above) 141ff.
[103] ibid 71.
[104] Rubery (n 77 above) 515.
[105] Pay Equity Taskforce (n 43 above) Chapter 5.

Ensuring that participants are representative is even more complex outside of the workplace. The guidance notes to the British race duty emphasize the need to include all in consultation, particularly those without a voice, such as older or rural ethnic minority members. One way of doing this is through 'listening events', or open meetings conducted in various parts of the country. Notably, however, the material does not specify how to ensure that these events are not captured by organized interests with loud voices. Nor does it confront the question of what role those who attend such events should play: is it to give information, gain information, or actually influence the decision? In all cases, the extent to which they are representative of the affected people as a whole is not addressed. Finally, and most complex, is the question of how to ensure that those whose identity falls within more than one group and who therefore suffer cumulative discrimination are properly represented. The Canadian Taskforce stresses the need to incorporate, as a separate sector, visible minority women, indigenous women, and disabled women.[106] How these different perspectives are brought together is not as yet made clear.

The participatory dimension of the positive model assumes a high degree of organization, commitment, and knowledge among potential participants. One way forward is to incorporate capacity building as part of the positive duty, making resources available for this purpose. Participants must have access to proper information, and training must be provided both to active participants and to all affected. For example, in Canada, the Status of Women Canada's *Women's Program* provides financial and administrative support to a wide range of community, regional, provincial, and national organizations.[107] A similar role is performed by the European Social Fund, which earmarks funds for the promotion of equal opportunities for all in a variety of contexts, including specific measures to improve the access and active participation of women in the labour market.[108] However, particular attention must be paid to the criteria for selecting the groups which are given access to the resources. The European Commission provides core funding for the European Anti Poverty network, but it is more difficult for NGOs or other groups which operate across a range of different areas. For example, the Platform of Social NGOs has had difficulty in raising funding from the Commission.[109]

---

[106] Pay Equity Taskforce (n 43 above) 228.
[107] MacKay and Bilton (n 48 above) 124.
[108] Regulation (EC) No 1784/1999 of the European Parliament and of the Council of 12 July 1999.
[109] Armstrong (n 76 above) 29.

D. Conclusion

The introduction of proactive models holds much promise, as well as many new challenges. Giving the initiative to those with power to bring about change is a key to genuine change. However, it is also subject to the vagaries of the political process and to the enlightened self-interest of key actors such as employers. Ultimately, then, it is crucial to recognize that new paradigms are not simply components of policy or practice. They are underpinned by clear and inderogable fundamental rights. Nor does this mean reversion to the individualist model of rights. As soon as it is acknowledged that rights give rise to positive duties as well as duties of restraint, it become clear that positive measures prescribed by proactive models are rooted in human rights rather than political choice.

8

Socio-economic Rights and
Positive Duties

It has been argued thus far instead of drawing distinctions between civil and political rights and socio-economic rights, it is preferable to focus on the positive duties
that arise from all human rights. The analysis in the book has therefore been devoted
to understanding and addressing the challenges of positive human rights duties.
This chapter aims to apply this approach to the familiar topics of socio-economic
rights, with a particular focus on housing, education, and welfare. In each of these
areas, I draw on comparative and international jurisprudence to examine the relevant duties in the light of the themes developed so far in this book.

A. Housing and Shelter

(i) Beyond the divide: human rights values and the right to housing

Rights relating to home and shelter fall on both sides of the notional divide between
civil and political rights and socio-economic rights. While socio-economic rights
documents refer to a right to shelter and housing, civil and political rights documents generally include a right to respect for one's home, family, and private
life. This distinction brings with it a separation between positive and negative
duties. The rights to respect for home and private life are said to give rise to char-
acteristically negative duties, protecting individuals' freedom from intrusion by
the State rather than requiring the State to protect individuals against homelessness. The fact that this right is rendered nugatory for those who do not have
a home is either ignored, or characterized as a distributive issue, outside of the
realm of human rights. This approach is strikingly evident in the interpretation
of the right to respect for home, family, and private life in Article 8 of the ECHR.
According to the Court in *Chapman*: 'While it is clearly desirable that every
human being has a place where he or she can live in dignity and which he or she
can call home, there are unfortunately in the contracting states many persons
who have no home. Whether the state provides funds to enable everyone to have
a home is a matter for political not judicial decision.'[1]

---

[1] *Chapman v United Kingdom* (2001) 33 EHRR 399 (European Court of Human Rights) para 99.

From the opposite perspective, the duty to provide housing is characterized as essentially a socio-economic right, giving rise to programmatic duties and enforceable generally through reporting requirements. At an international level, this is reflected in the positioning of the right to housing in the 'socio-economic rights' treaties, which, as we have seen, are generally given secondary status. Thus, there is a specific right to housing in the ICESCR and not the ICCPR.[2] The same is true of the right to housing in the European system, where it is found in the little known European Social Charter (ESC)[3], rather than in the much more powerfully validated ECHR.

By moving the focus to the duties that arise from the right, a very different picture emerges. The human rights values of freedom, solidarity, and equality set out in Chapter 1 point powerfully towards the need to recognize the positive duties that arise in respect of the right to a home, whether in the context of civil and political or socio-economic rights. Positive freedom to do and be what one values cannot be achieved if one is homeless. Homelessness leaves an individual exposed to a range of risks: physical assault, rape, illness, exposure to the elements, and severe discomfort. More than this, it undermines the basic dignity and respect which should be afforded to all as human beings. This is highlighted by the South African Court in *Grootboom*, when it declared that 'human dignity, freedom and equality, the foundational values of our society, are denied those who have no...shelter'.[4] As the United Nations Housing Rights Programme report points out:

To live in a place, and to have established one's own personal habitat with peace, security and dignity, should be considered neither a luxury, a privilege nor purely the good fortune of those who can afford a decent home. Rather, the requisite imperative of housing for personal security, privacy, health, safety, protection from the elements and many other attributes of a shared humanity, has led the international community to recognize adequate housing as a basic and fundamental human right.[5]

Homelessness is not only a threat to the person concerned; it also undermines the value of solidarity which holds communities together. Sachs J articulated this vividly in a recent South African case: 'It is not only the dignity of the poor that is assailed when homeless people are driven from pillar to post in a desperate quest for a place where they and their families can rest their heads. Our society as a whole is demeaned when State action intensifies, rather than mitigates, their marginalization.'[6] Also directly engaged is the value of equality, both in its redistributive and recognition senses. It is generally the poor who are most exposed

---

[2] ICESCR, Article 11(1).

[3] ESC, Article 31.

[4] *Republic of South Africa v Grootboom (1)* 2001 (1) SA 46 (South African Constitutional Court) para 23.

[5] *United Nations Housing Rights Programme, Report No 1* 'Housing Rights Legislation: Review of International and National Legal Instruments' (2002) at 1.

[6] *Port Elizabeth Municipality v Various Occupiers* 2005 (1) SA 217 (South African Constitutional Court) per Sachs J at para 18 (228).

to homelessness; and within this group, ethnic minorities, asylum seekers, and women are most at risk. For women facing domestic violence, the lack of alternative housing makes them particularly vulnerable.

It is not only in jurisdictions that explicitly recognize socio-economic rights that these values are articulated. Even in the steadfastly civil and political rights environment of the UK, the House of Lords regarded it as a breach of the right not to be subjected to cruel and inhuman or degrading treatment to leave people with no choice but to live rough. 'The exposure to the elements that results from rough-sleeping, the risks to health and safety that it gives rise to, the effects of lack of access to toilet and washing facilities and the humiliation and sense of despair that attaches to those who suffer from deprivations of that kind' are all relevant indicators of a potential breach of this right.[7] Residence can also be the key to access to a range of other rights and benefits, including the right to bail on arrest, social security benefits, and schooling. In addition, homelessness sets up a vicious circle, in that it is very difficult to be presentable enough to find paid employment and therefore to improve one's own condition.

(ii) Sources of positive duties in respect of housing

The infusion of the values of positive freedom, solidarity, and equality into the interpretation of fundamental rights opens up the possibility of recognizing positive duties even in relation to civil and political rights. At the forefront of such an approach is the Indian Supreme Court's interpretation of the right to life. Here positive duties flow directly from the Court's affirmation of the central values for which the right to life stands, particularly the value of positive freedom. This is summed up in the *Ahmedabad* case,[8] where the Court stated: 'In any organised society, the right to live as a human being is...secured only when he is assured of all facilities to develop himself and is freed from restrictions which inhibit his growth.' Shelter is more than just a protection against danger; it is a 'home where he has opportunities to grow physically, mentally, intellectually and spiritually'. This immediately gives rise to a range of positive duties: 'The right to life implies the right to food, water, decent environment, education, medical care and shelter, since no civil, political, social or cultural rights either in the Universal Declaration or the Indian constitution could be exercised without them.' A similar approach has been taken by the UN Committee on Human Rights. In its concluding remarks in respect of Canada in 1999, the Committee expressed its concern at the fact that homelessness in Canada has led to serious health problems and even

---

[7] *R (on the application of Limbuela) v Secretary of State for the Home Department* [2005] UKHL 66; [2006] 1 AC 396 (HL) para 71.
[8] *Ahmedabad Municipal Corporation v Nawab Khan Bulab Khan* (1997) 11 SCC 121 (Indian Supreme Court).

death. Article 6, the right to life, therefore required the State to take positive steps to address this problem.[9]

The strong endorsement of freedom as agency is further reflected in the link between the right to housing and the right to livelihood. The Court in *Olga Tellis* proclaimed in ringing terms:[10] 'The [pavement-dwellers] do not contend that they have a right to live on the pavements. Their contention is that they have a right to live, a right which cannot be exercised without the means of livelihood . . . In a word, their plea is that the right to life is illusory without a right to the means by which alone life can be lived.'[11] Thus, the duty is facilitative, one which treats the subject of the right as an active agent, opening up the possibility of furthering her own welfare.

As well as the right to life, positive duties in respect of housing could emanate from the right to respect for home, family, and private life. In its classic civil and political form, this is found in Article 8 of the ECHR, which provides: 'Everyone has the right to respect for his private and family life, his home and his correspondence.' On its own, this has been limited to a duty of restraint, preventing the State from interfering with the individual's home or family life. We saw above that the ECHR has refused to interpret Article 8 as giving rise to a positive duty to provide housing. However, there have been some glimmerings of a positive duty deriving from the Court's expansive interpretation of the value of personal autonomy inherent in the particular combination of a right to home, family, and private life. Rather than simply seeing it as freedom of invasion, the ECHR has understood autonomy as including the right to personal development, and the right to establish and develop relationships with other human beings and the outside world.[12] The values of family and dignity of children have also been used to trigger a positive duty to provide adequate housing under Article 8. In one British case, it was held that failure to provide adequate accommodation for a disabled mother, leaving her in a position of both intense discomfort and degradation, made it impossible for her to enjoy a normal private and family life. The High Court held that there was a clear breach of Article 8. Although there is no duty to provide a house, the State was under a positive duty to adapt the plaintiff's home in order to restore her dignity as a human being.[13]

It is when allied with the equality guarantee in Article 14 that Article 8 has constituted the most potent source of positive duties. As was seen in the previous chapter, the ECtHR has held that Article 8 need not be breached, but only 'engaged', for Article 14 to come into play. This means that if a State does in fact

---

[9] Concluding Observations of the Human Rights Committee: Canada, UN Doc CCPR/C/79/Add.105 (7 April 1999).

[10] *Olga Tellis v Bombay Municipal Corporation* AIR 1986 SC 180 (Indian Supreme Court).

[11] ibid.

[12] *Botta v Italy* (153/1996/772/973).

[13] *R (on the application of Bernard) v Enfield LBC* [2002] EWHC 2282 (High Court); see also *R (on the application of Anufrijeva) v Southwark LBC* [2003] EWCA Civ 1406 (CA).

take on responsibility for housing, it would be in breach of Article 8 combined with Article 14 if it provided housing in a discriminatory way. As Baroness Hale put it in *Ghaidan*:

Everyone has the right to respect for their home. This does not mean that the state—or anyone else—has to supply everyone with a home. Nor does it mean that the state has to grant everyone a secure right to live in their home. But if it does grant that right to some, it must not withhold it from others in the same or an analogous situation. It must grant that right equally, unless the difference in treatment can be objectively justified.[14]

This compromise is understandable from the point of view of a court which is cautious about distributive decisions. The court need not adjudicate on the difficult questions of how much housing, and to what standard, should be provided. The State sets the benchmark for provision; and the court's role is no more than to require that standard to be applied to a wrongfully excluded group. The weakness of this approach, however, is that a State which provided no housing to anyone would have fulfilled its duties under the Convention because everyone was equally badly off.

By contrast, socio-economic rights in respect of housing make it explicit that the right gives rise to positive duties on the State as well as negative duties of restraint. Article 11(1) of the ICESCR reads:

The States parties to the present Covenant recognize the right of everyone to an adequate standard of living for himself and for his family, including adequate food, clothing and housing, and to the continuous improvement of living conditions. The States Parties *will take appropriate steps* to ensure the realization of this right, recognizing to this effect the essential importance of international co-operation based on free consent.[15]

The ESC configures the rights and duties somewhat differently. Article 31 states: 'With a view to *ensuring the effective exercise* of the right to housing, the Parties *undertake measures* designed to promote access to housing of an adequate standard; to prevent and reduce homelessness with a view to its gradual elimination; and to make the price of housing accessible to those without adequate resources.'[16] There is also a duty to provide family housing,[17] suitable housing for elderly people,[18] and access to housing to those who live in poverty or are socially excluded.[19] At a domestic level, South Africa is the only country in the present study with a justiciable right to housing. This is contained in section 26, which states:

(1) Everyone has the right to *have access to adequate housing.*

---

[14] *Ghaidan v Godin-Mendoza* [2004] UKHL 30, [2004] 2 AC 557 (HL) at [135].
[15] Italics added.
[16] Italics added.
[17] ESC, Article 16.
[18] ESC, Article 23.
[19] ESC, Article 30.

(2) The state must take reasonable legislative and other measures, within its available resources, to achieve the progressive realisation of this right.

(3) No one may be evicted from their home, or have their home demolished, without an order of court made after considering all the relevant circumstances. No legislation may permit arbitrary evictions.[20]

Section 28 gives an unqualified right to shelter to children and there is also a duty to take reasonable steps to foster conditions which enable equitable access to land.[21]

(iii) Positive and negative duties: distinctions and relationships

A further advantage of focussing on duties is that it facilitates clearer distinctions between different types of duties. Failure to distinguish between duties of restraint and positive duties can lead courts to reject claims for the wrong reasons. This can be seen in the UK, where the assumption that housing inevitably gives rise to positive duties has led to rejection of claims which are in reality duties of restraint. Thus in *Poplar*,[22] a tenant of social housing claimed that her right to respect for home and family had been breached by legislation which obliged courts to issue a possession order without examining the reasons.[23] In fact, the claimant was not claiming breach of any positive duty to provide housing, but only of her negative duty not to be evicted without proper reasons. Nevertheless, the Court of Appeal justified its rejection on the ground that social housing was a resource-based issue, and questions of priority over resources were for Parliament, not the court.

At the same time, there are very close links between the duty of restraint against eviction and the positive duties to provide adequate housing. Many cases arise in the form of a defence against eviction proceedings, where the duty to provide suitable alternative housing is presented as the only way to justify lifting the duty of restraint against eviction. This was the scenario in *Olga Tellis*,[24] where pavement- and slum-dwellers turned to the courts for protection against eviction and demolition of their homes. The Court's failure to insist on the link in subsequent cases arguably led to its betrayal of the basic rights of slum-dwellers, where orders of eviction were not matched by duties to provide alternative housing.[25]

In South Africa, where the desperate housing shortage has led to numerous instances of land invasion and squatting, courts have had to grapple with the painful dilemma of whether to issue eviction orders in the absence of proper

---

[20] Italics added.
[21] South African Constitution, s 25(5).
[22] *Poplar Housing and Regeneration Community Association Ltd v Donoghue* [2001] EWCA Civ 595, [2002] QB 48.
[23] Housing Act 1988, s 21(4).
[24] *Olga Tellis* (n 10 above).
[25] See Chapter 5.

guarantees of adequate alternative housing. The Supreme Court of Appeal demonstrated the need to link the duty of restraint with the positive duty to provide in the *Modderklip* case,[26] in which it had to adjudicate on the conflicting rights of a private landowner and the 40,000 people who had settled on five hectares of its land. The Court held that the State was in breach of its duty to provide adequate housing. Its duty of restraint would also be breached if it carried out an eviction order against the settlers. Although the Constitutional Court made its decision on other grounds, it endorsed the remedy, which was that the residents should be entitled to occupy the land until alternative land was made available.[27] The result was to endorse the need to link the duty of restraint and the duty to provide. Nevertheless, the Constitutional Court has stopped short of holding that there is an unqualified duty to ensure that no home be destroyed unless alternative accommodation or land is made available. Instead, it has held that a Court should be reluctant to grant an eviction order against relatively settled occupiers unless it is satisfied that a reasonable alternative is available.[28]

The duty of restraint is not limited to preventing evictions; it also prevents the State from obstructing access to adequate housing.[29] But what amounts to adequate housing is contentious. In the recent *Rand Properties* case, the local authority defended its decision to evict squatters in derelict buildings, on the grounds that the buildings were unsafe under health and safety regulations. The claimants argued that, although of very poor quality, the derelict buildings were better than living on the pavements. As we have seen, the deliberative solution reached in the case explicitly accepts this view, placing a positive obligation on the State, to make the premises reasonably safe while alternatives are found.[30]

(iv) Participation and deliberative democracy

A key element of positive duties is the extent to which they foster deliberative democracy. The duty to consult is explicit in several provisions creating housing rights, and in other contexts could be said to be implied from basic natural justice principles. However, the duty to consult does not necessarily fulfil the conditions of deliberative democracy. It is all too easy to go through the motions of consulting without genuinely involving others in decision-making. To come closer to a deliberative framework, it is necessary to set up the consultative process with several key elements. First, it needs to impart information so that all involved can make an appropriate input. Secondly, it needs to be set in motion from the

---

[26] *Modderfontein Squatters, Greater Benoni City Council v Modderklip Boerdery* 2004 (6) SA 40 (South African Supreme Court of Appeal).
[27] *President of the Republic of South Africa and Another v Modderklip Boerdery (Pty) Ltd* CCT20/04 (South African Constitutional Court).
[28] *Port Elizabeth* (n 6 above) para 28.
[29] *Jaftha v Schoeman and Others; Van Rooyen v Stoltz and Others* 2005 (2) SA 140 (CC) at para 34.
[30] *Occupiers of 51 Olivia Road v City of Johannesburg, Rand Properties and others* CCT 24/07; see Chapter 4.

start of the decision-making process, and extend throughout to include monitoring of implementation. Thirdly, it should incorporate all those with power to make decisions; and those affected, including, in particular, marginalized groups who would not normally have a voice. While consultation with those affected is increasingly common, all too often it does not include all those who are genuinely able to make decisions or to influence decision-makers. In jurisdictions with multi-level governance structures, this should include all relevant tiers of government. In South Africa, for example, it has proved increasingly difficult to incorporate municipal, provisional, and national government in a meaningful consultative forum. Also crucial is the participation of those involved in delivery. Finally, there must be a genuine openness within the process to the views of participants. This is helpfully highlighted in the International Eviction Guidelines which require the following:

> States should explore fully all possible alternatives to evictions. All potentially affected groups and persons, including women, indigenous peoples and persons with disabilities, as well as others working on behalf of the affected, have the right to relevant information, full consultation and participation throughout the entire process, and to propose alternatives that authorities should duly consider.[31]

The key importance of participation was highlighted in the *Rand Properties* case above. Prior to instituting its eviction application, the City did not approach the occupiers to discuss possible steps to improve health or safety on the property or the question of suitable alternative accommodation for the occupiers. This was upheld by the Supreme Court of Appeal on the grounds of urgency, because of the dire state of the properties. However, this is to ignore the meaning and importance of consultation. It is not simply a gesture towards those involved; it is a central means of achieving deliberative solutions. As the applicants in the *Rand Properties* case deposed, eviction is the most drastic response to health and safety issues. With their full participation and cooperation, different solutions could have been reached which addressed their need for housing without putting them in unnecessary danger. Recognizing this, the Constitutional Court, as was seen in Chapter 4, has attempted to jump start such deliberation, by ordering the parties to enter into discussions and if possible agree a formula for the Court to endorse.[32]

The importance of anchoring participation in a fully deliberative context can be seen in *Olga Tellis*.[33] At one level, the Court's approach could be interpreted as endorsing participatory democracy. The Court declared that the slum-dwellers should not be removed until they had been properly consulted. This went some of the way to recognizing that without the active participation of those affected no solution would be either legitimate or effective. This was allied with a strong

---

[31] International Eviction Guidelines, 20, paras 38–40.
[32] *Rand Properties* (n 30 above).
[33] *Olga Tellis* (n 10 above).

endorsement of the fundamental right to livelihood which consultation should advance. However, none of the basic conditions for proper deliberative democracy were secured by the Court. The inequality of power between slum-dwellers and government was not addressed, and no measures were put in place to ensure that discussions took place in a deliberative rather than a bargaining spirit. Ultimately, then, the result is a flimsy procedural one.

(v) Determining the content

There are many who would argue that even if the duty in respect of housing exists, it is too indeterminate to qualify as a positive human rights duty. However, the fundamental values informing the right make it possible to derive its content. The duty to ensure that an individual can genuinely exercise her freedom, as well as the inherent dignity of the human person, means that housing must be affordable, accessible, habitable, close to sources of income, and culturally adequate. In addition, there should be sustainable access to safe drinking water, energy for cooking, heating and lighting, sanitation and washing facilities, means of food storage, refuse disposal, site drainage, and emergency services.[34] A similar approach to adequate housing is found in both the Indian and the South African Courts, which, in addition to the above elements have stressed the importance of adequate living space, safe and decent structure, civic amenities like roads,[35] and access to land.[36] Both Courts have highlighted the State's duty to construct houses at reasonable cost and make them easily accessible to the poor.[37]

The values of solidarity and equality further point to the need to ensure that housing does not reinforce social exclusion. This has arisen forcefully in Europe in the context of the Roma people and Irish travellers who frequently live in segregated settlements in dire conditions. This was starkly illustrated in a recent case against the government of Greece brought on behalf of over 100,000 Roma. The applicants were living in substandard housing in segregated settlements with inadequate infrastructure and limited or no access to basic amenities (such as water or electricity) or public services. Settlements were often in unsafe or unsanitary locations.[38] The content of the duty was directly deduced from the underlying values. The ESC Committee emphasized that one of the underlying purposes of the Charter is to express solidarity and promote social inclusion. 'It follows that States must respect difference and ensure that

---

[34] CESCR General Comment 4. *The Right to Adequate Housing* (Art. 11(1): 13/12/91).

[35] *Ahmedabad* (n 8 above).

[36] *Grootboom* (n 4 above).

[37] *PG Gupta v State of Gujarat* (1995) Supp 2 SCC 182 (Indian Supreme Court). See also *Shantistar Builders v Narayan Khimalal Totame* (1990) 1 SCC 520 (Indian Supreme Court) where surplus urban-vacant land was directed to be used to provide shelter to the poor. See also *Grootboom* (n 4 above) para 35.

[38] *European Roma Rights Centre v Greece* Complaint No 15/2003 (European Committee of Social Rights).

social arrangements are not such as would effectively lead to or reinforce social exclusion.'[39] The positive duty has also been formulated in the context of the civil and political rights found in the ECHR. The ECtHR has recognized that: 'The vulnerable position of gypsies as a minority means that some special consideration should be given to their needs and their different lifestyle... There is thus a positive obligation imposed on the Contracting States by virtue of Art. 8 to facilitate the gypsy way of life.'[40] For Roma who continue to follow the traditional nomadic lifestyle, the duty to provide adequate housing implies that adequate stopping places be provided.

The South African Court has used a different approach to specifying the duty, relying on the broad concept of reasonableness. In eschewing a set of specific requirements, the Court has been keen to stress the need for flexibility and responsiveness to the immediate context.[41] The criteria for reasonableness established in *Grootboom* are now reproduced in the reports of the Human Rights Commission as a way of assessing compliance with the duty to fulfil the right of access to housing.[42] First, there should be proper coordination between various tiers of government. A comprehensive and workable plan should be drawn up with full participation of both central and local agents to ensure that it is context sensitive and effective. It should allocate responsibilities and tasks and ensure that appropriate human and financial resources are available.[43] As summed up in the *TAC* case, the magnitude of the challenge facing the country 'calls for a concerted, co-ordinated and co-operative national effort in which government in each of its three spheres and the panoply of resources and skills of civil society are marshalled, inspired and led. This can only be achieved if there is proper communication.'[44]

Secondly, there is a strong emphasis on actual implementation. Legislation is not sufficient. The State is obliged to act to achieve the intended result. Thirdly, the programme must be flexible and context specific and be subject to continuous review, so that it can be adjusted to changing circumstances. Fourthly, it must be inclusive and pay appropriate attention to short-, medium-, and long-term needs.[45] But most particularly, it must include a component that responds to the urgent needs of those in desperate situations. In confronting the painful conflict between medium-term and short-term needs, the Court rejects a purely utilitarian approach, declaring that a statistical advance in the realization of the right may not meet the test of reasonableness. 'A society must seek to ensure that the basic necessities of life are provided to all if it is to be a society based on

---

[39] ibid para 19.
[40] *Connors v United Kingdom* (2005) 40 EHRR 9 (European Court of Human Rights) para 84.
[41] *Grootboom* (n 4 above) paras 37, 39, 40.
[42] Report of South African Human Rights Commission 2002–2003, 5.
[43] *Grootboom* (n 4 above) para 39.
[44] *Minister of Health v Treatment Action Campaign (no 2)* (2002) 5 SA 721 (South African Constitutional Court) para 123.
[45] *Grootboom* (n 4 above) para 42–43.

human dignity, freedom and equality.'[46] Progressive realization means that the State parties must move 'as expeditiously and effectively as possible'.[47] Finally, it stresses that both the rate of achievement of the obligation and the reasonableness of the measures employed are governed by the availability of resources.[48]

(vi) Monitoring compliance

The above methods of determining the content of the duty make it possible to devise appropriate means of monitoring it. As with other socio-economic rights, the trend is towards the specification of indicators, which can provide a consistent and internationally comparable set of data to measure the extent to which the relevant duties are being complied with. UN Habitat identifies six dimensions of the right to housing: housing adequacy, security of tenure, scope and scale of homelessness, adherence to international standards, national legislation, and non-discrimination. Each of these is measured according to set indicators. For example, housing adequacy is measured by collecting data on six specific indicators: (i) the number per 1,000 households with potable water; (ii) the number per 1,000 households with sanitation facilities; (iii) the median monthly household housing payment as a proportion of median monthly household income; (iv) the number per 1,000 households with more than two people per room; (v) the number per 1,000 households living in dilapidated or temporary structures; and (vi) whether there is legislation ensuring disabled accessibility to multi-occupancy buildings. Security of tenure, is measured both by examining numbers of secure occupiers (the number per 1,000 of households with legally enforceable protections), and those who have been forcibly evicted, those who are living in informal settlements, and the number of displaced persons. The scale and scope of homelessness is measured according to the number per 1,000 people who have been homeless in the past 12 months. Non-discrimination and equality are simply measured by the existence of non-discrimination legislation, particularly the equal right of men and women to housing. This is a surprising approach, given the widespread recognition that legislation on its own is not sufficient. As was seen in the previous chapter, discrimination can have a range of meanings, from the very limited notion of like treatment, through indirect discrimination to positive duties to promote equality. For the fifth element, national legal protection, the existence of national legislation on the right to housing is one of two indicators, the other being the existence of officers responsible for housing rights. Finally, the acceptance of international obligations is measured by indicators relating to ratification of the ICESCR and the fact of regular reporting. Here

---

[46] ibid para 44.
[47] CESCR General Comment No 3 The nature of States parties obligations (Fifth session 1990) para 9.
[48] *Grootboom* (n 4 above) para 46.

there is no reference to whether there is any actual responsiveness to ICESCR norms or recommendations.

Monitoring the duty to provide adequate housing also requires that attention be paid to disparities in housing between different social groups. This requires data to be disaggregated to capture inequalities with regard to gender, age, income level, race, and ethnicity. Most important is to disaggregate by gender. Women's lack of access to land and property remains widespread and contributes significantly to women's poverty. By monitoring change in respect of women, and incorporating women into the deliberative circle, deep institutional change is more likely to be achieved. In this respect, the traditional approach to gathering data in terms of heads of household will invariably obscure inequalities between women and men in respect of housing.

This means that as well as the primary duty to implement the right to adequate housing, there are important subsidiary duties to monitor progress, to continually review, and to adjust where not effective. The CESCR committee has pointed to the duty to monitor as one of the aspects of the duty of immediate effect. Similarly, in the ESC Roma rights case, the contracting State was rebuked for not having effective data collection.[49] At the same time, data collection raises its own difficulties. Some European countries regard data collection as an infringement of the duty of restraint in respect of personal privacy.[50] In other countries, the effort and resources expended on data collection are thought to consume the resources needed for other purposes.

B. Education

(i) Beyond the divide: human rights values and the right to education

Like housing, duties in respect of education fall on both sides of the divide between civil and political and socio-economic rights, with the concomitant division between negative and positive duties. In its civil and political formulation, the right to education manifests as a restraint on the State from interfering with education, and particularly with parental choice of religious instruction. Thus, the ECHR states: 'No person shall be denied the right to education...the State shall respect the right of parents to ensure such education and teaching in conformity with their own political and religious convictions.'[51] No positive duty has been implied from this provision. The Court in the *Belgian Linguistics* case confirmed that: 'The negative formulation indicates...that the Contracting

---

[49] *Roma Rights* case (n 38 above).
[50] See further T Makonnen *Measure For Measure Data Collection and EU Equality Law* (European Communities, 2007) <http://www.migpolgroup.com/documents/3645.html>.
[51] ECHR First Protocol, Article 2.

Parties do not recognise such a right to education as would require them to establish at their own expense, or to subsidise, education of any particular type or at any particular level.'[52]

Yet the human rights values of positive freedom, democracy, and solidarity show convincingly that positive duties should also be recognized. Positive freedom entails individual agency, freedom to do and be what one values. Education is essential for such individual agency. The right to education has been called a multiplier right, facilitating other rights such as freedom of speech, freedom from child labour, the right to health, and freedom of occupation. 'Education is both a human right in itself and an indispensable means of realising other human rights. As an empowerment right, education is the primary vehicle by which economically and socially marginalized adults and children can lift themselves out of poverty and obtain the means to participate fully in their communities.'[53] In addition, education directly enhances individuals' capabilities to exercise their democratic rights. This is reinforced by the value of solidarity. Positive duties to provide education are not merely to the advantage of the recipient. The community as a whole benefits from an educated population.

(ii) Positive and negative duties: distinctions and relationships

Even if the right to education is limited to its civil and political sense of protecting free choice of education, it is clear that it gives rise to both duties of restraint and positive duties. Protecting freedom of choice of education is meaningless without the ability to access education in the first place. This in turn highlights the important inter-relationships between duties of restraint and positive duties. A State which erects obstacles to accessing education is in breach of the basic duty to refrain from interfering with peoples' right to education. Even the *Belgian Linguistics* case recognized that obstructing access to existing provision would constitute a breach of the duty of restraint. A closer analysis of the interaction between different types of duty also illuminates the relationship between responsibility on the State and responsibilities on others, such as parents. Placing responsibility on parents is a ready pretext for a State abdicating its own duties to provide education. While reciprocal responsibilities are part of the concept of active citizenship, this should not permit a transfer of the State's duties onto parents. At most, reciprocal responsibilities on parents should consist of duties outside of the State's reach, such as ensuring that learners attend school, or do their homework.

The above analysis enables us to resolve the highly contentious issue of whether education should be free to all. Even the duty of restraint prevents the State from

---

[52] *Belgian Linguistic Case (No 2)* (1968) 1 EHRR 252 (European Court of Human Rights) 281.
[53] United Nations Economic and Social Council, The right to education (Art.13), 08/12/99, E/C.12/1999/10 (General Comments) 1.

creating obstacles to access to education. Fees and charges constitute such an obstacle; so does discrimination. A State which denies access to those who are unable to pay would be in breach of this duty. Free education is particularly important for girls. Since their labour is needed at home, families in many countries regard it as economically problematic to send their daughters to school.[54] However, this does not in itself argue for universally free education. Would the State be fulfilling its positive duties if it provided exemptions from school fees for those who were unable to pay? Although universal free education is provided for by most international documents,[55] the South African Constitution gives everyone the right to a basic education but does not specify that it should be free.[56] Legislation therefore permits fees to be charged but provides exemptions for those who cannot afford them.[57] This is defended on the grounds that, first, if parents are responsible for paying fees, they will take more responsibility for their children's education. It is difficult to discover any concrete evidence for this view. Secondly, it is argued that by charging fees to wealthier parents, the government is able to cross-subsidize poorer learners. However, a fairer and more efficient approach would be to use general taxation, where the poorest, who do not earn enough to be liable for taxation, are exempt. In any event, individual exemptions are costly to administer.[58]

The exemption policy cannot therefore be defended in terms of effectiveness. Nor can it be defended on principle. This is because, despite appearing as a benefit to the poorest in society, exemptions in effect discriminate against them. Although, in South Africa, it is unlawful to exclude learners because of parental inability to pay fees,[59] and although schools are required to grant full or partial exemptions for learners whose families fall within the prescribed means test,[60] the State does not provide corresponding subsidy for the resulting absence of fee revenue. The rational response of any individual school is to attempt to maintain its fee income by minimizing its intake of exempt children. Schools across the country have taken this path. They have done so in various ways: by concealing from learners their right to claim exemptions; by charging registration fees which poor learners are unable to afford; by insisting on birth certificates, in the

---

[54] K Tomaševski *Preliminary Report of the Special Rapporteur on the Right to Education* (Human Rights Commission 1999) para 60.

[55] Universal Declaration of Human Rights, Article 26 (free and compulsory education in the elementary fundamental stages); ICESCR, Article 13 (free and compulsory primary education); Convention on the Rights of the Child, Article 28 (free and compulsory primary education); African Charter on the Rights and Welfare of the Child, Article 11 (free and compulsory basic education).

[56] South African Constitution, s 29(1). See F Veriava and S Wilson 'A Critique of the Proposed Amendments on School Funding and School Fees' (2005) 6(3) ESR Review 9.

[57] South African Schools Act No 84 of 1996 as amended.

[58] Tomaševski (n 54 above) para 35.

[59] South African Schools Act No 84 of 1994, s 5.

[60] Exemption of Parents from the Payment of School Fees Regulations Government Notice 1293 (Government Gazette 19347) October 1998.

full knowledge that children from informal settlements will not have one, and even by suing parents in court for defaults in fees. Even if a child succeeds in gaining an exemption, or the parents can scrape together sufficient money to pay the fees, there remain transport costs, school uniforms, and books. In addition, the quality of the school reflects the fee-paying ability of its pupil body, so that schools serving poorer communities are inevitably providing a lower quality of education.

More recently, an amended framework was put in place whereby schools which service very poor communities can be declared 'fee free'.[61] But this brings its own problems of classification, since schools in middle class areas frequently serve children from severely deprived neighbouring areas, such as informal settlements. In addition, the decision as to whether schools are fee free depends on individual provinces' ability to provide adequate funding. Although the national government has granted more financial support, it remains up to the provincial government to allocate adequate subsidies. Thus selective exemptions from fees will inevitably breach both the duty not to obstruct access to education and the duty to discriminate.

(iii) Positive duties and distributive consequences

This is not to deny the difficult distributive consequences arising from the imperative to provide universal free education. A State with a shortage of resources might have to reduce standards in order to make some education available to everyone. Similarly, funds to primary education may compete with funding for secondary and tertiary education. It is this which leads many to argue that school funding is a distributive decision, for the government of the day, rather than a positive human rights duty. The costs to governments of providing education have also been subject to the chill winds of the globalization era. During the 1980s, education was seen as an unaffordable luxury, and although some effort was made in the 1990s, there was still a faction within the World Bank which encouraged the use of school fees to decrease fiscal deficits.[62]

The analysis in earlier chapters suggests some responses to this. Even more so than other positive duties, investment in education is an investment in society. Educated individuals are able to contribute both to their own and to the community advancement. This means that expenditure on education should be viewed as a social investment, or a productive factor, rather than merely a question of redistributive justice. This argument arises from the republican

---

[61] Education Laws Amendment Act 2005; Veriava and Wilson (n 56 above).
[62] Tomaševski (n 54 above) para 20, 80; Economic and Social Council *Annual Report of the Special Rapporteur on the Right to Education, Katarina Tomaševski* E/CN.4/2001/52 (11 January 2001) para 35.

emphasis on solidarity and active citizenship, rather than a narrow utilitarian view of the functional nature of education. It is not simply a question of calculating the net contribution of education to economic advancement, with the result that education could be trumped by market forces. Instead, it is a recognition that the welfare of society as a whole is enhanced by investment in education, whether in facilitating self-sufficiency on the part of its members, or in ensuring that they have access to other dependent rights, or in augmenting democracy. This means that the right to education cannot be trumped by narrow economic concerns, but should have first demand on budgetary allocations.

At the same time, a functional analysis assists in the argument against pressures from globalized free trade. An educated population is an asset in attracting inward investment and stimulating a competitive economy. This is recognized in the EU, which sees education as one of the key elements in its goal of becoming 'the most competitive and dynamic knowledge-based economy in the world capable of sustainable economic growth with more and better jobs and greater social cohesion'.[63] In a 2003 report on the strategy for creating jobs, it was concluded that: 'The productivity of enterprises, and the overall competitiveness of our economy, is directly dependent on building and maintaining a well-educated, skilled and adaptable workforce.'[64]

This analysis, which makes it mandatory for budgetary allocations to be based on human rights, rather than human rights being conditional on budgets, is powerfully endorsed by recent groundbreaking case law in the New York courts. The litigation has been based on the New York State Constitution, which states: 'The legislature shall provide for the maintenance and support of a system of free common schools, wherein all the children of this state may be educated.'[65] In a case brought by the Campaign for Fiscal Equity in the early 1990s, the applicants argued that New York State was failing in its constitutional obligation to provide a sound basic education to thousands of its schoolchildren. In a series of decisions, the New York Court upheld the claim. Noting that 'the political process allocates to City schools a share of State aid that does not bear a perceptible relation to the needs of City students', the Court directed the State to ensure, by means of '[r]eforms to the current system of financing school funding and managing schools... that every school in New York City would have the resources necessary for providing the opportunity for a sound basic education'.[66] This culminated in a landmark decision in March 2006, in which the Appellate Division of New York State held that 'the State, in enacting a budget for the fiscal year commencing

---

[63] Lisbon Accord 2000.

[64] W De Kok *Jobs, Jobs, Jobs: Creating More Employment in Europe (Report of the Employment Taskforce)* (European Commission, 2003) 8 <http://ec.europa.eu/employment_social/employment_strategy/pdf/etf_en.pdf>.

[65] New York State Constitution, Article XI, S 1.

[66] *Campaign for Fiscal Equity v State of New York* 100 NY2d at 930.

April 1, 2006, must appropriate the constitutionally required funding for the New York City schools'.[67]

Also considered as an obstacle to positive duties is the difficulty in giving content to a right to education. Possibly more than any other socio-economic right, education can be provided according to a range of different models, with differing emphases on syllabus, teacher–learner ratio, distance of school from home, teacher training, urban–rural balance, and mother tongue instruction. Nevertheless, as the analysis in Chapter 3 demonstrates, there is no need for a single fixed answer to these questions. Instead, the relevant prima facie principles need to be identified. These have helpfully been identified by the former UN Special Rapporteur for Education, Katarina Tomaševski, in terms of a 4-A scheme for primary schools: availability of infrastructure and teachers, accessibility for all in a non-discriminatory manner, acceptability in terms of culture, language, and religion, and adaptability to changing circumstances.[68] Similarly, the New York Court derived the content of the duty directly from the underlying value which it attached to education, namely the ability to undertake civil responsibilities meaningfully. This allowed the Court of Appeals to set the standards for a 'sound basic education', as required by the State Constitution, as consisting of 'the basic literacy, calculating, and verbal skills necessary to enable children to eventually function productively as civic participants capable of voting and serving on a jury'. The duty on the State therefore required 'minimally adequate' physical facilities, and teaching by adequately trained teachers.[69] New York City public schools had breached this duty.[70]

(iv) Equality and education

The focus on duties also assists in understanding the interaction between the equality principle and the right to education. The role of equality is particularly central in Europe and the US, where there is already well-established provision; but there are wide disparities reflecting patterns of segregation by race, ethnicity, or socio-economic status. In Europe, these disparities are most acutely experienced by Roma people.[71] Disproportionate numbers of Roma children in many Eastern European countries are placed in remedial 'special' schools for mentally disabled children, having been subjected to psychological testing premised on proficiency in the majority language or culture. Residential segregation also leads

---

[67] *Campaign for Fiscal Equity Inc v State of New York* 2006 NYSlipOp 02284 (Appellate Division, First Department).

[68] Tomaševski (n 54 above) paras 51–74.

[69] *Campaign for Fiscal Equity v State of New York,* 86 NY2d 307, 316, 317 [1995] (New York State Court of Appeals);100 NY2d at 908.

[70] 100 NY2d at 909–912.

[71] See generally, Farkas L *Segregation of Roma Children in Education: Addressing Structural Discrimination through the Race Equality Directive* (EU Commission 2007).

to a high concentration of Roma in poorer schools. In Western European countries, schooling does not accommodate travelling communities. The result is a high level of absenteeism, early drop out, and underachievement. This has led the European Monitoring Centre on Racism and Xenophobia to conclude that 'in many EU Member States, the Roma/Sinti/Gypsies/Travellers group constitutes the most vulnerable group in education'.[72]

The role of equality in respect of a positive right to education was tested in a major case against the Czech Republic, brought on behalf of children who had been placed in special schools after psychological testing. Figures produced by the applicants showed that a vastly disproportionate number of Roma children were assigned to special schools. These provided substantially inferior education to that in ordinary primary schools, and had long-term consequences such as the denial of access to secondary education other than vocational training. The applicants claimed that results were distorted because the tests were adapted to the Czech language and cultural environment. The Government claimed that the tests simply reflected the lower intellectual attainment of the children, and that in any event, the parents had consented to their children being placed in special schools. The Chamber of the European Court of Human Rights refused to consider the broader social situation, insisting instead on concentrating on the position of the 18 actual applicants before them. It rejected the claim largely on the basis that parental consent had been given both to the testing and to the transfer to special schools.[73]

However, the Court's assumption that the role of human rights is to protect freedom of choice obstructed its ability to pay proper attention to the conditions which are necessary before choice can be genuinely considered to be free. The context in which choices were made in this case makes it clear that it was at best a case of adaptive preferences, where limited possibilities, lack of information, and most importantly a sense of disempowerment led parents to follow options which were not optimal for themselves or their children. This was recognized by the Grand Chamber, which reversed the decision. In a ground-breaking decision in November 2007, the Court acknowledged that the principle of indirect discrimination applied to Article 14 of the Convention. Importing the concept from the EU, the Court set out several key principles in determining whether indirect discrimination had occurred. First, there is no need to prove intention to discriminate. Instead, it is sufficient to show that a policy or measure, although couched in neutral terms, has had a disproportionately prejudicial effect on the claimants' group. Secondly, once a prima facie case of indirect discrimination has been established, the burden of proof shifts to the State to justify the difference. Thirdly, statistics could be relied on in order to establish a prima facie

---

[72] European Monitoring Centre on Racism and Xenophobia, Annual Report 2005, Part II (EUMC I) 68.
[73] *Case of DH and Others v The Czech Republic* (Application no 57325/00) para 10–11 and 49–51 respectively.

case, although this was not mandatory. Finally, the State could only justify such
a disparity if it could show that the aim was objectively and reasonably justified
and that there existed a reasonable relationship of proportionality between the
means used and the aim pursued. All these elements were established in the case.
In particular, the Court held that parental consent could not be considered to be
a waiver of the right not to be discriminated against, because parents were not
fully informed of the range of alternatives. Equally importantly, the Court was
prepared to accept that the applicants as members of that community necessarily
suffered the same discriminatory treatment and therefore that there was no need
to examine their individual cases.[74]

This can be contrasted with the failure by the US Supreme Court to accept
that differential educational provision could breach the basic right to equality. As we saw in the previous chapter, the US Supreme Court in *San Antonio*
refused to hold that the Fourteenth Amendment was breached when children
in a low income neighbourhood received a lower standard of education than
their better-off neighbours.[75] In regarding this as an instance of a positive
duty of provision, which was for the political process rather than a question
of human rights, the Court failed to take into account that the disparity was a
direct result of action by the State in setting up a funding regime which based
school funding on local rates.

(v) Justiciability and compliance

This leaves the question of justiciability and other compliance methods to be
addressed. To what extent can the analysis in Section B be used to critically assess
judicial approaches to positive duties to provide education, and to point towards
improvement? The New York litigation is instructive in this regard. Particularly
striking is the extent to which the New York Courts were prepared to deal with
distributive questions, holding that the State had failed in its duty to provide
sound basic education because of its unsatisfactory budgetary allocation to
education.[76] This was directly facilitated by its deliberative approach to remedies.
During the first round of appeals, the Court of Appeal stressed that the courts
'have neither the authority, nor the ability, nor the will, to micromanage education financing'.[77] Nevertheless, it directed the State to ascertain the actual cost of
providing a sound basic education, to reform the current system of school funding and management, and to furnish every school in the City with the resources
necessary for providing the opportunity for a sound basic education. This

---

[74] *Case of DH and Others v The Czech Republic* (Application no. 57325/00) Grand Chamber,
13 November 2007.
[75] *San Antonio Independent School District v Rodriguez* 411 US 959, 93 SCt 1919 (US
Supreme Court).
[76] Contrast *Board of Educ, Levittown Union Free School Dist v Nyquist* 57 NY2d 27, 49 n 9
[1982], appeal dismissed 459 US 1139 [1983].
[77] *Campaign for Fiscal Equity v State of New York* 100 NY2d 893, 906, 908 [2003] [*CFE II*]) at 925.

included a crucial element of review: the State was required to 'ensure a system of accountability to measure whether the reforms actually provide the opportunity for a sound basic education'.[78] The State was given a deadline of 30 July 2004 by which to implement the necessary measures—a process which the lower court was given jurisdiction to supervise.[79]

When the deadline passed without the order being implemented, the Court was faced with a greater challenge. The trial judge, adopting a model closer to that of the Indian Supreme Court, appointed a panel of referees to recommend a model for determining how much was needed per learner to ensure an adequate education. This, however, was regarded by the Supreme Court of Appeals as stepping beyond the mandate of the Court. It was for the State to ascertain the cost of a sound basic education. The Court's role was to decide whether the State's estimate was reasonable; and whether the State had produced a plan which provided for sound basic education expenditure and which ensured a system of accountability.[80] It was this which the Appellate Court proceeded to do. Having held that this standard was met it went on to declare this to be the constitutionally required funding for the New York City School District. Of importance too is the fact that, in the shadow of the litigation, the budget for capital spending on schools was in fact uprated in line with the earlier courts' decisions, so that by the time the case came to final appeal, the parties were all agreed that there was no further necessity for a court order. The final point of interest is the rejection, by the highest New York court, of the trial court's attempt to keep the deliberative process of review going by requiring the Supreme Court to call for state costing-out studies every four years and its requirement that the New York City Department of Education prepare a comprehensive 'sound basic education' plan, to ensure accountability. Instead the Court saw this as a costly layer of city bureaucracy and not constitutionally required. The 'minimally adequate accountability mechanisms' for the evaluation of New York schools were seen as sufficient.

By contrast with the head-on challenge of State funding in New York, South African litigation has concentrated on the failure of schools to ensure that eligible learners were provided with appropriate exemptions. A test case class action was brought against a school in Durban, for failing to inform learners and their parents of their rights to claim fee exemptions and of how to apply.[81] Although not situated in an area of extreme poverty, the school attracted a significant number of learners from nearby informal settlements who would in principle qualify for exemption. The case was settled in June 2007, with a consent order requiring the school to inform all parents of their rights in respect of school fee exemptions;

[78] ibid at 930.
[79] *Campaign for Fiscal Equity* (n 77 above) at 932.
[80] *Campaign for Fiscal Equity Inc v State of New York* (2006 NYSlipOp 08630) 11.
[81] *Centre For Applied Legal Studies v Hunt Road Secondary School Case* No:10091/2006.

including their rights of appeal if refused. The school was also required to properly process all applications.

Targeting the school, however, demonstrates some of the problems which can arise when a polycentric problem is dealt with as if it were a dispute between two parties to be settled by adversarial court proceedings. In particular, the court could not order the State to provide subsidies to recompense schools for providing fee exemptions. Since there was no way to make up for the resulting shortfall in fees, the consequences for the school of providing all eligible fee exemptions, was potentially devastating. Although the province and central governments were joined, they simply agreed to abide by the decision or the settlement, rather than coming to court to justify their actions. The judge could do no more than express his concern that the national and provincial governments were not represented and his dissatisfaction that the school was not properly funded.

The limited success in the case itself should not, however, be seen as the end of the matter. The case was used as part of a broader public awareness campaign which led to large numbers of learners claiming exemption. This in turn created political pressure on the government to reconsider the question of subsidies for schools with large numbers of exempted learners. Following the legal action, the Department of Education declared that it was working out how to compensate schools for fee exemptions.[82] In addition, public interest litigants have been part of a broader process of reform of the school fees policy, which led to the further legislation, mentioned above, declaring the lowest quintile of schools 'fee free'. It is notable that the Minister of Education went so far as to commit herself to the goal of universal free education, stating that the aim of the new statutory framework is to 'breach the barrier [to education for many children] and set us on the road to free and compulsory education'.[83] The problems raised by the new scheme for schools in relatively well-off areas who draw pupils from nearby informal settlements are now being addressed by further test case litigation.

What should the appropriate role of the court be in a synergistic approach? As seen in the New York case, the court should not be expected to give a fixed solution to the complex issues that arise. There is no reason to believe that a court is better at problem-solving than the other participants in the decision-making process. However, the court is uniquely capable of insisting on a deliberative response. This entails, first, requiring the State to come to the process with the aim of giving a convincing and evidence based justification of its chosen formula. This enhances the accountability of the State as well as facilitating full deliberative debate, both within the court and in the broader political process. In the South African instance, the State would be required to justify the assertion that parents take more responsibility for schooling if they have to

[82] D MacFarlane 'Government to Act on School Fees' *Mail* and *Guardian* 30 July 2007.
[83] Plenary Speech by the Minister of Education, Naledi Pandor, MP, Education Laws Amendment Bill debate, National Council of Provinces 16 November 2005.

pay fees especially in the light of models in other countries which give universal free education in the State system without an apparent loss of parental commitment. Similarly, it should be able to defend the model based on charging fees in order to cross-subsidize poorer schools in the light of competing models, such as free education for all combined with progressive taxation of better-off individuals.

As well as accountability, the Court can trigger deliberation by requiring the State to enter into deliberative debate with other stakeholders on the basis that all parties are genuinely open to the perspectives, information, and arguments of others. The State's solution, instead of being imposed, will therefore be able to be absorbed into the systems it is addressing. The problems raised by the exemption regime are a good example. A command by the State to schools to provide exemptions will lead to avoidance behaviours in the absence of proper alternative funding, since this is a rational response from the perspective of any individual school. Widespread breach of the law is therefore not unexpected. As the judge in the Hunt Road case intimated, an opportunity was lost for the State to come to the situation open to doing more than enforcing an exemptions policy which had perverse effects. Thirdly, then, the Court should require the establishment of deliberative and problem-solving structures within schools, together with a potentially coordinating role for the municipal or provincial authorities. Its own role would be to set timetables and judge reasonableness.

The emphasis so far has been on the potential role of the court. Consideration also needs to be given to mechanisms outside of the court. Sabel describes new compliance mechanisms, based on local problem-solving, which have been designed as a constructive alternative to the unrewarding struggle for educational desegregation and equality which was fought through the courts for many years.[84] The broad goals to which the duty is aimed are set out in a federal statute known as the No Child Left Behind Act. This does not in itself prescribe standards of education, but instead leaves it to States to do so by setting 'challenging' academic content and achievement standards for local schoolchildren. The goal is for all students to meet the State standard of adequacy within 12 years. Monitoring implementation and accountability is required through reporting obligations and using the results of tests and indicators to review the progress of schools. Technical assistance should be provided to schools which have persistently failed to meet the annual goals, and awards are provided to those who succeed in closing educational gaps. Schools that fail to meet their obligations must present a plan for doing so, and parents and staff must actively participate in the planning process. There are undoubtedly problematic issues in the implementation and design of this scheme, but to the extent that it builds on the model of

[84] J Liebman and C Sabel 'A Public Laboratory Dewey Barely Imagined: The Emerging Model of School Governance and Legal Reform' (2002–03) 23 NYU Journal of Law and Social Change 183–304.

deliberative local problem-solving, it has the potential to address some of the difficulties in securing an adequate standard of educational provision for all learners.

Also of importance is the role of Human Rights Commissions. Education is perhaps a paradigm example of the possibilities of a Commission instituting a process similar to the Open Method of Coordination, whereby participants at all levels of governance are encouraged to enter into discussion with the Commission and each other in order to appraise their own functioning, discover alternative possibilities, and, most important in this context, air common problems of coordination in order to search for an ever-improving set of solutions. The South African Human Rights Commission conducted a public hearing in 2005 on the right to basic education, thus constituting a potential deliberative forum along the lines described above.[85] The Commission in its report stresses that a public hearing is not a court of law, but a platform for dialogue. The public hearing concluded that the lived daily reality for many children in South Africa was incongruous with the State's legislation and policies. Township, poor, and rural schools were marginalized and the most disadvantaged children lacked the social power to claim their rights. The Commission recommended that the right to primary education should be free; that poor learners should receive State transport assistance; and that reliable monitoring systems be established.

While these findings were relatively hard-hitting, the public hearing did not have the capacity to promote directly deliberative coordinated approaches. Few government departments or local authorities participated in the process and only a handful gave oral evidence. Nor was there a sense of a dynamic ongoing interaction between the participants to achieve mutual learning and peer review. At most, the results could be fed into the political process; but without activism in the political field, this may have no impact.

C. Welfare Rights

(i) Human rights values and the right to welfare

The status of welfare in human rights discourse remains highly contested. Few acknowledge welfare as a fundamental human right but most accept that the State has a basic responsibility to provide the existential minimum. The shape and form of welfare is itself subject to strongly divergent approaches. However, seen through the prism of positive duties, the question of whether there is a right to welfare is transformed. Instead of balancing precariously on the margins of human rights discourse, it should be integral to human rights frameworks. This is a direct consequence both of the positive conception of freedom and the

---

[85] South African Human Rights Commission 'Report of the Public Hearing on the Right to Basic Education' 2006.

substantive conception of equality. Without an existential minimum, freedom and equality become liberal gestures without substance. These values, together with that of solidarity, also generate principles to shape the duty.

The status of welfare in human rights is directly related to the underlying meaning attributed to freedom, choice, and responsibility. Nineteenth-century notions of individual responsibility characterized poverty and destitution as the fault of the individual, and liberal ideas of a non-interventionist State saw the State's role as confined to law and order issues. A good example are nineteenth-century Poor Laws in Britain, which attributed unemployment and poverty to individual idleness,[86] placing responsibility squarely on the shoulders of the individual. State maintenance was punitive and disciplinarian, requiring destitute able-bodied persons to enter the workhouse and be put to work as a condition of relief. It was not until the end of the nineteenth century that unemployment came to be seen as a social and economic problem. This opened the way to acceptance that the State should be under positive duties to contribute to individual welfare. In his seminal work, TH Marshall[87] recognized that under formal juridical equality, the market undermines individuals' ability to exercise their civic rights to the full. Thus, rights should extend beyond the civil and political, to the granting of social rights. This necessarily enlists the positive contribution of the State, to ensure that citizens enjoy 'the whole range from a modicum of economic welfare and security to the right to share to the full the social heritage and to live the life of a civilised being according to the prevailing standards'.[88] Thus, social democracy recasts the State's role to include a positive responsibility to intervene to promote individual welfare.

However, in its attempt to counter the liberal view of the individual as responsible for her own misfortune, the social democratic tradition tends to place the responsibility wholly on the State. This is problematic in several respects. First, it casts the individual in the role of passive beneficiary, rather than an active citizen. This assumes that the definition of need is technical, rather than one which requires democratic discussion.[89] Secondly, its emphasis on transfers of wealth gives the impression that improving the position of the poor can only be achieved at a cost to the wealthy. The implication is that welfare is an indulgence rather than a right. Thirdly, its primary concern is with redistributing material resources or income, rather than addressing the social structures and institutional contexts which underlie these distributive outcomes.[90] Finally, placing the

---

[86] Royal Commission Report in 1834, S Webb and B Webb *English Poor Law Policy* (Longmans 1910) 277.

[87] TH Marshall 'Citizenship and Social Class' in TH Marshall and T Bottomore (eds) *Citizenship and Social Class* (Pluto 1992).

[88] ibid 7.

[89] P Jones 'Universal Principles and Particular Claims: From Welfare Rights to Welfare States' in A Ware and R Goodin (eds) *Needs and Welfare* (Sage London 1990); A Sen *Development as Freedom* (OUP Oxford 1999) 78–81.

[90] IM Young *Justice and the Politics of Difference* (Princeton Paperbacks Princeton 1990) 22.

full responsibility on the State makes it difficult to address broader questions of the role of community and the responsibility of individuals to each other.

Reaction to the idea of the State as wholly responsible for welfare provision for the poor or needy has flowed in two different directions. The first is a throwback to nineteenth-century conceptions of individual and State responsibility. Although there is now a greater acknowledgement of the structural causes of unemployment, there is still ready resort to the notion that welfare beneficiaries are idle scroungers. Individuals should provide for themselves by pursuing their self-interest in the free market, and those who do not succeed are seen as a burden on those who do. Thus, asserts Mead, 'people regard the non-working poor, not just as free riders, but as parasites, even betrayers of their society'.[91] Wax reports a widespread resurgence in the US of the distinction between the deserving and undeserving poor. This 'finds expression in the popular view that the able-bodied should work and that public assistance should be available only to those who are unable to support themselves'.[92] Far from advancing equality, unconditional assistance to the poor is considered as special treatment.[93] On this view, the Welfare State quickly becomes a 'nanny' State, which, far from facilitating freedom, stifles initiative and individual autonomy.

The alternative to the neo-liberal reversion has been to attempt to strike out in a new direction, a 'Third Way', which seeks to produce a new pattern of rights and responsibilities within the Welfare State.[94] The Third Way follows social democracy in acknowledging that real freedom of choice requires active State intervention. On the other hand, it resists the social democratic tendency to place total responsibility on the State. Instead, the architects of the Third Way argue for a 'facilitative' or 'enabling' State.[95] 'The Welfare State is not a safety net but a springboard', declares Gordon Brown.[96] This means that the role of the State is not based on redistribution of material goods to passive recipients, but on a politics of 'empowerment'.[97] Thus, Supiot has argued that the function of welfare should be to give individuals the resources to equip themselves with 'active security to cope with risks',[98] giving real freedom, backed by the means to make it effective, to take full part in social and economic life.

[91] L Mead 'Welfare Reform and Citizenship' in L Mead and C Beem (eds) *Welfare Reform and Political Theory* (Russell Sage Foundation New York 2005) 187.
[92] A Wax 'The Political Psychology of Redistribution: Implications for Welfare Reform' in Mead and Beem (n 91 above) 200 at 201.
[93] ibid 216.
[94] T Blair *The Courage of Our Convictions* (Fabian Society London 2002); A Giddens *The Third Way and Its Critics* (Polity Press London 2000); S White 'The Ambiguities of the Third Way' in S White (ed) *New Labour: The Progressive Future?* (Palgrave New York 2001).
[95] S Fredman 'The Ideology of New Labour Law' in C Barnard, S Deakin, and G Morris (eds) *Essays in Honour of Bob Hepple* (Hart Oxford 2004).
[96] G Brown in D Miliband (ed) *Reinventing the Left* (Polity Press London 1994) 114.
[97] D Held 'Inequalities of Power, Problems of Democracy' in D Miliband (ed) *Reinventing the Left* (Polity Press London 1994) 47.
[98] A Supiot *Beyond Employment* (OUP Oxford 2001) 197–198.

The Third Way directly challenges the neo-liberal assumption that positive duties on the State impose an unfair burden on productive members of society. Instead: 'Well targeted social protection is essential for adapting the economy to change and providing for an efficient and well-trained labour force.'[99] But just as importantly, 'raising the employment rate will underpin the sustainability of the financing of social protection systems'.[100] Gender equality is specifically promoted as pursuing these dual aims: 'Tapping the potential of female participation is both an issue of gender equality and a matter of economic effectiveness.'[101]

The Third Way goes some way towards realizing the ideals of positive freedom, solidarity, and equality at the basis of positive human rights. However, there are dangerous ambiguities in the approach, taking some Third Way thinkers perilously close to a neo-liberal vision of rights and responsibilities. This can be seen from the current and highly contentious debate about 'welfare-to-work', or policies which make eligibility for benefits conditional on the acceptance of paid work or vocational training in some form. Welfare to work policies have generally been part of a neo-liberal policy approach. Captured in the popular slogan, 'no rights without responsibilities', this approach calls for a return to the Victorian sense of individual responsibility. As one of its foremost proponents Laurence Mead puts it, the use of conditionality is 'an effort to return to the earlier view—to hold the dependent once again responsible for at least some behaviours, especially employment'.[102] Thus, instead of giving aid on the basis of 'impersonal economic criteria such as income', it was argued, it should be 'conditioned in some way on good behaviour'.[103] Good behaviour is primarily defined as undertaking paid work, but US legislation also expressly encourages States to promote marriage as a solution to welfare and poverty.[104]

Perhaps the most strident example of conditionality is the 1996 US legislation, aptly entitled the Personal Responsibility and Work Opportunity Reconciliation Act of 1996. Welfare in the US has traditionally been limited to families with dependent children, and its beneficiaries were predominantly single mothers and their children. Welfare reform is deliberately aimed to move 'welfare mothers' off welfare and into work by setting stringent work requirements as a condition of welfare. Families are limited to five years on welfare rolls, counted cumulatively over various spells on or off welfare, and paid work in exchange for benefits is required after two years of income support. The focus of welfare correspondingly shifted to the provision of in-work tax benefits in the form of wage subsidies, a

---

[99] Commission of the European Communities *Social Policy Agenda* COM (2000) 379 final (henceforth *Social Policy Agenda*) para 1.2; and see 'Mid term Review' para 3.3.

[100] *Social Policy Agenda* para 1.2.

[101] Draft Joint Employment Report 2003/2004 (2004) 18.

[102] L Mead 'Summary of Welfare Reform' in L Mead and C Beem (eds) *Welfare Reform and Political Theory* (Russell Sage Foundation New York 2005) 13.

[103] ibid 12.

[104] L Mead 'Welfare Reform and Citizenship' in Mead and Beem (n 102 above) 173.

slightly higher minimum wage, and a small expansion in childcare and health coverage. Individual States can design their own welfare schemes, subject to loose federal rules. Wisconsin, for example, confined almost all cash aid to parents who were employed.[105]

Advocacy of 'no rights without responsibility' has not only come from neo-liberal quarters. It has also been central to the attempt by 'Third Way' British and EU policy-makers to strike out in a new direction. 'No rights without responsibilities,' argues Giddens, is 'a prime motto for the new politics.'[106] 'People should not only take from the wider community,' he continues, 'but give back to it too.' Resonating with civic republican notions of civic virtue, Gordon Brown declares that the true role of government is to 'foster personal responsibility, not substitute for it'.[107] Aimed at countering right-wing accusations that the Welfare State is no more than a nanny State, generating dependency, the Third Way stresses that individuals should take primary responsibility for themselves and their children. While the State should provide the basic opportunities for all, it is up to individuals to make the best use of these. Policies should therefore harness self-interest for the public good.[108] According to the leading blueprint on the Welfare State, issued soon after New Labour came to power in the UK: 'It is the government's responsibility to promote work opportunities and to help people take advantage of them. It is the responsibility of those who can take them up to do so.'[109] With this come certain penalties: benefits can be withdrawn if people do not take up job opportunities.[110]

It is here that the problematic ambiguity in Third Way ideology needs to be uncovered. At its best, the focus on the facilitative State, equality of opportunity and community bonds chimes with the positive momentum towards active citizenship. But it can easily slip into neo-liberal notions of individual responsibility for their own destitution. Thus, Giddens focusses primarily on the duty of the individual recipient to reciprocate. Far preferable is the approach of Vandenbroucke, who insists that individual responsibility should not consist only of the 'easy rhetoric about the moral responsibilities of the poor and powerless'.[111] Instead, the web of interlocking responsibilities[112] includes the rich and

---

[105] L Mead 'Summary of Welfare Reform' in Mead and Beem (n 102 above) 15–19; D King 'Making People Work' in Mead and Beem (n 102 above) 66, 67.

[106] A Giddens *The Third Way and Its Critics* (Polity Press London 2000) 65.

[107] Brown (n 96 above) 114.

[108] See, for example, F Field *Stakeholder Welfare* (Institute for Economic Affairs London 1997); C Oppenheim 'Enabling Participation? New Labour's Welfare to Work Policies' in S White (ed) *New Labour: The Progressive Future?* (Palgrave Great Britain and New York 2001) 78.

[109] Green Paper *New Ambitions for Our Country: A New Contract for Welfare* (Cm 3805 1998) 24, 31.

[110] *Preventing Social Exclusion* the 2001 report of the Social Exclusion Unit (Cabinet Office London 2001) 8.

[111] F Vandenbroucke 'European Social Democracy and the Third Way' in S White (ed) *New Labour: The Progressive Future?* (Palgrave Great Britain and New York 2001) 170–171.

[112] ibid.

the powerful, as well as the State, to intervene where the market is not a true reflection of personal responsibility and effort.

It is from this last direction that a theory of positive duties to provide welfare must proceed. The understanding of positive freedom elaborated here makes it clear that the State has a positive duty to ensure that individuals can exercise their freedoms and rights. At the same time, this responsibility need not be conceived of wholly in terms of the unidirectional provision of a package of benefits, or a transfer of wealth from rich to poor. The analysis thus far demonstrates that positive duties are richer and more complex. Instead, the State's role is to facilitate and empower individuals; and, correspondingly, the rights bearer is characterized as an active agent instead of a passive recipient. This means that positive duties include both direct provision and the facilitation of conditions which make it possible for people to provide for themselves through paid work without exploitation and under decent terms and conditions.

However, the duty on the State to facilitate agency through paid work should not be confused with a duty on the individual to undertake paid work, as advocates of welfare to work would have it. It is here that the distinction between different kinds of duties is important. The positive duty on the State to facilitate agency coexists with a duty of restraint on the State, preventing it from interfering in individuals' choices. Opening up genuine possibilities for paid work would fulfil the positive duty; but forcing an individual to take up those opportunities under threat of the loss of welfare is a breach of the State's duty of restraint. This demonstrates the clear conceptual difference between active labour market measures, which are at the basis of the new European social model, and the duty to work in conditionality schemes. Active labour market measures function, not as an obligation on the citizen, but as an obligation on the State to provide the means of empowerment. The rejection of conditionality does not imply individuals have no responsibilities to themselves or the community; only that it cannot be acceptable to enforce those responsibilities by the sanction of withdrawing the basic means of existence.

There are also strong arguments against welfare to work from the value of substantive equality. Those who have enough means (through inheritance or otherwise) to live without undertaking paid work may share in the fruits of social cooperation without paying the same dues.[113] In addition, by privileging paid work, welfare to work devalues all the other activities that individuals should be valued for, most prominently caring work. The US statute, in requiring single mothers to undertake paid work as a condition of welfare, leaves entirely out of account their contribution to society in the form of caring for their children. It can also entrench inequalities by paying too little attention to quality of work.

---

[113] See, for example, A Deacon 'An Ethic of Mutual Responsibility? Toward a Fuller Justification for Conditionality in Welfare' in Mead and Beem, 127–150; S White 'Is Conditionality Illiberal' in Mead and Beem (n 102 above) 92.

While paid work can be liberating, it can also be exploitative; paid work does not guarantee an adequate income or freedom from poverty. This is not countered by placing a duty on the State to safeguard conditions of work:[114] conditionality undermines the element of choice which is essential to giving workers any bargaining power. If lay-off, dismissal, or failure to find work carries with it the risk of starvation, workers are in no position to insist on their rights, even if they exist on paper. Indeed, welfare payments are often characterized as a reservation wage which is essential to underpin terms and conditions of workers in the paid labour market.

A theory of positive duties to provide welfare is also shaped by the value of solidarity. Critics of positive duties to provide welfare argue that they impose a burden on productive members of society in order to benefit the unproductive. However, as was argued in Chapter 1, State responsibility for ensuring all reach a minimum capability threshold should be viewed as a contribution to the community as a whole,[115] not simply to particular individuals. Thus, Ritchie argued at the end of the nineteenth century that fundamental or natural rights were 'mutual claims which cannot be ignored without detriment to the well-being and in the last resort to the very being of a community'.[116] Even more forceful is the statement of Mokgoro J in the recent South African social security case of *Khosa*. As she stressed, 'sharing responsibility for the problems and consequences of poverty equally as a community represents the extent to which wealthier members of the community view the minimal well-being of the poor as connected with their personal well-being and the well-being of the community as a whole'.[117]

(ii) The content of the positive duty

The Welfare State comes in many shapes and forms. While all types make provision of some sort, not all further the values of freedom as agency, substantive equality, and solidarity. The value of substantive equality is particularly important, in that, as the previous chapter demonstrated, it is possible for redistributive measures to reinforce status inequalities. This is especially true in relation to gender. Particular models of Welfare State can also entrench socio-economic inequalities both through stigmatizing welfare recipients, and through keeping benefit levels low.

These arguments can be elaborated by considering the three prototype Welfare State regimes described by Esping-Anderson: the liberal-individualist, social

---

[114] White (n 111 above).
[115] M Freeden 'Rights, Needs and Community: The Emergence of British Welfare Thought' in A Ware and R Goodin (eds) *Needs and Welfare* (Sage London 1990) 55.
[116] D Ritchie *Natural Rights* (Allen & Unwin London 1894) 87.
[117] *Khosa and Mahlaule v Minister for Social Development* 2004 (6) BCLR 569 (South African Constitutional Court) at para 74.

democratic, and conservative.[118] Each provides a specific trade-off between the market, the family, and the State as a source of welfare, with the liberal model placing primary emphasis on the market, the conservative on the family, and the social democratic on the State. Although he associates different models with different countries, it is more usual to view the Welfare State as consisting of an amalgam of traits drawn from all three models.

The 'liberal regime' is readily recognizable. It adheres to the principle that freedom consists in lack of intervention by the State, leaving individuals to pursue their self interest through the free market. It is only when the market fails that the State has a role, and then only to provide a safety net. It has three main characteristics. First, it provides means-tested benefits, targeting only the poor. As a result, benefits are not cast in the form of rights. Secondly, only a limited range of risks are considered to be a social responsibility, excluding, in the case of the US, so basic a risk as health. Thirdly, it is strictly limited to welfare rights, and does not extend to employment rights or labour market regulation.[119] Means-tested benefits are increasingly used in place of universal benefits.

The needs-based principle has the advantage of targeting those in need unconditionally and regardless of their ability to contribute. However, to avoid the charge of over-taxing those who provide for themselves through productive work, benefit levels are generally inadequate. Thus, while providing a safety net against destitution, they do not positively contribute towards greater equality in society. These disadvantages are particularly apparent in the US, where the Welfare State provides means-tested assistance for the poor, while the middle classes make their own private provision. This is coupled with few genuinely social or public services, such as a health service. Many middle class Americans therefore feel little commitment to the principle of welfare rights.[120]

This means that means-tested benefits fail to advance the value of solidarity. They are also problematic in respect of substantive equality, making some distributive gains, but at the cost of deepening recognition inequalities. While means of survival might be guaranteed, this is at the cost of respect and esteem in a society where individual achievement is valorized. It is an easy step from here to portraying welfare beneficiaries as scroungers and then to welfare to work policies. In addition, means-tested benefits can reinforce gender inequality. In Britain, for example, the means test has always been based on an aggregation of all the resources of a married or cohabiting couple, with the attendant assumption that these resources are equally distributed within the family. Yet it is now well established that inequalities of earning power within the family can replicate

---

[118] G Esping-Anderson *Social Foundations of Post Industrial Economies* (OUP Oxford 1998).

[119] ibid 74–76.

[120] G Esping-Anderson *Social Foundations of Post Industrial Economies* (OUP Oxford 1998) 171.

social power structures, and that male partners do not necessarily share their income with the rest of the family.[121]

As well as means-tested benefits, many Welfare States have contributory or employment based benefits, based on Esping-Anderson's second model, the 'conservative or familial' model of welfare. Unlike the 'liberal model', this approach does not see welfare as a safety net for those who have failed in the market, but a reward for those who have been industrious. Benefits are contributory, functioning as an insurance against risks that may befall everyone: retirement, redundancy, and sickness or injury while working. The amount payable depends on contributions accrued and therefore favours those in continuous and long-term employment in a stable job situation. Those who cannot actively participate in the paid labour market are expected to depend on the family on the assumption that the primary breadwinner will maintain the family through paid work, or if necessary, contributory benefits. The British Welfare State at its inception was heavily influenced by this model and it remains a central tenet both in Britain and in other European countries, such as Italy.[122]

Insurance-based regimes escape the criticism that positive duties on the State unfairly burden some in order to provide for others because they appear to be no more than individuals helping themselves. Thus, welfare critics such as Mead draw a strict line between benefits of this sort and 'welfare' benefits, characterized as support provided by government to people who are unable to support themselves.[123] In reality, however, insurance-based benefits are also dependent on duties on the State to provide. Even in the US where much social insurance is apparently provided privately through the market, private provision, such as personal or occupational health insurance, is heavily tax financed.[124] Thus, the State does in fact support provision, although it is largely the middle classes who benefit, rather than the poor.[125]

This model while advancing substantive equality as between working class and middle class men, creates serious conflicts in respect of gender equality. Its egalitarianism lies in what it means to the industrial working class, in that society takes care of the risks faced by those without resources to fall back on when paid employment fails. However, this very focus conflicts head on with equality for women. In the traditional male-breadwinner family, the reliance on the family as the basic unit of support perpetuates inequality by assuming that any measure to improve male welfare is shared by women and children. Apart from the dubious

---

[121] K Bellamy, F Bennett, and J Millar *Who Benefits? A Gender Analysis of the UK Benefits and Tax Credits System* (Fawcett Society 2005) 5; S Fredman *Women and the Law* (OUP Oxford 1998) 171–173.

[122] Fredman (n 122 above) at 27ff; G Esping-Anderson *Social Foundations of Post Industrial Economies* (OUP Oxford 1998).

[123] L Mead 'A Summary of Welfare Reform' in Mead and Beem (n 102 above) 10.

[124] G Esping-Anderson *Social Foundations of Post Industrial Economies* (OUP Oxford 1998) 171.

[125] ibid 175–178.

assumption that all family units are composed of father and mother, this assumes that women in such households have access to a male partner's income.[126] In fact, there is clear evidence that women's poverty may well be hidden by unequal distribution of income within the household.[127]

Now that the male-breadwinner family has been superseded, the contributory model reinforces gender inequality in a different way. Because women are expected to be both breadwinners and home-makers, many women have to engage in non-standard working, which limits their ability to amass sufficient contributions. A combination of low earnings, irregular working patterns, and time spent out of the labour market has meant that large numbers of women are excluded from the realm of contributory benefits. Particularly problematic is the effect on pensions of the bias in favour of male patterns of work. Non-standard working carries with it all the factors associated with low pension income: low earnings, time not spent in full-time work, low or irregular private pension contributions, and earlier retirement.[128] Among newly retired women in Britain in 2005, only 23% had a full basic pension on the basis of their own contributions as against 77% of men.[129]

The model which comes closest to expressing the values of positive freedom, solidarity, and substantive equality is the 'social democratic' paradigm. Instead of the isolated individual in the 'lonely market', the social democratic model views individuals as essentially social. This is not at the expense of individual autonomy but instead a way of achieving individual autonomy: social progress is viewed as the best way to achieve individual well-being. Social rights are viewed as integral to citizenship and community membership, avoiding the stigmatic 'we-they' divide which characterizes the liberal welfare regime. This is reflected in its universal quality: instead of targeted means-tested assistance, the emphasis is on public goods, such as health, education, childcare, leisure, and public spaces. The market is regarded as a harsh and arbitrary means of achieving basic welfare. Instead of leaving individuals to purchase basic needs, such as health care or childcare, in the market, it aims at a comprehensive socialization of risks. In the UK, this can be seen in the form of the NHS, in Scandinavian countries it includes a comprehensive service structure related to family needs. Particularly importantly, it is premised on an active rights-bearing citizen, rather than a passive recipient of State welfare. Rights are geared towards facilitating productive and constructive individuals, through the provision of education, training, health care, and work opportunities. The result is that the community as a whole

---

[126] S Fredman 'Women at Work: The Broken Promise of Flexicurity' (2004) 33 Industrial Law Journal 299.

[127] J Bradshaw et al *Gender and Poverty in Britain* (EOC 2003) Lewis 92.

[128] Pensions Policy Institute *The Under-pensioned: Women* (2003) 8.

[129] K Bellamy, F Bennett, and J Millar *Who Benefits? A Gender Analysis of the UK Benefits and Tax Credits System* (Fawcett Society 2005) 4.

is viewed as both providing and benefiting from the basic socio-economic rights necessary to function as a full-scale citizen.[130]

The social democratic model is most attuned to achieving both substantive equality and solidarity. By collectivizing family needs, it frees women from an undue burden of unpaid labour, facilitating a dual earner household. This has been shown to have other positive consequences, such as reducing child-poverty through dual earner households.[131] Crucial too is the community solidarity which comes from giving everyone a stake in the Welfare State. Access to public services, such as vocational training, health care, transport, education, and child-care, are considered as collective benefits, giving individuals real rather then formal opportunities.[132] Nor is there an unbridgeable divide between those in need of State provision and those who are not. Disability, retirement, illness, and child and family responsibilities are all risks facing everyone, even the most productive.

(iii) Sources of duties

The South African Constitution is unusual in having an express right to social security. As with other socio-economic rights, this gives rise to a duty to take reasonable steps within available resources to progressively realize the right. However, as in the case of education and housing above, the positive duty to provide welfare need not arise solely from express rights to social security. Positive duties have also arisen from perhaps the most fundamental civil and political right: the right not to be subjected to cruel and inhuman treatment. In the UK, the judicial recognition of such duties has come in response to claims by asylum seekers faced with the deliberate refusal of the political process to accept responsibility for even the basic existential minimum. In *Limbuela*,[133] they met a cautious but definite recognition from the UK House of Lords of the State's basic responsibilities to prevent destitution. The claimants challenged the policy of withdrawing entitlement to basic social support from any asylum seekers who had not applied for asylum immediately on arrival. Asylum seekers were also denied the right to undertake paid employment. As a result, they were left wholly destitute. They claimed breach of their right not to be subjected to inhuman or degrading treatment or punishment under Article 3 of the ECHR. The House of Lords unanimously held that in order to avoid a breach of Article 3, the Secretary of State was obliged to provide support.

There were two crucial elements to this decision. The first was that the meaning of 'inhuman and degrading' in Article 3 was held to cover the denial of

---

[130] Esping-Anderson (n 124 above) at 78–80.
[131] ibid at 178–179.
[132] Supiot (n 98 above) 144.
[133] *R on the Application of Hooper v Secretary of State for Work and Pensions* [2005] UKHL 29 (House of Lords) at [7].

the most basic needs of any human being to a seriously detrimental extent. Secondly, and particularly importantly, was the recognition that the State was responsible for their destitution because it was the legal structure itself which rendered the individuals destitute, by prohibiting them from obtaining paid work while simultaneously withdrawing the social support which would otherwise be available to destitute asylum seekers. This finding is especially significant in that Article 3 states that no one shall be subject to degrading treatment, wording which is capable of being read as requiring only a duty of restraint on the State. Nevertheless, the House of Lords recognized that it was unhelpful to analyse Article 3 according to whether it gave rise to a negative or positive duty. 'Time and again these are shown to be false dichotomies', Lord Brown declared. Instead, the real issue is whether the State is 'properly to be regarded as responsible for the harm inflicted (or threatened) upon the victim'.[134] This responsibility was not limited to direct infliction of violence or punishment. The State is also regarded as responsible when the statutory regime it has established leaves individuals in a position of inevitable destitution. In this case it was the statutory regime which removed any source of social support while at the same time prohibiting asylum seekers from supporting themselves through paid work. 'It seems to me one thing to say, as the ECtHR did in *Chapman*, that within the contracting states there are unfortunately many homeless people and whether to provide funds for them is a political, not judicial, issue; quite another for a comparatively rich (not to say northerly) country like the UK to single out a particular group to be left utterly destitute on the streets as a matter of policy.'[135] This constitutes a crucial recognition of one of the main themes in this book.

A further source of positive duties in the field of welfare is the equality principle, where, as in other areas, it is capable of generating positive duties from traditional civil and political rights. The ECHR has no direct right to social security. Strikingly, however, it is the property provision which has been used to generate positive duties to provide social security. This is despite its formulation as a duty of restraint. Protocol 1 Article 1 provides: 'Every natural or legal person is entitled to the peaceful enjoyment of her possessions. No one shall be deprived of her possessions except in the public interest and subject to the conditions provided for by law and by the general principles of international law.' This does not give rise to a right to social security on its own. However, the Court has gradually recognized that social security benefits, when provided by statute in contracting States, should be viewed as generating proprietary rights. At first this was confined to benefits for which an individual could claim some interest because of her contributions. But by 2005, the Court recognized that the provision should reflect

---

[134] *Limbuela* (n 7 above) at [92] and see Lord Hope at [53].
[135] *R (on the application of Limbuela) v Secretary of State for the Home Department* [2005] UKHL 66; [2006] 1 AC 396 (HL).

the reality of welfare provision within contracting States, where many individuals are, for all or part of their lives, completely dependent for survival on social security and welfare benefits. Many domestic legal systems recognized that such individuals required a degree of certainty and security, and provided for benefits to be paid to eligible individuals as of right. The position was explained thus:

> 54.... [Article 1 of the First Protocol] does not create a right to acquire property. It places no restriction on the Contracting State's freedom to decide whether or not to have in place any form of social security scheme, or to choose the type or amount of benefits to provide under any such scheme... If, however, a Contracting State has in force legislation providing for the payment as of right of a welfare benefit—whether conditional or not on the prior payment of contributions—that legislation must be regarded as generating a proprietary interest falling within the ambit of [Article 1 of the First Protocol] for persons satisfying its requirements...[136]

What then is the role of the court? Beyond requiring the minimum necessary to survive, courts struggle to give appropriate shape to positive duties in the welfare field. Given the polycentric nature of social security and its wide distributive consequences, it is inappropriate for courts to insist on one model rather than another. However, it is through the principle of equality that courts should have the most helpful impact. At the very minimum, courts can play an important role where a policy, aimed at advancing distributive equality, in practice entrenches recognition or status-based inequalities. This is facilitated by the conceptual structure of the equality principle, whereby categorizations which impact disproportionately on a status group constitute prima facie discrimination, unless justified by the State. This justification requirement places the court in a position to insist on accountability and transparency. The extent to which this is taken forward in a deliberative sense depends on the level of stringency with which the Court is prepared to test the State's justification and the extent and nature of participation demanded by the Court.

We have already seen that in the Canadian case of *Gosselin*,[137] which concerned a welfare to work policy which discriminated against claimants under 25, the Court expected only a cursory justification from the State. In particular, it was prepared to accept without evidence the State's argument that younger people had better job prospects than those over 25. A similar pattern is evident in respect of the ECHR. The ECtHR has accepted a substantive view of equality to the extent that 'Article 14 does not prohibit a Member State from treating groups differently in order to correct "factual inequalities" between them; indeed in certain circumstances a failure to attempt to correct inequality through different treatment may in itself give rise to a breach of the article'.[138]

---

[136] *Stec and others v UK* Application nos 65731/01 and 65900/01 (2005) (Admissibility decision 6 July 2005) para 54.
[137] *Gosselin v Quebec* 2002 SCC 84 (Canadian Supreme Court).
[138] *Stec v UK* [2006] ECHR 65731/01 (European Court of Human Rights) para 51.

A difference of treatment is, however, discriminatory if it has no objective and reasonable justification; in other words, if it does not pursue a legitimate aim or if there is not a reasonable relationship of proportionality between the means employed and the aim sought to be realized. This in principle gives the Court a significant role in achieving both accountability and deliberation in situations in which social security is challenged on grounds of gender equality or other prohibited ground. However, the ECtHR is caught between its relatively robust approach to recognition claims and its deferent approach to distributive decisions. Like the Canadian Court, its response has been one of deference. 'Because of their direct knowledge of their society and its needs, the national authorities are in principle better placed than the international judge to appreciate what is in the public interest on social or economic grounds, and the Court will generally respect the legislature's policy choice unless it is "manifestly without reasonable foundation".'[139]

More complex has been the South African Court's response. In the *Khosa* case, permanent residents who were not yet citizens challenged the fact that old age pensions and child benefit were confined to South African citizens. The South African Constitution provides that everyone is entitled to social security, bringing in both the substantive right and the equality principle. The Court was prepared to scrutinize the State's justification closely and decided that it could not be sustained in the light of the constitutional values of dignity and solidarity. Unlike its Canadian and European counterparts, it was not daunted by distributive decisions, holding that the cost to the State of extending the benefit to permanent residents was not too onerous a drain on the country's budget. On the other hand, its analysis of the recognition dimension of the claim was scanty. The Court simply held that the exclusion of permanent residents breached the right of everyone to social security. What it did not do is discuss whether this was limited to permanent residents, or whether a very different sort of reasoning would apply to the far more numerous group of temporary residents.[140] Its reasoning focussed on the fact that permanent residents were on track to become citizens, thus apparently confining the recognition dimension to a concept of citizenship, whether legal or social. However, more explanation would be needed to justify limiting the expansive concept of 'everyone' to those on whom the State chooses to confer citizenship or quasi-citizenship. On the other hand, the distributive dimension becomes even more challenging, given the large numbers involved. Human rights principles nevertheless require, as the House of Lords recognized in the British asylum seekers case, that the State has a duty to provide, at the very least, the existential minimum to prevent total destitution.

---

[139] ibid.
[140] I am indebted to Geoff Budlender for this point.

D. Conclusion

Positive duties arising from human rights can no longer be ignored, or hidden behind artificial distinctions between different categories of rights. The fundamental values of freedom, equality, democracy, and solidarity which underpin all human rights entail the recognition of both positive duties and duties of restraint. The challenge is to fashion those duties in a way which is not only coherent and sustainable, but which advances those values. Above all, human rights duties must enhance democracy. In a globalizing world, this is a task which has particular salience, as trade values and regulatory duties on the State threaten to inhabit the whole space of feasible measures. It is this challenge which this book has attempted to address. It is hoped that a small contribution has been made to a task which is both daunting and essential.

Index

Lightning Source UK Ltd.
Milton Keynes UK
UKOW06f0346161015

260679UK00004B/103/P